GEO YEAR BOOK

An Overview of
Our Changing Environment

2004/5

Produced by the GEO Section
Division of Early Warning and Assessment (DEWA)
United Nations Environment Programme
P.O. Box 30552
Nairobi 00100
Kenya

Tel: +254 20 623562
Fax: +254 20 623944
Email: geo@unep.org
UNEP web site: http://www.unep.org
GEO Year Book web site: http://www.unep.org/geo/yearbook

Internet references cited in the GEO Year Book are available on the GEO Year Book web site.

Editor: Paul Harrison
Graphics and layout: Bounford.com
Coordination of Production: United Nations Office for Project Services (UNOPS)
Printing: Interprint Ltd. Malta
Distribution: SMI (Distribution Services) Ltd. UK

This publication is available from Earthprint.com http://www.earthprint.com

This book is printed on 100 per cent recycled, chlorine free paper.

G E O
Y E A R
B O O K

An Overview of
Our Changing Environment   2004/5

UNEP

Contents

Preface iii

2004 Overview 1

Global 2

Africa 12

Asia and the Pacific 17

Europe 22

Latin America and the Caribbean 27

North America 32

West Asia 37

Polar 42

The Global International Waters Assessment 47

Indian Ocean Tsunami 50

Feature Focus: Gender, Poverty and Environment 55

Gender Matters 56

Gender, Poverty and Environment: A Three-way Interaction 62

Challenges for the Future 69

Emerging Challenges – New Findings 71

Emerging and Re-emerging Infectious Diseases: Links to Environmental Change 72

Abrupt Climate Change: Ocean Salinity Changes and Potential Impacts on Ocean Circulation 80

GEO Indicators 85

Atmosphere 86

Disasters Caused by Natural Hazards 87

Biodiversity 88

Coastal and Marine Areas 89

Freshwater 90

Urban Areas 91

Global Environmental Issues 92

Acronyms and abbreviations 95

Acknowledgements 96

Preface

There is much to be optimistic about when we review the state of the global environment, and how it has fared in 2004. Efforts towards environmental sustainability at the local, regional and global level are bearing fruit. As the links between environmental and human well being become clearer, many people and governments are taking action to move environmental protection centre-stage.

Concrete recognition of the central role of good environmental management reached a new peak in 2004. For the first time, the Nobel Peace Prize was awarded to an environmentalist. Wangari Maathai won the award for promoting peace and democracy through environmental protection and regeneration. Professor Maathai's work has provided tangible proof that a healthy environment, and democratic and sustainable management of our natural resources, is a powerful key to overcome poverty and deliver a more stable and peaceful world.

Despite our best efforts, however, we cannot always avoid the bad news. By early December, following a series of hurricanes and typhoons, the global insurance industry had already declared 2004 the most expensive year for damage caused by weather-related disasters. There was much worse to come. Just as the Year Book was ready to go to press at the end of 2004, disaster struck in the form of the Indian Ocean earthquake and resulting tsunami.

Over 220 000 people were killed in Indonesia, India, Sri Lanka, Thailand, the Maldives and other countries as far away as Somalia on the east coast of Africa. Millions more were rendered homeless. The full scale of the disaster was still not clear as the year came to a close. First assessments of the devastation revealed that affected areas could take years to recover and that a substantial increase in the death toll was likely if diseases spread through flooding, contaminated water and lack of sanitation in the aftermath.

A UNEP Asian Tsunami Disaster Task Force was established immediately after the disaster to identify and help alleviate the environmental impacts of the disaster, and support efforts of the affected countries. At the same time we 'stopped the press' on the Year Book to insert an additional section on the Indian Ocean tsunami in the **2004 Overview**, although information of the full human and environmental impact of the disaster was just trickling in.

Following a positive response to the first volume of the Year Book series, UNEP has retained the same formula for the *GEO Year Book 2004/5,* providing a global and regional overview of key environmental events and developments, including policy. A regional network of collaborators has been instrumental in identifying the most important issues, to fit a whole year's coverage into the slim Year Book format. There have been some innovations, however. We have introduced a full-page spread of satellite images at the end of each of the regional sections of the Overview chapter. Taking advantage of the latest technology, these images provide a vivid record of our rapidly changing environment.

The **Feature Focus** of the Year Book series analyses a crosscutting issue of universal relevance and increasing concern. It is designed to inform the deliberations of the UNEP Global Ministerial Environment Forum (GMEF), which takes place in the first quarter of every year, and thereby contribute to the formulation of UNEP's input to the Commission on Sustainable Development (CSD). Keeping this in mind, we chose to look at the links between gender, poverty and environment in this volume – key crosscutting issues in the CSD thematic cluster of water, sanitation and human settlements for 2004/5.

Science plays a vital role in understanding our increasingly complex world, helping us to deal with ongoing problems and to identify emerging issues. In preparing the Year Book, UNEP works with the Scientific Committee on Problems of the Environment (SCOPE) to select and present important new policy-relevant findings from scientific research for the chapter on **Emerging Challenges**. The two topics for *GEO Year Book 2004/5* are strongly linked to environmental change. The first explores how environmental change can trigger the emergence or re-emergence of infectious diseases, demonstrating the role of good environmental management in minimizing adverse trends. The second presents recent evidence of changes in ocean salinity and a step-by-step explanation of why this could have serious consequences.

The **GEO Indicators** chapter draws upon the most recent available data to present a range of key pressure, state, impact and response indicators. Many of them have featured in previous GEO reports. Time series and graphics are used to present a continuous picture of both positive and negative changes in the global environment. This year we have also introduced some new indicators, including on air quality, marine protected areas, and ozone protection.

UNEP is more than ever aware of its responsibility to keep the state of the global environment under close scrutiny, and bring positive and negative changes, unexpected trends and emerging threats to public attention – particularly to the attention of policy makers. The GEO Year Book series, part of a set of products developed within UNEP's GEO process for integrated environmental assessment, is one of our principal tools for doing just this. Along with the GEO Report, published every five years, the Year Book reaches out across the globe in different formats and languages, and is designed to appeal to a variety of audiences. I hope that you find it interesting and informative. As always, your feedback is very welcome.

Klaus Töpfer
United Nations Under-Secretary General
and Executive Director,
United Nations Environment Programme

2004 Overview

● GLOBAL ● AFRICA ● ASIA AND THE PACIFIC
● EUROPE ● LATIN AMERICA AND THE CARIBBEAN
● NORTH AMERICA ● WEST ASIA ● POLAR
● INTERNATIONAL WATERS ● INDIAN OCEAN TSUNAMI

Global

A year of extreme weather events presented clear indications of our increasing pressure on the planet while a devastating tsunami revealed our continuing vulnerability (see Indian Ocean Tsunami section). An unprecedented rise in carbon dioxide levels coincided with stronger evidence of melting glaciers and ice-caps. Alarming surveys of the rates of species loss converged with studies showing just how hard our numbers and consumption are pressing on the planet's capacity to supply our needs.

Human responses moved in parallel. International measures to control invasive marine species and hazardous chemicals, and to share the benefits of plant genetic resources for food security and sustainable agriculture entered into force, and the Kyoto Protocol received sufficient ratifications for it to do so in early 2005. And to symbolize our growing recognition of the link between environmental well-being, conflict prevention and long-term

human security, the Nobel Peace Prize was awarded for the first time to an environmentalist, Kenya's Wangari Maathai.

GROWING PRESSURES
Indicators of climate change in 2004

The year 2004 strengthened the evidence of global warming and underlined the impacts of climate change on economies and the environment, as well as on human health and well-being. Four severe hurricanes in sequence brought havoc, tragedy and huge economic losses to the Caribbean and southern United States. While not all extreme weather events can be attributed directly to climate change, the intensity of such events is likely to increase as a result of global warming (Knutson and Tuleya 2004).

Measurements in 2004 recorded an unprecedented surge in atmospheric carbon dioxide (CO_2) levels. The value of 379 parts per million registered in March 2004 was 3 parts higher than in 2003 (NOAA 2004). The average annual increase in the 1960s, soon after measurements began, was less than one part per million, while over the past decade it has been approximately 1.8 parts per million (**Figure 1**).

A number of studies published during the year found worrying impacts of climate change. Only half of the CO_2 that human activity released over the last 200 years has remained in the atmosphere. A 15-year-long study of the role of anthropogenic CO_2 in the Earth's oceans found that oceans had absorbed 30 per cent of the other half, causing an acidification process. Calcium carbonate plays an important role in regulating carbon sequestration in oceans. Increased CO_2 uptake gives rise to fears that acidification and dissolution of marine carbonates from corals, algae and carbonate shells of marine plankton could have significant impacts on the biological systems in the oceans in ways we are only beginning to understand (Feely and others 2004). A further study warned that climate change could drive over a million species into extinction by 2050 (Thomas, Cameron and others 2004).

The European Environment Agency found clear trends of climate change impacts on glaciers, snow and ice, marine systems, terrestrial ecosystems and biodiversity, water, agriculture, human health and economy (EEA 2004).

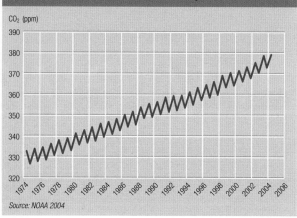

Figure 1: Increase in atmospheric carbon dioxide levels registered at the Mauna Loa Observatory

CO_2 (ppm)

Source: NOAA 2004

2004 **JANUARY** **FEBRUARY**

Cyclone Heta strikes the island of Niue, causing severe damage to the West Coast. Residential and commercial sectors in the capital Alofi are devastated.

A study published in *Nature* reports that climate change could drive over a million species into extinction by 2050.

Tropical Cyclone Ivy affects more than 54 000 people in Vanuatu. Early warning by the Bureau of Meteorology limits deaths and injuries to two persons killed and one seriously injured. Over 95 per cent of water supply systems in the affected islands are damaged, along with 11 000 houses and about half of the health centres.

The Rotterdam Convention on the Prior Informed Consent Procedure for Certain Hazardous Chemicals and

Pesticides in International Trade enters into force.

The International Convention for the Control and Management of Ships' Ballast Water and Sediments is adopted at the International Conference on Ballast Water Management, in London. The convention aims to halt the global spread of alien aquatic organisms carried in ships' ballast waters.

The Agreement on the Conservation of Albatrosses and

Petrels enters into force. It aims to stop or reverse population declines through conservation measures, including research and monitoring, reducing mortality in fisheries, eradicating non-native species at breeding sites, and reducing disturbances, habitat loss and pollution.

The seventh meeting of the Conference of the Parties to the Convention on Biological Diversity (CBD COP 7), in Kuala Lumpur, Malaysia, adopts a programme to

establish and maintain protected areas in representative ecosystems by 2010 for terrestrial areas, and by 2012 for marine areas. CBD COP 7 decides to develop indicators to assess and report on progress in achieving the 2010 target, and adopts the Global Strategy for Plant Conservation.

CBD COP 7 also serves as the First Meeting of the Parties to the Cartagena Protocol on Biosafety. The meeting sets up a

framework to implement the Protocol, and adopts mechanisms to promote compliance.

The Cartagena Protocol on Biosafety adopts a new system of identification and labels for all bulk shipments of Genetically Modified Organisms and Living Modified Organisms.

Hundreds of researchers launch 'SPLASH – Structure of Populations, Levels of Abundance and Status of Humpbacks', the

A number of other reports on the impacts of global warming found significant increases in the rate of melting of land and sea ice from the Arctic to Mount Everest to the Antarctic, with major implications for humans and biodiversity (see Polar section; Bøggild and others 2004; Chinese Academy of Sciences 2004; Thomas, Rignot and others 2004). Meanwhile, evidence for the dominant human role in climate change continued to accumulate. Some scientists suggested that recent variations in solar activity have only had a minor influence in global warming (Krivova and Solanki 2004).

A further investigation concluded that emissions during the past century doubled the chances of the heat wave that hit Europe last summer, and predicted that by the 2040s, more than half of Europe's summers will be warmer than that of 2003 (Scott and others 2004). The finding could make it easier to bring lawsuits against large emissions-producers. Eight US states and New York City have a lawsuit against five of the country's power companies. The plaintiffs want a federal judge to force five power producers to reduce emissions 3 per cent annually for ten years (SFC 2004).

Changing human and natural populations

The latest revision of the United Nations Population Division's World Urbanization Prospects, published in 2004, reveals an increasingly urban future. By 2007, for the first time in human history, the urban population will form more than half of the total. Almost all population growth in the next 30 years will be concentrated in urban areas, and most of this

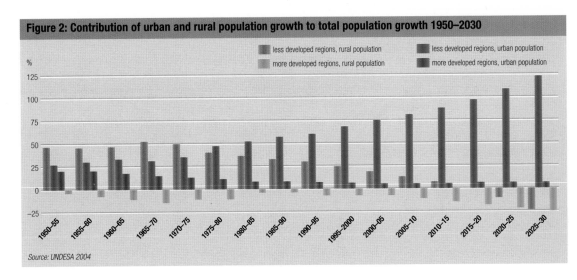

Figure 2: Contribution of urban and rural population growth to total population growth 1950–2030

less developed regions, rural population
more developed regions, rural population
less developed regions, urban population
more developed regions, urban population

Source: UNDESA 2004

growth will occur in less developed countries. The rural population will decline between 2003 and 2030, from 3.3 billion to 3.2 billion, so that the share of growth due to rural populations (as well as to the populations of some developed countries) will be actually negative (**Figure 2**) (UNDESA 2004).

According to UN-HABITAT: "if nothing is done to check the current trend, the number of people living in slums will rise from one billion today to some 1.5 billion by the year 2020." This will make it difficult to achieve the Millennium Development target of significantly improving the lives of at least 100 million slum-dwellers by 2020 (UN-HABITAT 2004).

While the international community has pledged to achieve by 2010 a significant reduction of the current rate of biodiversity loss at the global, regional and national level (CBD 2004a), studies provided new indications that biodiversity loss is increasing.

Amphibians are declining at an unprecedented rate. Their permeable skin makes them particularly vulnerable to pollution and climate change, so they serve as a good indicator of environmental health. The Global Amphibian Assessment found that just under one third of the world's 5 743 amphibian species are threatened with extinction (**Figure 3**). This is considerably higher than the comparable figures for birds

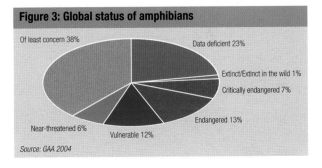

Figure 3: Global status of amphibians

Of least concern 38%
Data deficient 23%
Extinct/Extinct in the wild 1%
Critically endangered 7%
Endangered 13%
Vulnerable 12%
Near-threatened 6%

Source: GAA 2004

MARCH

most comprehensive ongoing study of endangered humpback whales to date.

In a statement released at the Annual Meeting of the American Association for the Advancement of Science and at CBD COP7, over one thousand marine scientists from 69 countries call for urgent action from governments and the UN to protect deep sea coral and sponge ecosystems.

United States Pentagon officials warn that abrupt climate change poses a major worldwide security threat that could result in wars, nuclear conflict, large-scale droughts, famine, and other disasters.

UNEP-WCMC publishes the Cloud Forest Agenda – a first mapping of all the world's tropical montane cloud forests – to encourage new conservation actions for the forests. More than 60 countries have cloud forests.

The Mauna Loa Observatory registers an unprecedented increase in carbon dioxide concentration in the atmosphere to 379 parts per million.

Arctic Environment: European Perspectives is released by UNEP and the European Environment Agency. The report highlights Europe's growing dependence on the Arctic's resources, and the increasing pressures on them.

Saudi Arabia launches a US$200 000 prize to promote

scientific research in environment management in the Arab region. It will be awarded every two years.

Canada launches the One-Tonne Challenge, encouraging Canadians to cut their annual greenhouse gas emissions by one tonne.

Republic of Korea hosts the first UNEP Governing Council/Global Ministerial Environment Forum to be held in Asia, attended by close to 100 ministers and delegations from over 120

countries. Main issues under discussion: delivering safe and sufficient water, providing better sanitation services, and dust storms.

An Extraordinary Meeting of the Parties to the Montreal Protocol on Substances that Deplete the Ozone Layer in Montreal, Canada, addresses methyl bromide issues, left unresolved at the 15th Meeting of the Parties in November 2003. Compromise is reached on the

levels of production and consumption of methyl bromide necessary to satisfy critical needs of some parties.

UN Secretary-General Kofi Annan announces the establishment of an Advisory Board on Water and Sanitation to mobilize funds for water and sanitation projects, and to raise awareness and develop new partnerships on these issues.

Box 1: Human appropriation of Net Primary Production

A new assessment based on satellite and statistical data found that, globally, humans are already consuming 20 per cent of Earth's total net primary production (NPP) on land (Imhoff and others 2004). NPP is the amount of plant material generated through photosynthesis that remains after respiration. The study calculated the amount of NPP required to produce all the land-based products consumed in the base-year 1995, including plant foods, meat and dairy, natural fibres and wood-based products.

The balance between supply of and demand for NPP varies considerably on a geographic basis (see figure). Western Europe and South Central Asia consume the equivalent of more than 70 per cent of their regional NPP supply, while East Asia consumes 63 per cent. Human use of NPP in other regions is much lower, ranging from 24 per cent in North America down to only 12 per cent in Africa and 6 per cent in South America (see table). At more local scales, spatial differences are even more striking, ranging from over 30 000 per cent of local NPP in large urban centers down to almost nothing in sparsely populated areas. This share is likely to rise as human demands for food, fibre and fuel grow.

Human appropriation of net primary production (NPP), as a per cent of total NPP. The local consumption rate of NPP is compared to the local production rate of NPP. Highly populated areas (yellow and red) consume up to 300 times their local production.

Source: Imhoff and others 2004

Human-appropriated net primary production (NPP) of selected regions (intermediate estimate) calculated on a per capita basis.

Region	Area (million km²)	Population (millions)	NPP supply ('000 million tonnes)	Human appropriation of NPP ('000 million tonnes)	Human appropriation (as % of regional NPP)	Human appropriation per capita (tonnes)
Africa	31.1	742	12.50	1.55	12.4	2.08
East Asia	11.9	1400	3.02	1.91	63.3	1.37
South-Central Asia	10.9	1360	2.04	1.64	80.4	1.21
Western Europe	1.2	181	0.72	0.52	72.2	2.86
North America	19.7	293	6.67	1.58	23.7	5.40
South America	18.4	316	16.10	0.98	6.1	3.11

Source: Imhoff and others 2004

(12 per cent) and mammals (20 per cent), the only other groups for which comprehensive assessments have been completed (see GEO Indicators section). At least nine amphibian species have gone extinct since 1980. Another 113 species have not been reported from the wild in recent years and are considered to be possibly extinct (GAA 2004). Some 43 per cent of all amphibian species are in population decline, while fewer than one per cent are increasing (Stuart and others 2004).

THE INTERNATIONAL ENVIRONMENTAL AGENDA

Along with increasing pressures on the natural environment came some encouraging responses from the political realm. A number of new global environment agreements entered into force, while the Kyoto Protocol, a critical driver of global negotiations on climate change, will enter into force in early 2005. Other political achievements covered the areas of chemicals management, plant genetic resources, and ballast water management. Meanwhile the growing role of biotechnology in agriculture offered both promise and challenge.

The international community succeeded in reaching various targets for the year, agreed at the 2002 World Summit on Sustainable Development (WSSD) – particularly in the areas of biodiversity and chemicals management. However it missed the target of establishing a process for regular global reporting and assessment of the state of the marine environment. It also missed a number of goals for Small Island Developing States (SIDS) on waste and pollution, sustainable tourism, and energy supply and services.

MARCH continued

The Executive Board of the Kyoto Protocol's Clean Development Mechanism (CDM) begins registering projects.

A study published in *Nature* finds that the growth patterns of forests in the Amazon have changed over the past two decades: both tree mortality and tree growth have increased over time, possibly due to rising levels of carbon dioxide in the atmosphere.

Brazil announces a new plan to reduce deforestation, based on satellite monitoring systems.

APRIL

The Arab Water Council is established to promote better management of water resources in the 22 Arab states.

The *Greater Mekong Subregion Atlas of the Environment*, covering Cambodia, Laos, Myanmar, Thailand, Vietnam and the Chinese province of Yunnan, is published by UNEP and the Asian Development Bank.

Ecuador, Colombia, Panama and Costa Rica set up a linked chain of marine protected areas

covering 211 million ha, including the Galápagos Islands. It is considered the first ever attempt to pursue integrated ecosystem management across political jurisdictions.

In New York the 12th session of the UN Commission on Sustainable Development reviews implementation of water, sanitation and human settlement goals.

The OECD's Development Assistance Committee meets in Paris to review progress toward

the goals set under the United Nations Millennium Declaration. It notes that Overseas Development Aid has increased by 11 per cent over the last two years, reversing declines in the previous decade.

The Environmental Vulnerability Index is launched by the South Pacific Applied Geoscience Commission. The index integrates both ecological fragility and economic vulnerability.

MAY

UNEP-WCMC launches the *Bamboo Biodiversity* report, indicating that as many as half of the world's 1 200 woody bamboo species may be in danger of extinction as a result of massive forest destruction.

The African Ministerial Meeting on Energy, in Nairobi, Kenya, adopts an African Statement on Renewables, calling on development partners to help Africa develop and manage its renewable resources sustainably.

The Antarctic Treaty Consultative Meeting XXVII, in Cape Town, South Africa, appoints an inaugural Executive Secretary, more than 10 years after consensus was reached, at ATCM XVII in 1992, to establish a Secretariat.

A cyclone hits the state of Rakhine in Myanmar, killing an estimated 220 people and leaving more than 18 000 homeless.

The incorporation of environmental priorities into the mainstream of development concerns has been an ongoing process. But the year 2004 saw the global environmental agenda increasingly integrated with the global development agenda. Donor support for environmental concerns is shifting towards issues linked to international development goals – especially those agreed at the 2000 Millennium Summit and the 2002 Monterrey International Conference on Financing for Development (OECD 2004). This shift prepares the ground for the 2005 High-Level Plenary meeting, to be held during the 60th session of the UN General Assembly, which will review progress towards the commitments of the Millennium Declaration. Also in a first for multilateral environmental agreements, the Conference of the Parties to the Convention on Biological Diversity (CBD) adopted at its seventh meeting a decision on the Millennium

Wind energy has seen a sharp increase over the last decade.
Source: PROSOR-UNEP/Still Pictures

Development Goals, reinforcing the recognition of the inseparable link between biodiversity and the wider sustainable development agenda (CBD 2004b).

International environmental governance saw other advances both inside and outside the UN system. The 8th Special Session of the UNEP Governing Council/Global Ministerial Environment Forum decided to develop an Intergovernmental Strategic Plan for Technology Support and Capacity Building related to UNEP's work. In June at Renewables 2004, an initiative on global renewable energy was launched (**Box 2**). In April over 40 countries in the Group on Earth Observations adopted a ten-year framework plan to share data to improve understanding of the Earth's systems. Initiatives like these strengthen government commitment to environmental issues, and increase synergies and cooperation.

Climate initiatives
The entry into force of the Kyoto Protocol had appeared to be in question following the United States' rejection of the Protocol in 2001. In order to come into force it required the ratification of at least 55 countries accounting for at least 55 per cent of total emissions. In 2004 the Russian Federation joined over 120 other

countries in ratifying the treaty, thus ensuring that the instrument will enter into force on 16 February 2005.

Although it is not part of the larger multilateral approach to addressing climate change, the United States government

---

JUNE

Brazil introduces an emergency plan against the invasion of the freshwater mussel (*Limnoperna fortunei*), which has become a plague in the Rio de la Plata estuary.

The EU expands from 15 to 25 member countries. The new members are Cyprus, the Czech Republic, Estonia, Hungary, Latvia, Lithuania, Malta, Poland, the Slovak Republic and Slovenia.

The Stockholm Convention on Persistent Organic Pollutants enters into force on 17 May. A 'dirty dozen' of industrial chemicals blamed for causing deaths and birth defects are now outlawed.

The Wastewater Emission Targets – Water, Sanitation and Hygiene campaign (WET-WASH), aimed at reducing pollution of the world's seas, is launched by UNEP and the Water Supply and Sanitation Collaborative Council.

FAO releases its *State of Food and Agriculture* report, endorsing agricultural biotechnology and highlighting its potential benefits for developing countries.

Monsanto, the world's largest distributor of GM seeds, announces it will defer efforts to introduce Roundup Ready wheat.

World Environment Day, which annually promotes worldwide awareness of the environment, embraces the theme '*Wanted! Seas and Oceans – Dead or Alive?*'

The UN Secretary-General's Panel of Eminent Persons on UN-Civil Society Relations releases its report, *We the Peoples: Civil Society, the United Nations and Global Governance*. The report says the UN should foster 'multi-constituency' processes that

incorporate the perspectives and abilities of citizen groups, policy advocates, businesses, local governments and parliamentarians. It sees dialogue and collaboration with non-state actors as a powerful way to reinvigorate the intergovernmental process.

The worst monsoon flooding in 15 years hits Bangladesh, Nepal and parts of east India. More than 1 800 people are killed and more than 42 million affected.

The 4th Ministerial Conference on Environment and Health is held in Budapest, Hungary. The WHO Conference focuses on the future of our children.

The first meeting of environment ministers from Southern Common Market (MERCOSUR) countries (Argentina, Brazil, Paraguay, Uruguay, and Chile) is held in Buenos Aires, Argentina. The MERCOSUR Framework Agreement on the Environment enters into force.

continues to track the issue. In 2004 a report from the US government's Climate Change Science Program acknowledged that global warming is the result of human activities (CCSP 2004).

The United States took some steps in international fora towards addressing the problems of climate change. It belongs to the Carbon Sequestration Leadership Forum. Launched in 2003, this forum engages 16 government partners to focus on the development of carbon capture and storage technologies. A ministerial meeting of the forum in January 2004 in Rome endorsed ten joint projects. The US is also playing a lead role in the Methane to Markets partnership, a new agreement between nations designed to reduce methane emissions.

Chemical waste storage of a soap and vegetable-oil factory in Lusaka, Zambia.
Source: Ron Giling/Still Pictures

Chemicals management comes of age

Chemicals management has been a longstanding area of international cooperation, but the global regime for more systematic management 'came of age' in 2004 with the completion of a trio of instruments controlling their trade and movements.

One of the goals set at the WSSD was to achieve, by 2020, that chemicals are used and produced in ways that minimize significant adverse effects on human health and the environment. Work towards that goal accelerated in 2004. Two major agreements entered into force as global, legally-binding instruments regulating the life cycle of chemicals. The Rotterdam Convention on the Prior Informed Consent (PIC) Procedure for Certain Hazardous Chemicals and Pesticides in International Trade came into force on 24 February, and the Stockholm Convention on Persistent Organic Pollutants (POPs) on 17 May. These two join the Basel Convention on the Control of Transboundary Movements of Hazardous Wastes and their Disposal as complementary international agreements, significantly expanding the legal regime that governs the movement and use of chemicals.

The provisions of the three agreements are complementary. The Stockholm Convention deals with the evaluation and regulation of existing and new POPs (see also Box 1 in Polar section). The Rotterdam Convention covers the import and export of hazardous chemicals, while the Basel Convention establishes principles for the environmentally-sound movement and disposal of hazardous wastes. Trade provisions and hazard communication are important aspects of all three conventions.

Work continued during the year on developing these instruments. The first Conference of Parties (COP-1) to the Rotterdam Convention, held in Geneva in September, broadened the Convention's scope by including an additional 14 chemicals to its existing list of regulated substances. The seventh COP of the Basel Convention, which met in October, took key decisions to increase focus on waste minimization and to apply the terms of the Convention to the dismantling of ships.

The year 2004 also saw steps to link important elements of the chemicals life cycle into a coherent management regime for a safer future. Since 2003, international organizations, governments and stakeholders have been drafting a Strategic Approach to International Chemicals Management (SAICM) designed to enhance synergies and coordination among regulatory instruments and agencies. In October, over 300 government representatives meeting in Nairobi took significant steps to clarify the scope and purpose of a SAICM. They agreed that it would consist of an overarching policy strategy, a global plan of action, and a high-level declaration. The work of the SAICM preparatory process will culminate in an International Conference on Chemicals Management in 2006.

JUNE continued

The International Treaty on Plant Genetic Resources for Food and Agriculture enters into force. Its objectives are the conservation and sustainable use of plant genetic resources for food, food security and agriculture, and the fair and equitable sharing of benefits derived from their use.

The International Conference for Renewable Energies takes place in Bonn, Germany. The resulting International Action Programme contains over 156 concrete actions and commitments.

The International Conference on Fifty Years of Nuclear Power meets in Moscow and Obninsk, Russian Federation. This meeting marks 50 years since electricity produced by nuclear power was first fed into a national grid at Obninsk.

The G8 Summit meets in Georgia, US. Governments agree to launch in 2005 the 'Reduce, Reuse, and Recycle Initiative', to cut down on waste, promote recycling, reduce barriers to trade in goods and materials for recycled and remanufactured products, and promote relevant science and technologies.

The United Nations University opens the Institute for Environment and Human Security in Bonn, Germany, with the aim of enhancing the capacity of governments to respond to disasters.

German-based chemicals and healthcare company Bayer AG agrees to support UNEP's strategy to involve youth in environment issues through a US$ 1.33 million a year partnership.

JULY

More than 500 children from over 40 countries attend the Fifth Tunza International Children's Conference on the Environment in Connecticut, US. The four main themes are: endangered species; indigenous peoples and their healing ways; oceans, rivers and waterways; and resource conservation.

The 56th session of the International Whaling Commission, in Sorrento, Italy, agrees to keep its 18-year long moratorium on commercial whaling, though calls to establish new whale sanctuaries in the South Pacific or the South Atlantic are rejected.

The Third Science Conference of the Large-scale Biosphere-Atmosphere Experiment in Amazonia convenes in Brasilia, Brazil. Key studies show that: the Amazon is a net emitter rather than absorber of greenhouse gases; and approximately two-thirds of the carbon dioxide-equivalent gases produced annually in Brazil come from logging and burning of the forest.

UNEP launches the 'Responsible Investment Initiative', under which it will work with major institutional investors to develop a set of globally recognized principles for responsible investment by September 2005.

Frozen Ark – the first tissue bank aiming to freeze and preserve genetic material from endangered species around the world – is established in the United Kingdom. The first

Box 3: Methyl bromide heats up ozone talks

The Montreal Protocol on Substances that Deplete the Ozone Layer is widely recognized as one of the most successful of all multilateral environmental agreements. Since it was adopted in 1987, the treaty has ensured the gradual phase-out of a number of substances responsible for depleting the ozone layer (see GEO Indicators section). The consumption of ozone depleting substances has decreased significantly, allowing some scientists to predict that the ozone layer would recover by the middle of the 21st century if all the control measures of the Montreal Protocol were adhered to by all countries (UNEP 2000).

In spite of this success, challenges still remain. In 2004 the Protocol faced one of its biggest tests in recent years. Major disagreements surfaced in late 2003 over the ozone-depleting pesticide methyl bromide. Under the Protocol, developed countries were required to phase-out methyl bromide use by 1 January 2005. However, some parties called for exemptions to permit its ongoing use, arguing that there are as yet no cost-effective alternatives.

For the first time in the protocol's history, an extraordinary meeting of parties was convened in March 2004 to help resolve the issue. The meeting secured a compromise on critical-use exemptions for 11 developed country parties in 2005 (UNEP 2004a). The matter was not fully resolved, and required further work throughout the year. In spite of lengthy discussions the Sixteenth Meeting of the Parties to the Montreal Protocol, which took place in late November 2004, was not able to agree on methyl bromide exemptions for 2006. Parties decided to hold an additional 'extraordinary' meeting in mid-2005 to revisit the issue (UNEP 2004b).

Rain forest, Australia.

Source: Eugene Cisneros http://www.minresco.com/australia/dn_under.htm

The future of global forests governance

The future of the international governance of forests featured prominently in 2004. Discussions proceeded on the future of global forest processes due for renewal or replacement over the next two years: the International Tropical Timber Agreement (ITTA), the International Arrangement on Forests (IAF), and the United Nations Forum on Forests (UNFF).

The UNFF was set up in 2000 as part of the IAF designed to promote the management, conservation and sustainable development of forests and to strengthen long-term political commitment to this end (Economic and Social Council 2000). The

Forum's initial five-year mandate will expire in 2005. The ITTA, first negotiated in 1983 and renegotiated in 1994 to provide a framework for cooperation on issues concerning tropical timber, is scheduled to expire at the end of 2006.

The UNFF's future was the focus of the UNFF *Ad Hoc* Expert Group on Consideration with a View to Recommending the Parameters of a Mandate for Developing a Legal Framework on All Types of Forests (AHEG-PARAM), which met in September 2004 (UNFF 2004a). This issue was also discussed at the UNFF's fourth session in May (UNFF 2004b).

To date there is no all-embracing and legally binding international instrument regulating all aspects of sustainable forest use in all parts of the world. Two major options were proposed during the AHEG-PARAM. One is to build on the existing IAF. Experts in the AHEG-PARAM reached common ground on the objectives and content of a future IAF. Many emphasized the need to strengthen the IAF, and to fully implement existing commitments in the global forests policy arena. The instrument to accomplish these goals will be decided on at UNFF's fifth session in May 2005.

AUGUST

SEPTEMBER

animals to enter the Frozen Ark will include the yellow seahorse, scimitar horned oryx and Partula snails.

Australia's Great Barrier Reef becomes the world's largest marine protected area. A new zoning plan increases the Marine Park and World Heritage Area's 'no-take' zones, where all types of extraction are banned, from 4.5 per cent to 33.3 per cent of the reef.

The Olympic Games take place in Athens, Greece. The games' environmental strategy includes efforts to improve green spaces, environmental awareness and performance, waste management and recycling, environmentally friendly transportation, and biodiversity protection initiatives.

The Economic Cooperation Organisation (ECO) – a regional trading group in Central and Western Asia – and UNEP agree to joint action to promote

renewable energy sources, toughen green laws and encourage eco-friendly tourism in the area.

The first assessment of the state of the environment of the Democratic People's Republic of Korea (DPRK) is launched by UNEP and DPRK officials.

The Joint Monitoring Programme on Water Supply and Sanitation of WHO and UNICEF releases *Meeting the MDG Drinking-Water and Sanitation Target: A Mid-*

Term Assessment of Progress. The report provides the latest data on how countries are making progress on their national commitments to improve international water and sanitation goals.

Earthdive, an initiative in which professional and amateur divers will help record the health of the marine environment including coral reefs, mangrove swamps and coastal waters, is launched by UNEP-WCMC.

Environment ministers and senior officials from around the Pacific meet in Pape'ete, French Polynesia, to discuss the critical challenges facing Pacific countries and territories. The meeting strongly endorses a new action plan for managing the environment of the Pacific islands region.

The Antarctic Treaty Secretariat is established and begins work in Buenos Aires, Argentina.

The first Conference of the Parties to the Rotterdam Convention meets in Geneva, adding 14 additional chemicals to the Convention, and successfully adopting decisions required to make the legally binding PIC Procedure operational.

The other option is to develop a new legally-binding international instrument, such as a Forest Convention, or a Forest Protocol to an existing instrument like the CBD. Many participants in the debate recognize that a combination of both these approaches could be developed (Mankin 2004).

Meanwhile a number of endangered timber species received international protection. The 13th meeting of the Conference of the Parties of the Convention on International Trade in Endangered Species of Wild Fauna and Flora (CITES) decided to control trade in several Asian yew trees and ramin, a major export timber (CITES 2004).

PROTECTING BIODIVERSITY AND BIOSAFETY

A number of new initiatives were strengthened in 2004 aimed at preserving biodiversity on land and in marine ecosystems, both in wild species and those cultivated in human agriculture. With the conclusion of negotiations on the ballast water convention (**Box 4**), the entry into force of the International Treaty on Plant Genetic Resources for Food and Agriculture (ITPGRFA) and the outcomes of the first Meeting of the Parties to the Cartagena Protocol on Biosafety (**Box 5**), the international community has added new dimensions to global efforts in protecting biodiversity.

The year 2004 also saw some developments in the areas of biotechnology, including a signaling of support for the use of biotechnology by the UN Food and Agriculture Organization (FAO) and emerging political interest, particularly for boosting agricultural productivity in Africa.

The International Treaty on Plant Genetic Resources for Food and Agriculture

Following seven years of negotiations, ITPGRFA entered into force in June. This represents a milestone in international efforts to conserve plant genetic resources.

Genetic diversity of food plants is the basis for food production throughout the world. But agricultural biodiversity is in sharp decline due to the effects of modernization, changes in diets and increasing population density. Today, only 150 crops feed most of the world's population, and just 12 crops provide 80 per cent of dietary energy from plants. Rice, wheat, maize, and potato alone provide 60 per cent, and often just a few modern varieties dominate (FAO 2004a).

Farmers in developing countries often cannot afford expensive external inputs such as fertilizers, pesticides or hybrid seeds. Plant genetic diversity of both wild and semi-domesticated food sources is therefore a crucially important part of their farming systems (Goote and Lefeber 2003). It allows them to select varieties adapted to local conditions such as drought or low nutrients, or crops that can serve as alternatives in times of scarcity (Koziell and McNeill 2002). It also provides the genetic storehouse for development of future food crops and varieties.

The ITPGRFA is a legally-binding instrument, aiming to ensure that plant genetic resources will be conserved, used for sustainable agriculture and food security, and that their benefits will be fairly distributed (Commission on Genetic Resources for Food and Agriculture 2004).

The following interest groups benefit from the treaty:
- Consumers, because of a greater variety of foods and other agriculture products, as well as increased food security;

Genetic diversity in maize.
Source: CIMMYT

The Third International Nitrogen Conference, in Nanjing, China, issues the Nanjing Declaration urging policy makers to optimize nitrogen management in food and energy production, while minimizing its environmental impacts, such as eutrophication of ecosystems and damage to the ozone layer.

The first Global Women's Assembly on Environment: Women as the Voice for the Environment (WAVE) is held at UNEP headquarters in Nairobi, organized by the Network of Women Ministers for Environment and UNEP.

The Nobel Committee announces that Professor Wangari Maathai, Assistant Minister of Environment and Natural Resources of Kenya and founder and chair of the Green Belt Movement, is the 2004 Nobel Peace Prize winner.

The 13th Meeting of the Convention on International Trade in Endangered Species of Wild Fauna and Flora is held in Bangkok. Some 1 200 participants from 154 governments and numerous observer organizations agree to strengthen wildlife management, combat illegal trafficking and update the trade rules for a wide range of plant and animal species.

The US introduces new policies to reduce the emission of tiny particulates in recognition of the harmful effects they pose to human health.

The seventh meeting of the Conference of the Parties to the Basel Convention on the Control of Transboundary Movements of Hazardous Wastes and their Disposal meets in Geneva, and decides to apply the terms of the Convention to ship dismantling.

The second session of the Preparatory Committee for the Development of the Strategic Approach to International Chemicals Management (SAICM) takes place in Nairobi. PrepCom2 decides that the SAICM will consist of an overarching policy strategy for international chemicals management, a global plan of action, and a high-level declaration.

The IUCN 3rd World Conservation Congress, held in Bangkok, Thailand, calls for a moratorium on the further release of genetically modified organisms, and establishes the World Conservation Learning Network to build capacity of conservation and development professionals.

First Heads of State Summit on the International Conference on the Great Lakes region of Africa is held in Dar es Salaam, Tanzania.

Launch of the *Arctic Climate Impact Assessment* (ACIA) report by the Arctic Council and the International Arctic Science Committee. The assessment finds that the Arctic is warming much more rapidly than previously known, at nearly twice the rate of the rest of the globe.

Launch of the *Arctic Council's Arctic Human Development Report*, the first comprehensive assessment of human conditions in the entire circumpolar region.

- The scientific community, through access to the plant genetic resources crucial for research and plant breeding;
- International Agricultural Research Centres, whose collections the treaty puts on a safe and long-term legal footing;
- Public and private sectors, which are assured access to a wide range of genetic diversity for agricultural development;
- Farmers and their communities, through the Farmers' Rights provisions. These rights include: intellectual property protection of traditional knowledge relevant to plant genetic resources for food and agriculture; the right to participate equitably in sharing benefits from the use of plant genetic resources; and the right to participate in making decisions, at national level, on the conservation and sustainable use of plant genetic resources; and
- The environment, and future generations, because the treaty will help conserve the genetic diversity necessary to face unpredictable environmental changes, and future human needs.

Parties to the treaty must guarantee access to genetic resources and share the commercial and other benefits arising from their use. They have the right to receive seeds of crop species covered by the treaty from public institutions in any other contracting country, free of charge and not subject to individual bilateral negotiation. This represents a significant step forward from the provisions in the CBD, which required plant breeders to negotiate on a bilateral basis with the country of origin.

Another key aspect of benefit sharing is that, in some cases, people who commercialize plants bred with material from the Multilateral System for Access and Benefit Sharing (set up under the treaty and covering 35 food crops and 29 forage crops) will be required to pay an equitable share of the monetary benefits to a trust fund. Proceeds from the fund will be used to help developing countries improve the conservation and sustainable use of plant genetic resources (Commission on Genetic Resources for Food and Agriculture 2004).

Box 4: New regulations to keep invasive species out of ballast water

In February 2004, the International Convention for the Control and Management of Ships' Ballast Water and Sediments was adopted at a Diplomatic Conference attended by representatives from 74 states.

Every year an estimated 3 to 10 billion tonnes of ballast water is carried round the globe (IMO 2004). It is taken on by ships to provide balance and stability, but aquatic species are also inadvertently taken on board and can travel thousands of kilometres before being dumped at the port of destination. It is estimated that at least 7 000 different species are being carried in ships' ballast tanks around the world (Global Ballast Water Management Programme 2004). When organisms are dumped in waters similar to their origin, they can become established in the new environment (Wittenberg and Cock 2001). The problem is getting worse as globalization multiplies international trade – over 90 per cent of the world's traded goods are carried by sea (IMO 2004).

One the most infamous introductions via ballast water was that of the zebra mussel into the Great Lakes in North America. The mussel polluted local water supplies and damaged underwater infrastructure. Cleanup costs totalled almost US$1 billion between 1989 and 2000 (IMO 2004).

The new treaty, sponsored by the UN's International Maritime Organisation (IMO), was 10 years in the making. Its first tier of regulations applies to all ships, while the second tier gives countries the option to take additional precautions before allowing ships into their ports. Countries agreed on a phase-in period for different regulations, between 2009 and 2016, giving shipping companies time to comply. Starting in 2009 ships will have to ensure that ballast discharges contain fewer than 10 viable organisms larger than 50 μm/m^3. The challenge ahead is to achieve the ratifications needed: for the treaty to enter into force, 30 countries representing 35 per cent of the world's shipping tonnage must approve it (IMO 2004).

Debating the role of biotechnology in agriculture

The issue of food security will continue to be a key global concern in coming decades, given declining investment in agricultural research and infrastructure, increasing water scarcity, and the challenges posed by HIV/AIDS and climate change.

The debate on the role of biotechnology continued to be highly polarized in 2004. Some consider biotechnology as the next Green Revolution, while others caution against potential risks for human health and the environment.

DECEMBER

The Russian Federation deposits its instrument of ratification for the Kyoto Protocol.

In Prague, Czech Republic, the 16th Meeting of Parties to the Montreal Protocol on Substances that Deplete the Ozone Layer fails to conclude discussions on methyl bromide and decides for the second time in its history to hold an additional 'extraordinary' MOP.

The Intergovernmental Panel on Climate Change meets in New Delhi to discuss the scope, content and process for its Fourth Assessment Report.

The United Nations Secretary General's High-level Panel on Threats, Challenges and Change recommends policies and UN changes to improve human security. Among its recommendations are incentives for the further development of renewable energy sources, a phasing out of environmentally harmful subsidies, and negotiations on a new long-term strategy for reducing global warming beyond the period covered by the Kyoto Protocol.

The AMAP Assessment *Heavy Metals in the Arctic* reports increasing mercury levels in marine birds and mammals in the Canadian Arctic and West Greenland. It argues that excess exposure to mercury must be addressed by reducing worldwide emissions.

World observes the 20th anniversary of the Bhopal disaster that took place on 2 December 1984.

In Buenos Aires, Argentina, the tenth session of the UN Framework Convention on Climate Change marks the tenth anniversary of the entry into force of the UNFCCC. COP-10 adopts the Buenos Aires Programme of Work on Adaptation and Response Measures and opens the way for new types of Clean Development Mechanism projects related to small-scale forestry.

An undersea earthquake measuring 9.0 on the Richter scale takes place in the Indian Ocean off the northern coast of Sumatra, Indonesia, generating tsunami waves and causing one of the deadliest natural disasters in modern history. The tsunami waves devastate the shores of Indonesia, Sri Lanka, India, Thailand, the Maldives and other countries as far as the east coast of Africa killing over 220 000 people and leaving millions homeless.

Box 5: Protecting against the risks of Living Modified Organisms

The Cartagena Protocol on Biosafety is the only international instrument dealing exclusively with living modified organisms (LMOs). It aims to protect biodiversity from the potential risks of LMOs. It focuses specifically on transboundary movements, and takes into account risks to human health. The protocol establishes an advance informed agreement procedure for imports of LMOs for intentional introduction into the environment, and also incorporates the precautionary approach and mechanisms for risk assessment and risk management. The protocol establishes a clearinghouse to facilitate information exchange. It contains provisions on capacity building and financial resources with special attention to developing countries and those without domestic regulatory systems. By November 2004 there were 110 parties to the protocol.

The Meeting of the CBD COP, serving as the first meeting of the parties to the protocol, in Kuala Lumpur in February 2004, established a framework for implementation. The parties adopted an interim identification system to strengthen the safe handling of genetically engineered organisms. This system requires identification and contact information for all bulk shipments of genetically modified or living modified organisms intended for processing, feed or food.

Key issues that still need to be resolved include the percentage of modified material that these shipments may contain and still be considered GMO-free, and the inclusion of any additional detailed information. These matters will be considered at the next meeting of the parties in June 2005. The first meeting also adopted procedures and mechanisms for promoting compliance with the protocol and assisting countries in cases of non-compliance. A 15-member Compliance Committee will submit regular reports and recommendations to the meeting of the parties. A negotiating group of legal and technical experts on liability and redress for damages resulting from transboundary movements of LMOs was also launched and requested to develop a regime by 2008.

Source: CBD 2004d

In its 2003–04 *State of Food and Agriculture* report, the FAO signalled qualified support for the potential benefits of agricultural biotechnology in improving agricultural productivity for developing countries (FAO 2004b). A letter to FAO, signed by more than 650 civil society organizations and 800 individuals from over 80 countries, criticized the report for supporting the biotech industry, arguing that access and distribution play a far greater role than technology in food security (GRAIN 2004).

This statement sparked a counter-response, signed primarily by free enterprise institutes and biotechnology stakeholders. This letter commended FAO for its balanced approach, and for acknowledging biotechnology's potential to increase food security, food safety and economic opportunities for smallholder farmers in developing countries (International Consumers 2004). The Ecological Society of America has also recognized the potential of genetically engineered organisms in sustainable agriculture, though it strongly recommends a cautious approach to releasing such organisms into the environment (ESA 2004).

The year 2004 also saw shifting governmental responses to the biotechnology issue. The European Union ended its *de facto* moratorium on genetically modified organisms, while the United States increased its promotion of biotechnology as a valuable weapon in the fight against hunger. The US Embassy to the Holy See organized a conference entitled Fighting a Hungry World: The Moral Imperative of Biotechnology. The aim was to influence the Vatican, which has not yet taken a position on the issue (US Embassy to the Holy See 2004).

Possibly the most significant shift in favour of agricultural biotechnology was seen in Africa. A number of key initiatives and meetings took place, including the launch of the African Agricultural Technology Foundation and the convening of the Conference on Assuring Food and Nutrition in Africa by 2020 in Kampala (IFPRI 2004).

At the sub-regional level, four West African presidents signalled cautious support for genetically modified crops in solving food production problems, at the Ministerial Conference on Science and Technology held in Ouagadougou in June (USDA 2004). More mixed views on the issue were expressed by Southern African countries during the African Policy Dialogues on Biotechnology held in Harare in September (APDB 2004). Underscoring the need to move forward on policy options, the Secretariat of the New Partnership for Africa's Development (NEPAD) and the African Union Commission agreed in July to establish a high-level panel of experts to prepare a comprehensive African strategy on biotechnology (NEPAD 2004).

Box 6: Global community urges efforts to protect deep sea ecosystems

It is only in the last decade that scientists have had the technology needed to study deep sea ecosystems. These environments have high and often endemic biodiversity, but they are slow-growing and fragile. This makes them especially vulnerable to physical damage, particularly by bottom trawl fishing, deep-sea oil and gas development, and mining (Freiwald and others 2004; Gianni 2004; Rogers 2004).

A growing number of governments, scientists and conservation organizations are working towards protecting these vulnerable habitats. In February 2004, 1 136 scientists from 69 countries endorsed a statement calling for urgent action to protect deep sea ecosystems. The scientists appealed to the UN and other international bodies to establish a moratorium on high seas bottom trawling and called on governments to ban the practice in deep sea ecosystems within their Exclusive Economic Zones (MCBI 2004). Australia, Canada, New Zealand and Norway have already begun implementing such measures.

The Seventh Conference of Parties of the Convention on Biological Diversity also called for urgent action to address threats to marine biodiversity in deep sea areas and urged the UN General Assembly to take relevant measures (CBD 2004c). During the IUCN World Conservation Congress in November, governments and NGOs alike voted in favour of urging the UN General Assembly to adopt a resolution calling for a moratorium on high seas bottom trawling.

CHALLENGES FOR THE FUTURE

2005 will see the United Nations completing ten-year reviews of key environmental and sustainable development agreements on disaster reduction and Small Island Developing States. There will also be key meetings of the Conferences of Parties of conventions on wetlands, migratory species and desertification. 2005 also sees the start of the United Nations Decade of Education for Sustainable Development, with UNESCO as the lead agency and UNEP as a key partner.

During the next two years the future of international forest governance will need to be determined. As new technologies come on line the issue of biotechnology is likely to present broadening challenges. Though Kyoto is an important step, responses to climate change will remain a perennial issue in coming decades.

As always, the effort towards sustainable development is a continuing struggle, and if it is to succeed it must be a collective one, involving international bodies, individual governments, civil society and the private sector in all nations.

REFERENCES

APDB (2004). Second Session of the African Policy Dialogues on Biotechnology, http://www.ifpri.org/africadialogue/events/20040920.asp

Bøggild, C.E., Mayer, C., Podlech, S., Taurisano, A. and Nielsen, S. (2004). Towards an assessment of the balance state of the Greenland Ice Sheet. *Geological Survey of Denmark and Greenland Bulletin*, 4, 81-4. http://www.geus.dk/departments/quaternary-marine geol/icemon/icemon_publ_2004_1.pdf

CBD (2004a). *CBD COP Decision VI/26: Strategic Plan for the Convention on Biological Diversity*. http://www.biodiv.org/decisions/default.aspx?m=COP-06&id=7200

CBD (2004b). *CBD COP Decision VII/32: The programme of work of the Convention and the Millennium Development Goals*. http://www.biodiv.org/decisions/default.aspx?m=COP-07&id=7769&lg=0

CBD (2004c). *CBD COP Decision VII/5: Marine and coastal biological diversity. Convention on Biological Diversity*. http://www.biodiv.org/decisions/default.aspx?m=COP-07&id=7742&lg=0

CBD (2004d). *Report of the First Meeting of the Conference of the Parties serving as the Meeting of the Parties to the Protocol on Biosafety*. http://www.biodiv.org/doc/meetings/bs/mop-01/official/mop-01-15-en.pdf

CCSP (2004). *Our Changing Planet: U.S. Climate Change Science Program for Fiscal Year 2004 and 2005*. U.S. Climate Change Science Program. http://www.usgcrp.gov/usgcrp/Library/ocp2004-5/default.htm

Chinese Academy of Sciences (2004). *Chinese Glacier Inventory*. World Data Center for Glaciology and Geocryology, Lanzhou. http://wdcdgg.westgis.ac.cn/DATABASE/Glacier/glacier_inventory.asp

CITES (2004). Decisions concerning the proposal to uplist Gonystylus spp. *13th meeting of the CITES COP. Convention on International Trade in Endangered Species of Wild Fauna and Flora*. http://www.cites.org/eng/cop/13/sum/E13-ComIRep9.pdf

Commission on Genetic Resources for Food and Agriculture (2004). *The International Treaty on Plant Genetic Resources for Food and Agriculture*. http://www.fao.org/ag/cgrfa/itpgr.htm

Economic and Social Council (2000). *Report of the fourth session of the Intergovernmental Forum on Forests*. Economic and Social Council of the United Nations. 18 October 2000, E/2000/L.32. http://ods-dds-ny.un.org/doc/UNDOC/LTD/N00/660/38/PDF/N0066038.pdf?Open Document

EEA (2004). *Impacts of Europe's Changing Climate*. European Environment Agency. http://reports.eea.eu.int/climate_report_2_2004/en/tab_content_RLR

ESA (2004). *Genetically Engineered Organisms and the Environment: Current Status and Recommendations*. Ecological Society of America. http://www.esa.org/pao/esaPositions/Papers/geo_position.htm

FAO (2004a). *Treaty on Biodiversity to become Law*. Food and Agriculture Organization. http://www.fao.org/newsroom/en/news/2004/39887/index.html

FAO (2004b). *The State of Food and Agriculture 2003-2004*. Food and Agriculture Organization. http://www.fao.org/docrep/006/Y5160E/Y5160E00.HTM

Feely, R.A., Sabine C.L., Lee K., Berelson W., Kleypas J., Fabry V.J., and Millero, F.J. (2004). Impact of Anthropogenic CO_2 on the $CaCO_3$ System in the Oceans. *Science*, 305, 362-6.

Freiwald A., Fossa J., Grehan A., Koslow T. and Roberts J. (2004). *Cold-water Coral Reefs: Out of Sight – No Longer Out of Mind*. United Nations Environment Programme/World Conservation Monitoring Centre. http://www.unep-wcmc.org/press/cold-water-coral-reefs/CWC_LR.pdf

GAA (2004). *Global Amphibian Assessment*. http://www.globalamphibians.org/

Gianni, M. (2004). *High Seas Bottom Fisheries and their Impact on the Biodiversity of Vulnerable Deep-Sea Ecosystems*. IUCN/NRDC/CI/WWF. http://www.iucn.org/themes/marine/pdf/MattGianni-CBDCOP7-Impact-HS-BottomFisheries-Complete.pdf

Global Ballast Water Management Programme (2004). *The Problem*. GEF/UNDP/IMO Global Ballast Water Management Programme, Programme Coordination Unit, International Maritime Organization. http://globallast.imo.org/index.asp?page=problem,htm&menu=true

Goote, M. and Lefeber R. (2004). *Compliance Building under the International Treaty on Plant Genetic Resources for Food and Agriculture*. Background paper 20. FAO Commission on Genetic Resources for Food and Agriculture, Rome.

GRAIN (2004). *NGOs' open letter to Mr. Jacques Diouf, FAO Director General: FAO declares war on farmers, not on hunger*. http://www.grain.org/nfg/?id=180

IFPRI (2004). *Conference on Assuring Food and Nutrition in Africa by 2020*. International Food Policy Research Institute. http://www.ifpri.org/2020 africaconference/index.htm

Imhoff, M. L., Bounoua, L., Ricketts, T., Loucks, C., Harriss, R. and Lawrence, W. (2004). Global patterns in human appropriation of net primary productivity, *Nature*, 429, 24 June 2004, 870-3.

IMO (2004). International Convention for the Control and Management of Ships' Ballast Water and Sediments. http://www.imo.org/Conventions/mainframe.asp?topic_id=867

IEA (2004). Renewable Energy – Markets and Policy Trends in IEA Countries. International Energy Agency. http://www.iea.org/Textbase/press/pressdetail.asp?PRESS_REL_ID=128

International Consumers (2004). NGOs in support of FAO report, "Agricultural biotechnology: meeting the needs of the poor?" An open letter to Mr. Jacques Diouf, Director General of UN Food and Agriculture Organization. http://www.internationalconsumers.org/faoletter.htm

Knutson, T. and Tuleya, R. (2004). Impact of CO_2-Induced Warming on Simulated Hurricane Intensity and Precipitation: Sensitivity to the Choice of Climate Model and Convective Parameterization. *Journal of Climate*, 17, 18, 3477-95.

Koziell, I., and McNeill, C.I. (2002). *Building on hidden opportunities to achieve the Millennium Development Goals. Opinion: World Summit on Sustainable Development*. UNDP. http://www.undp.org/equatorinitiative/pdf/poverty_reduction.pdf

Krivova, N.A., and Solanki, S.K. (2004). Solar variability and global warming: A statistical comparison since 1850. *Adv. Space Res.*, 34, 361-4

Mankin, B. (2004). *The IAF at the crossroads: Tough choices ahead*. WWF Forests for Life Programme. http://www.panda.org/downloads/forests/iaftoughchoices 30aug04.pdf

MCBI (2004). *Scientists' Statement on Protecting the World's Deep-sea Coral and Sponge Ecosystems*. Marine Conservation Biology Institute. http://www.mcbi.org/DSC_statement/sign.htm

NEPAD (2004). *NEPAD/AU moving forward on science and technology – Panel of experts to prepare strategy*. NEPAD Communications and Outreach. http://isa-africa.com/english/nepad/news130804.htm#Article2

NOAA (2004). *Climate Monitoring and Diagnostic Laboratory Carbon Cycle Greenhouse Gases*. http://www.cmdl.noaa.gov/ccgg/iadv/index.php

OECD (2004). *Statement adopted by the OECD's Development Assistance Committee (DAC) at its High Level Meeting, 15-16 April 2004*. http://www.oecd.org/dataoecd/42/26/31505731.pdf

Rogers A. (2004). *The Biology, Ecology and Vulnerability of Deep-Water Coral Reefs*. International Union for the Conservation of Nature. http://www.iucn.org/themes/marine/pdf/AlexRogers-CBDCOP7-DeepWaterCorals-Complete.pdf

Secretariat of the International Conference for Renewable Energies (2004). *International Action Programme*. International Conference for Renewable Energies, 1-4 June 2004, Bonn. http://www.renewables2004.de/pdf/International Action Programme.pdf

SFC (2004). Global warming lawsuit accuses 5 power plants. *San Francisco Chronicle*. July 22 2004

Scott, P.A., Allen, M. R. and Stone, D.A. (2004). The human contribution to the European heatwave of 2003. *Nature*, 432:610-4

Stuart, S.N., Chanson, J.S., Cox, N.A., Young, B.E., Rodrigues, A.S.L., Fischman, D.L. and Waller, R.W. (2004). Status and Trends of Amphibian Declines and Extinctions Worldwide. *Science*, 2004 0: 11035381-0

Thomas, C., Cameron, A., Green, M., Bakkenes M., Beaumont L., Collingham Y., Erasmus B., De Siqueria M., Grainger A., Hannah L., Hughes L., Huntley B., Van Jaarsveld A., Midgley G., Miles L., Ortega-huerta M., Peterson A., Phillips O., and Williams S. (2004). Extinction risk from climate change. *Nature*, 427, 145-8

Thomas, R., Rignot E., Casassa, G., Kanagaratnam, P., Acuna, C., Akins, T., Brecher, H., Frederick, E., Gogineni, P., Krabill, W., Manizade, S., Ramamoorthy, H., Rivera, A., Russell, R., Sonntag, J., Swift, R., Yungel, J. and Zwally J. (2004). Accelerated Sea-Level Rise from West Antarctica. *Science*, 306, 255-8

UNDESA (2004). *World Urbanization Prospects: The 2003 Revision* http://www.un.org/esa/population/publications/wup2003/2003WUPHighlights.pdf

UNEP (2000). *Action on Ozone*. United Nations Environment Programme, Nairobi

UNEP (2004a). *Report of the First Extraordinary Meeting of the Parties to the Montreal Protocol on Substances that Deplete the Ozone Layer*. UNEP/OzL.Pro.ExMP/1/3. http://www.unep.org/ozone/Meeting_Documents/mop/Ex_mop/1ex_mop-3.e.doc

UNEP (2004b). *Advance Copy of the Report of the Sixteenth Meeting of the Parties to the Montreal Protocol on Substances that Deplete the Ozone Layer*. UNEP/OzL.Pro.16/17. http://www.unep.org/ozone/Meeting_Documents/mop/16mop/16mop-17.e.doc

UNFF (2004a). *Report of the Ad Hoc Expert Group on Consideration with a view to Recommending the Parameters of a Mandate for Developing a Legal Framework on All Types of Forests*. New York, 7-10 September 2004. United Nations Forum on Forests. http://www.un.org/esa/forests/adhoc-param.html

UNFF (2004b). *Report on the fourth session (June 2003 and 3 to 14 May 2004)*. E/2004/42; E/CN.18/200413. United Nations Forum on Forests. http://www.un.org/esa/coordination/ecosoc/report.forests.2004.pdf

UN-HABITAT (2004). *State of the World's Cities 2004/2005 – Globalization and Urban Culture*. UN-HABITAT, Earthscan, Nairobi

USDA (2004). *Ministerial Conference on Harnessing Science and Technology to Increase Agricultural Productivity in Africa: West African Perspectives*. Burkina Faso. http://www.fas.usda.gov/icd/stconf/event6.html

US Embassy to the Holy See (2004). *Feeding a Hungry World: The Moral Imperative of Biotechnology*. http://vatican.usembassy.it/policy/events/biotech.asp

Wittenberg, R., and Cock, M.J.W. (2001). *Invasive alien species. How to address one of the greatest threats to biodiversity: A toolkit of best prevention and management practices*. CAB International, Wallingford, Oxon, UK http://www.hear.org/pier/pdf/gisp_toolkit.pdf

Africa

When Professor Wangari Maathai, Kenya's Assistant Minister of Environment and Natural Resources, won the 2004 Nobel Peace Prize, Africa's environmental agenda gained international attention and environment was affirmed as key to peace and security. At the same time, natural disasters and conflicts competed for headline attention with the region's cooperative policy initiatives. Wildfires and the worst locust plague for 15 years recalled the challenges that constantly stalk sustainable development efforts in Africa.

Professor Wangari Maathai, with United Nations Secretary General Kofi Annan during his visit to Nairobi to attend a UN Security Council meeting in November.
Source: UNEP DCPI

Key Facts

- The number of people in Africa who depend on biomass fuels is expected to increase from an estimated 580 million in 2000 to about 820 million in 2030. Most of this demand is for cooking and heating.

- More than 500 million people in Africa have no electricity. This figure is projected to jump to approximately 650 million people by 2030.

- The region needs about US$210 billion investment in the electricity sector, over the next 30 years, to meet projected demand and improve current services.

- By the end of June 2004, a total of 19 African countries had ratified the Rotterdam Convention on the Prior Informed Consent Procedure for Certain Hazardous Chemicals and Pesticides in International Trade, which came into force on 24 February 2004. By the end of July 2004, 22 African countries had ratified the Stockholm Convention on Persistent Organic Pollutants.

Sources: African Union 2004a and b, AMCEN 2004, IEA 2002, PIC Secretariat 2004, POPs Secretariat 2004

WANGARI MAATHAI WINS NOBEL PEACE PRIZE

Professor Maathai scored several firsts with her Nobel Peace Prize: she was the first environmentalist to win; also the first African woman, and the first Kenyan to win the award. The prize acknowledged a passionate lifelong fight for the environment and justice, and remarkable contributions to sustainable development, democracy and peace.

"Peace on Earth depends on our ability to secure our living environment," the Norwegian Nobel Committee said on announcing the award in early October. "Maathai stands at the front of the fight to promote ecologically viable social, economic and cultural development in

Box 1: Wildfires in Africa

Every year, large parts of Africa experience widespread wildfires, and tens of thousands of fires are detected by satellite (see figure). On 5 August 2004, no less than 12 000 wildfires could be detected by satellite in Southern Africa alone (Earth Observatory 2004a). Many African farmers and herders intentionally set fire to dry savannah grasslands. Together with blazes touched off by lightning, these fires are necessary to maintain the fire-climax vegetation of the savannah ecosystem. In addition, nutrients are released from the ash and returned to the soil, and new grass growth is stimulated.

However, these fires are a major source of air pollution. A thick pall of smoke chokes regional skies for weeks during the fire season. The smoke is laced with gases such as nitrogen oxides, carbon monoxide, and hydrocarbons. Not only are these pollutants in their own right, they also react under the intense heat and sunlight to form ground-level ozone, which can lead to respiratory diseases and cause serious damage to crops (Earth Observatory 2004a).

Source: Earth Observatory 2004a

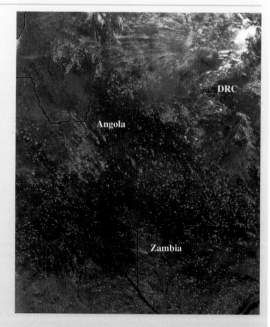

NASA's Moderate Resolution Imaging Spectroradiometer (MODIS) on NASA's Aqua satellite captured this image on 5 August 2004, showing fires across parts of Democratic Republic of Congo (top), Angola (left), and Zambia (bottom), in south-central Africa. Large-scale burning can have a strong impact on weather, climate, human and animal health, and natural resources.
Source: Earth Observatory 2004a
Image courtesy of MODIS Rapid Response Project at NASA/GSFC

Figure 1: The locust invasion in Western and Northern Africa in September and October 2004

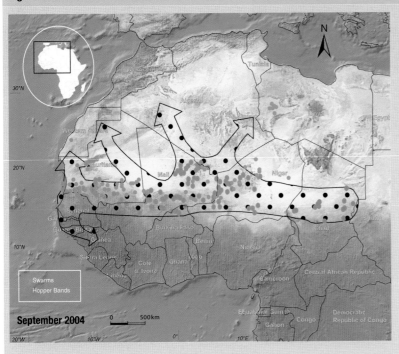

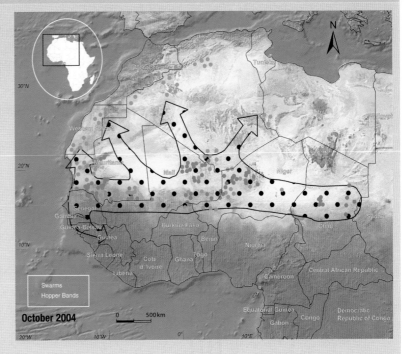

More than 10 countries in these African sub-regions were affected by the invasion – the worst since 1986–89.

Source: FAO-Desert locust information service 2004

Kenya and in Africa. She has taken a holistic approach to sustainable development that embraces democracy, human rights and women's rights in particular. She thinks globally and acts locally" (Nobel Committee 2004).

For decades, Professor Maathai has been a strong opponent of forest destruction and the private grabbing of public land, and a vigorous advocate for democracy and environmental protection. She founded Kenya's Green Belt Movement, which has planted more than 30 million trees throughout Africa (Green Belt 2004).

The Nobel Peace Prize goes alongside many other accolades Professor Maathai has received over the years, including a UNEP Global 500 award, the Goldman Environment Prize and the Sophie Prize, which she received in March 2004 "for her fearless fight for the protection of the environment, human rights and promotion of democratic governance in Kenya."

DESERT LOCUST INVASION

A locust invasion across much of Northern and Western Africa threatened millions of people in more than 10 countries with food insecurity (**Figure 1**).

Desert locusts periodically invade Northern Africa and the Sahel region – the last plague was between 1986–89. In 2004, locusts started invading the Sahel region from the end of June, with Mauritania, Mali, Senegal and Niger the worst affected. More than 2.5 million rural households were at risk of food shortages as over four million ha of crops and farmland were devastated by the swarms. In Mauritania about 1.6 million ha were invaded and an estimated 80 per cent of crops were destroyed (FAO 2004a). The invasion also affected national economies. For example, Morocco spent about US$30 million in defence of an agricultural sector worth US$7 billion in 2002, US$1 billion of which are export earnings (FAO 2004b).

Ironically, good rains, which would normally boost agricultural production, also provided

ideal weather conditions for the locusts to multiply. The desert locust has been described as a pest of unusually destructive powers (FAO 2004b). A tonne of locusts – just a small part of an average swarm – eats the same amount of food in a day as 2 500 people. Each swarm is composed of millions of insects, sometimes covering several square kilometres. One swarm spotted in northern Mauritania during the invasion was 70 km long. Adult locusts can fly over 200 km per day (FAO 2004a).

The Food and Agriculture Organization of the United Nations (FAO) appealed to the international community for US$100 million to help contain the locusts (FAO 2004a). Control involves spraying, and to reduce risks to human health and the environment FAO has promoted the use of pesticides that usually degrade in a week. FAO and governments in the region are seeking even safer replacements, testing a fungus that attacks locusts in the field, and a natural hormone that disrupts the insects' normal behaviour (FAO 2004a).

A goat herd runs away from a swarm of desert locust near Kaedi, Mauritania. Livestock are in competition with the insects for available grazing land.

Source: FAO Photo Gallery

The Centre for Ecotoxicological Research in the Sahel, established in Senegal in 1991 with FAO assistance, helps governments to monitor the risks to environmental and human health from pesticides. It also helps governments to establish safety measures, to check people's health, and to ensure the safe handling of pesticide residues. The centre also trains national environmental monitoring teams and collaborates with national chemical laboratories and other institutions such as universities (FAO 2004c).

POLICY INITIATIVES

Conflicts, particularly in the Western Sudanese region of Darfur, overshadowed other developments in the news headlines. However, positive and high profile efforts at environmental cooperation continued, such as the African Ministerial Meeting on Energy in May and the 10th regular session of the African Ministerial Conference on the Environment (AMCEN) in June. In the Great Lakes region, leaders of 11 countries met in Dar es Salaam in November at the International Conference on the Great Lakes.

A large range of issues was discussed including peace and security, democracy and good governance, economic development and regional integration, and humanitarian and social issues. Environment was a crosscutting theme in all these areas, and featured prominently in preparatory meetings and the conference itself.

Energy

More than 70 per cent of Africans still rely on traditional biomass fuels such as wood, charcoal, and plant residues to meet their domestic energy needs (African Union and others 2004). The numbers depending on these fuels are expected to increase from an estimated 580 million in 2000 to about 820 million in 2030 (IEA 2002). Fuelwood consumption is also growing, with charcoal use increasing even more rapidly because of urbanization (CIFOR 2003).

These developments have a powerful impact on biodiversity. Fuelwood collection, including charcoal production, and the harvesting of non-woody vegetation, are a key element in loss of habitat area, affecting 15 per cent of globally threatened birds (BirdLife International 2004).

The African Ministerial Meeting on Energy in May aimed to speed up the development and implementation of sound policies and

Box 2: Chemicals management

At a regional meeting in Nigeria in May 2004, African governments adopted a position on the Strategic Approach to International Chemicals Management (SAICM) – a tool to advance the sound management of chemicals for sustainable development in the region.

The African position emphasized that SAICM should, among other activities:

● Manage chemicals at all stages of their life cycle, using the principles of 'cradle-to-grave' life cycle analysis;

● Target the most toxic and hazardous chemicals as a priority;

● Ensure full integration of chemicals management and better coordination among stakeholders;

● Increase chemical safety capacity at all levels;

● Ensure that children and other vulnerable populations are protected from the risks of chemicals;

● Promote corporate social responsibility and develop approaches that reduce human and environmental risks for all, rather than transferring the risks to those least able to cope with them;

● Incorporate the principles of substitution, prevention, polluter pays, right to know, and greening of the industry; and

● Integrate the precautionary, life cycle, partnership, liability and accountability approaches.

The statement urges that SAICM should be established at national, regional and international levels as a coordinating structure for harmonizing legal instruments and organizations responsible for chemicals management.

Source: UNEP 2004

strategies for sustainably managing the region's energy resources. The meeting adopted an African Statement on Renewables, calling on development partners to help Africa develop and manage its renewable resources sustainably. The statement was targeted at the

International Conference for Renewable Energies in Bonn in June 2004 (African Union and others 2004). In the International Action Programme adopted at the conference, the African Development Bank committed itself to a programme to alleviate poverty by providing improved access to electricity in Africa, with special focus on renewable energy and energy efficiency (International Conference for Renewable Energies 2004).

Box 3: New law tackles genetically modified organisms

South Africa's National Environmental Management: Biodiversity Act 2004 kept the issue of genetically modified organisms (GMOs) high on the agenda. Most of the environmental concerns about GMOs are based on the possibility of gene transfer from one organism to another, possible undesirable effects of exotic genes or traits (for example, insect resistance or herbicide tolerance), and possible effects on non-target organisms.

The new law identifies the handling of GMOs, along with alien species, as a key management issue. It requires an environmental impact assessment to be approved before the government will permit any GMO to be released into the environment, either on a trial or a general basis.

Source: Government of South Africa 2004

Environment ministers address chemicals management

At the 10th African Ministerial Conference on the Environment (AMCEN) session held in the Libyan Mediterranean city of Sirte, African environment ministers adopted several important decisions. One of these concerned the development of a Strategic Approach to International Chemicals Management (SAICM).

The ministers noted the link between poverty and vulnerability to toxic chemicals, as well as the impact of toxic chemicals on biodiversity. They endorsed and encouraged participation of all stakeholders in developing a SAICM, especially in sectors such as agriculture, environment, health and industry. The AMCEN decision on chemicals endorsed recommendations made at the African regional meeting on international chemicals management (**Box 2**).

The year also saw significant policy successes at sub-regional and national levels, such as the establishment of the Zambezi Watercourse Commission, and South Africa's National Environmental Management: Biodiversity Act 2004 (**Box 3**).

Zambezi Watercourse Commission adopted

Following 23 years of on-and-off negotiations, seven of the eight riparian states in the Zambezi River Basin agreed to create the Zambezi Watercourse Commission (ZAMCOM). The signatory states are Angola,

Botswana, Malawi, Mozambique, Namibia, Tanzania, and Zimbabwe (Zambezi Watercourse Commission 2004). Only Zambia has yet to sign the agreement.

The commission will strengthen transboundary cooperation in the whole basin, which drains a total of about 1.3 million square kilometres (Nhamo 1998) and is home to more than 40 million people (Chenje 2000). The commission will facilitate collection, evaluation and dissemination of data and information on the basin, and promote, support, coordinate and harmonize water resources management and natural resource conservation (Zambezi Watercourse Commission 2004).

CHALLENGES FOR THE FUTURE
Policy decisions during the year represent real gains, but the major challenge is to transform policy into meaningful action. The implementation of the decisions of the energy ministers meeting and the 10th AMCEN session as well as the full establishment of ZAMCOM are some of the immediate needs.

REFERENCES

African Union (2004a). *List of Countries which have Signed, Ratified/Acceded to Bamako Convention on the Ban of the Import into Africa and the Control of Transboundary Movement of Hazardous Wastes within Africa*. http://www.africa-union.org/home/Welcome.htm

African Union (2004b). *List of Countries which have Signed, Ratified/Acceded to the Revised African Convention on the Conservation of Nature and Natural Resources*. http://www.africa-union.org/home/Welcome.htm

African Union, Uganda Ministry of Energy and Mineral Development, Kenya Ministry of Energy, UNEP, UNECA, Secretariat of the UN Convention to Combat Desertification, and the German Ministry of Economic Cooperation and Development (2004). Renewable Energy in Africa: Challenges and Opportunities. *African Ministerial Meeting on Energy, 7-8 May 2004*, Nairobi

AMCEN (2004). *Decisions of the 10th Regular Session of the African Ministerial Conference on the Environment*. United Nations Environment Programme, Nairobi

BirdLife International (2004). *State of the World's Birds 2004: Indicators for our changing world*. BirdLife International, Cambridge

Chenje, M. (ed.) (2000). *State of the Environment Zambezi Basin 2000*. SADC/IUCN/ZRA/SARDC, Maseru/Lusaka/Harare

CIFOR (2003). *Fuelwood Revisited: What Has Changed in the Last Decade?* CIFOR Occasional Paper No.39. Center for International Forestry Research, Jakarta.

Earth Observatory (2004a). Fires in Southern Africa. *Natural Hazards*. NASA. http://earthobservatory.nasa.gov/NaturalHazards/natural_hazards_v2.php3?img_id=12317

Earth Observatory (2004b). Betsiboka Estuary, Madagascar. NASA http://earthobservatory.nasa.gov/Newsroom/NewImages/images.php3?img_id=16512

FAO (2004a). *FAO intensifies locust campaign in West Africa*. Food and Agriculture Organization, http://www.fao.org/newsroom/en/news/2004/50990/index.html

FAO (2004b). *Hunger in their wake: inside the battle against the desert locust*. Food and Agriculture Organization. http://www.fao.org/newsroom/en/focus/2004/51040/

FAO (2004c). *New ways to tackle locusts – Research targets biological controls*. Food and Agriculture Organization. http://www.fao.org/newsroom/en/focus/2004/51040/article_51053en.html

FAO-Desert locust information service (2004). *The Latest Situation*. Food and Agriculture Organization. http://www.fao.org/news/global/locusts/locuhome.htm

Government of South Africa (2004). *National Environmental Management: Biodiversity Act 2004*. Government of South Africa, Pretoria

Green Belt (2004). *Major Achievements*. Green Belt Movement. http://www.greenbeltmovement.org/Achievements.htm

International Conference for Renewable Energies (2004). *International Action Programme* – International Conference for Renewable Energies, August 30, 2004. http://www.renewables2004.de/pdf/International_Action_Programme.pdf

IEA (2002). *World Energy Outlook 2002*. International Energy Agency. http://www.worldenergyoutlook.org/weo/pubs/weo2002/weo2002.asp

Nhamo, G. (1998). Eight SADC countries share Zambezi River Basin. *The Zambezi Newsletter*, 1, April-June 1998

Nobel Committee (2004). *The Nobel Peace Prize for 2004*. The Nobel Foundation. http://www.nobel.no/eng_lau_announce2004.html

PIC Secretariat (2004). *Signatures and Ratifications*. http://www.pic.int/en/ViewPage.asp?id=345

POPs Secretariat (2004). *Stockholm Convention on Persistent Organic Pollutants*. http://www.pops.int/documents/signature/signstatus.htm

UNEP (2004). *Report of the African Regional Meeting on the Development of a Strategic Approach to International Chemicals Management*, http://www.chem.unep.ch/saicm/meeting/afreg/AbujareportE.doc

Zambezi Watercourse Commission (2004). *Agreement on the Establishment of the Zambezi Watercourse Commission*. Southern African Development Community, Gaborone

Our Changing Environment

Betsiboka Estuary, Madagascar: Flooding and soil erosion

Tropical Cyclone Gafilo hit northern Madagascar on 7 and 8 March 2004. In the cyclone's wake, astronauts aboard the International Space Station documented widespread flooding and a massive red sediment plume flowing into the Betsiboka estuary and the ocean (bottom image). A comparative image (top) taken in September 2003 shows normal water levels in the estuary.

The Betsiboka is the largest river in Madagascar. Its estuary is one of the world's fast-changing coastlines, mainly due to sediment washed from most of the north of the island. Ocean-going ships were once able to travel up the Betsiboka estuary, but must now berth at the coast.

Extensive logging and clearing of Madagascar's rainforests and coastal mangroves have resulted in severe deforestation on Madagascar's western slopes, with very high rates of erosion. The situation is made worse when tropical storms bring severe rainfall, greatly accelerating the erosion and clogging of coastal waterways.

Source: Earth Observatory 2004b

04 Sep 2003

25 Mar 2004

Source: Earth Observations Laboratory, Johnson Space Center. Composition by UNEP/GRID – Sioux Falls

Asia and the Pacific

In 2004, Asia and the Pacific was struck by a massive tsunami (see Indian Ocean Tsunami section) in addition to serious environmental challenges ranging from air pollution and management of toxic wastes, to problems of freshwater and biodiversity. There were also positive policy developments in addressing priority issues through sub-regional cooperation.

DUST AND SAND STORMS

Dust and sand storms are plaguing North East Asia nearly five times as often as in the 1950s, and are also growing in intensity (UNEP 2004a). In April 2002 dust levels in Seoul exceeded 2 000 micrograms per cubic metre, twice the level considered hazardous to health (UNEP 2004a).

The storms originate in the dry regions of northern China and Mongolia and blow across the Korean peninsula and Japan. They cause considerable hardship through disruption of communications, respiratory problems and related deaths, loss of livestock and crops over large areas, and associated loss of income (UNEP 2004a).

To deal with this issue, governments of the region are working together with the Asian Development Bank, the UN Economic and Social Commission for Asia and the Pacific, the UN Convention to Combat Desertification, and the United Nations Environment Programme in monitoring and early warning.

A joint project has been set up to create an initial institutional framework and a master plan to guide regional cooperation to control dust and sand storms in North East Asia (UNEP 2004a).

WASTE MANAGEMENT

Electronic waste (e-waste) – from computers, televisions, telephones, cell phones, electronic toys, and other sources – is posing a new management challenge to Asia and the Pacific. E-waste is currently one of the fastest growing segments of solid waste.

The quantities involved are vast. Four million personal computers are discarded every year in China (UNEP RRCAP 2004). In India e-waste worth US$1 500 million was generated in 2003 (UNEP RRCAP 2004).

Disposal of e-waste is a serious problem, because it often contains toxic substances such as mercury, cadmium and lead which contaminate the environment and pose a danger to human health. It is often buried in

Dust and sand storms like this one in China have increased in North East Asia.

Source: Mylvakanam Iyngararasan/UNEP RRCAP

Key Facts

- The Asia and Pacific region extends over a total land area of 34.6 million km^2, 45 per cent of which is classified as deserts and dryland.

- With 15 per cent of the world's land surface area, Asia and the Pacific receives 22 per cent of global precipitation and has 28 per cent of internal renewable water resources. However, as the region is home to more than half of the world's population, the amount of water resources per inhabitant is around half the world average.

- Development is disparate across the region. Australia, Brunei, Hong Kong, Japan, New Zealand, Republic of Korea and Singapore figure in the list of high Human Development Index (HDI) countries in 2004, while Pakistan and East Timor were among the low HDI countries.

- In 2004, the urban population was 41 per cent of the total. The rate of urbanization was increasing at 2.4 per cent per annum.

- With a population of 3 600 million, this is also the most populous area in the world. Growing at 1.1 per cent a year, the population is projected to reach 4 690 million by 2025.

- In 2002 almost 18 per cent of the Asian population was living on less than US$1 a day, and 49 per cent was living on less than US$2 a day.

Source: ADB 2004, FAO 2004a and b, UNDP 2004a, UNESCAP 2004

Box 1: Regional Centre on Pacific Waste opens in South Pacific

Studies indicate that waste is fast becoming a key problem in Small Island Developing States (SIDS). The wastes threaten not only public health but also livelihoods.

The character of solid waste has changed over the last two decades, from organic wastes associated with agriculture to less biodegradable wastes produced by industry. It is estimated that since the early 1990s the levels of plastic wastes in SIDS has increased five-fold (UNEP 2004b and 2005).

To combat these problems in the South Pacific, a Regional Centre on Pacific Waste began work in July 2004, at the headquarters of the South Pacific Regional Environment Programme (SPREP) in Samoa. Its task is to implement the Basel Convention (on the control and disposal of transboundary movements of hazardous wastes) and the Waigani Convention (to ban the importation into member island countries of hazardous and radioactive wastesand to control the transboundary movement and management of hazardous wastes within the region). The Centre will initiate training, technology transfer and awareness raising for implementation of the Basel and Waigani Conventions in Australia, Cook Islands, Federated States of Micronesia, Republic of Fiji, Republic of Kiribati, Nauru, New Zealand, Niue, Papua New Guinea, Republic of Marshall Islands, Samoa, Solomon Islands, Tonga, and Tuvalu (SPREP 2004).

Giant panda threatened by deforestation and poaching.

Source: Fritz Polking/Still Pictures

landfills, where pollutants can leach into soils and groundwater, or burned in incinerators forming dangerous compounds (UNEP RRCAP 2004). The problem is compounded by unregulated informal sector enterprises which handle e-waste improperly, endangering themselves and the environment.

National level initiatives on e-waste exist in some countries of the sub-region including China, India and Japan. Most initiatives are at the initial stages and require technical assistance and intergovernmental cooperation. So far, there is no regional level intergovernmental initiative on e-waste management in Asia and the Pacific (UNEP RRCAP 2004).

BIODIVERSITY

The year 2004 was marked by favourable trends in sub-regional cooperation (**Box 1**) and the discovery of previously unknown populations of endangered animal and bird species.

A study carried out by United Nations Environment Programme–World Conservation Monitoring Centre, the World Conservation Union (IUCN) and UNESCO found that the majority of moist humid cloud forests are found in Asia and the Pacific, rather than in Latin America as had been previously believed (Bubb and others 2004). Around 60 per cent of the world's cloud forest is found in the region, with Papua New Guinea and Indonesia having high percentages.

As lowland forests are converted to agriculture, the significance of the less accessible cloud forests increases, because they provide forest goods and services, as well as refuges for once widespread forest species. Yet Asia's cloud forests are threatened by timber extraction, road building, collection of fuelwood and charcoal production. The report underlines the vital need for improved monitoring and conservation measures in Asia, including regeneration of damaged and degraded cloud forests, if these precious habitats are to survive the 21st century (UNEP 2004c).

Biodiversity remained under pressure (**Box 2**), but there were some encouraging discoveries and re-discoveries (**Box 3**). In June 2004, a survey carried out by the Chinese forest ministry and the World Wide

Box 2: Critically endangered saiga antelope

The saiga antelope (*Saiga tatarica*) faces imminent extinction. This herding antelope roams the dry steppes and semi-arid deserts of Central Asia and the Russian Federation. It featured prominently in the launch of the 2002 IUCN Red List of Threatened Species, where it was listed under the highest category of threat (CMS 2004).

Saiga numbers have plunged by 95 per cent, from about one million in 1990 to less than 50 000 today. The main cause of this catastrophic decline is poaching for the animal's horn and meat. Poaching is fuelled by widespread poverty arising from major changes in the rural economies of the saiga's main range states – Kazakhstan, Uzbekistan, Turkmenistan and the Russian Federation Republic of Kalmykia (IUCN 2004).

Conservation of the saiga antelope was an issue at the 13th meeting of the Convention on International Trade in Endangered Species (CITES). All the range states were urged to immediately sign the Memorandum of Understanding (MoU) and implement an Action Plan on the Conservation, Restoration and Sustainable Use of the Saiga Antelope. The range states are planning to sign the revised memorandum and Action Plan in early 2005. Only urgent action will protect the saiga from extinction in the wild. The meeting also recommended that the CITES secretariat assist with regular assessment of the implementation of the MoU and the Action Plan (CITES 2004).

Source: CMS 2004

Saiga antelope (*Saiga tatarica*).

Source: Anna Lushchekina

Fund for Nature (WWF 2004) showed that there are nearly 1 600 pandas in the wild – over 40 per cent more than were previously thought to exist. WWF experts believe that the difference is mainly due to better counting rather than an improved environment. The survey pinpointed a number of threats to the long-term survival of this endangered species, including continued deforestation and poaching (WWF 2004).

FRESHWATER

There were several alarming developments threatening freshwater resources. In July, UNDP warned that Lake Balkhash in Kazakhstan could dry up, creating another major environmental crisis in the region (UNDP 2004b). This is the second largest lake in Central Asia after the Aral Sea, which is already drying up.

Lake Balkhash is suffering from industrial pollution and from high usage in China of the river Ili, largest of the seven tributaries that feed into the lake. Kazakhstan's own heavy use of water, especially for irrigation, poses an additional threat (UNDP 2004b).

Box 3: New bird species and sightings

The world's largest population of the critically endangered Gurney's Pitta (*Pitta gurneyi*) has been found in forests adjacent to the proposed Lenya National Park in Southern Myanmar. This bird is sometimes called the 'Jewel-thrush' and is one of the most beautiful and rare birds on Earth. As recently as 2003, the known world population was less than 20 birds. Around 150 new sightings were recorded, suggesting that this new population may number several hundred pairs, offering renewed hope for the species (BirdLife 2004a).

Another welcome discovery was the sighting of at least 28 slender-billed vultures (*Gyps tenuirostris*) in northeast Cambodia – at least four times as many as the previous largest single count in Indochina. White-rumped vultures (*G. bengalensis*) were also seen in the same area. Both species are critically endangered. Altogether more than 120 vultures were seen at this site, the largest single gathering recorded in Indochina during the past 15 years.

Populations of both species, together with the Indian vulture, *G. indicus*, have declined dramatically over the past decade. Research has revealed that these declines are caused by veterinary use of the drug diclofenac. Vultures feeding on carcasses of cattle treated with diclofenac are poisoned and die within a short time (Birdlife 2004b).

In May, a new species of rail, which has been named the Calayan rail (*Gallirallus calayanensis*) was discovered by a team of specialists on the island of Calayan, one of the Babuyan Islands in the northernmost part of the Philippines archipelago. The new species appears to be almost flightless, like its closest relative, the Okinawa rail (*G. okinawae*) from Okinawa Island, 1 000 km to the north. On the basis of its small known population and range size, the Calayan rail appears to qualify as vulnerable on the IUCN Red List of Threatened Species (BirdLife 2004c).

Box 4: Philippines bans commercial logging in storms' wake

A series of tropical storms resulted in catastrophic flooding and massive loss of life across parts of the Philippines. As of 15 December 2004, the disasters left 1 060 people dead, 1 023 injured and 559 missing. An additional 3.6 million people were affected. Some 880 000 people were displaced by floods and are reliant on outside assistance to meet basic needs (WHO 2004).

Four serious storms struck northern and north-central Philippines in close succession, including Typhoon Muifa in mid-November, tropical storm Winnie on 29 November, and Typhoon Nanmadol on 2 December. By far the most damaging of these storms was Winnie, which accounted for over 1 200 of the dead and missing (NASA 2004).

Over the period 16 November to 3 December 2004 the island of Luzon received between 381 and 1 016 mm of rain. The typhoons caused massive and widespread flooding, flash floods and landslides. More than 12 000 homes were destroyed, and there was extensive damage to infrastructure and agriculture (UNICEF 2004).

Officials blamed widespread logging for the landslides that occurred in the wake of the typhoons. In response, the President of the Philippines banned all commercial logging. The government estimates the country's forest cover at seven million ha. The logging ban would affect 18 timber licensing agreements covering just over 800 000 ha (AFP 2004).

Satellite images showing the area around Alitas, north-eastern Philippines, before and after the storm.

Source: UNOSAT 2004

Box 5: Gangotri Glacier recedes

Gangotri Glacier is situated in the Uttarkashi District of Garhwal Himalaya, northern India. With its tributary glaciers, it is one of the largest glaciers in the Himalayas. It has been receding since 1780 although studies show its retreat quickened after 1971. It is currently 30.2 km long and between 0.5 and 2.5 km wide.

The blue contour lines drawn in the image show the recession of the glacier's terminus over time. They are approximate, especially for the earlier years. Over the last 25 years, Gangotri Glacier has retreated more than 850 metres with an accelerated recession of 76 metres from 1996 to 1999 alone.

The retreat is an alarming sign of global warming, which will impact local communities. Glaciers play an important role in storing winter rainfall, regulating water supply through the year, reducing floods, shaping landforms, and redistributing sediments.

Source: Earth Observatory 2004

Source: Image by Jesse Allen, Earth Observatory, based on data provided by the ASTER Science Team. Glacier retreat boundaries courtesy of the Land Processes Distributive Active Archive Center

Another worrying trend is the retreat of glaciers, which has important impacts on stable water resources and flooding in downstream areas (**Box 5**). A study by the Chinese Academy of Science (Tandong and others 2004) shows that glaciers in the High Asia region of Northwest China are retreating under the impact of global warming. The region includes the Tibetan Plateau, the Tien Shan Mountains and the Altai Mountains. The 1990s retreat was the most rapid of the 20th century, and caused an increase of more than 5.5 per cent in the runoff of glacial meltwater in Northwest China (Tandong and others 2004).

CHALLENGES FOR THE FUTURE

The year 2004 showed growing pressures on natural resources, as well as positive trends in conservation and cooperation. Government and civil society partnerships, together with regional agencies, have taken initiatives to promote environmental conservation in the region and these efforts need to be strengthened and multiplied.

REFERENCES

ADB (2004). *Key Indicators 2004: Poverty in Asia: Measurement, Estimates, and Prospects.* Asian Development Bank, Manila

AFP (2004). P*hilippines suspends all logging as aid rushed to storm victims.* Agence France-Presse New York, ReliefWeb. http://wwww.reliefweb.int/w/rwb.nsf/f303799b1 6d2074285256830007fb33f/d98504640aae55ca49256f620011eaf4?OpenDocument

BirdLife (2004a). *World's largest 'Jewel-thrush' population found.* BirdLife International. http://www.birdlife.net/news/news/2004/06/myanmar.html

BirdLife (2004b). *Record vulture count in Cambodia includes Asia's rarest.* BirdLife International. http://www.birdlife.org/news/news/2004/06/cambodia_vulture_news.html

BirdLife (2004c). *Remarkable rail discovered "just in time".* BirdLife International. http://www.birdlife.org/news/news/2004/08/calayan_rail.html

Bubb, P., May, I., Miles, L., and Sayer, J. (2004). *Cloud Forest Agenda.* UNEP-WCMC, Cambridge. http://www.unep-wcmc.org/resources/publications/UNEP_WCMC_bio _series/20.htm

CITES (2004). *Conservation of Saiga tatarica.* Convention on International Trade in Endangered Species of Wild Fauna and Flora. http://www.cites.org/common/cop/13/ raw-docs/IE06.pdf

CMS (2004). *Urgent action for the Saiga Antelope required.* Convention on Migratory Species. http://www.cms.int/news/PRESS/nwPR2004/260504_Saiga_Antelope.htm

Earth Observatory (2004). DAAC Study: Sizing Up the Earth's Glaciers. NASA http://earthobservatory.nasa.gov/Study/GLIMS/

FAO (2004a). TERRASTAT. Food and Agricultural Organisation. http://www.fao.org/ag/ agl/agll/terrastat/wsrout.asp?wsreport=2a&region=1&search=Display+statistics+%21

FAO (2004b). AQUASTAT. Food and Agricultural Organisation. http://www.fao.org/ag/agl/aglw/aquastat/regions/asia/index3.stm

IUCN (2004). *No respite for Critically Endangered Saiga Antelope.* Species Survival Commission. http://www.iucn.org/themes/ssc/news/saiga.htm

NASA (2004). NASA's Earth Observatory. http://earthobservatory.nasa.gov/Natural Hazards/natural_hazards_v2.php3?img_id=12612

SPREP (2004). *Regional Centre on Pacific Waste opens in SPREP.* South Pacific Regional Environment Programme. http://www.sprep.org.ws/article/news_ detail.asp?id=146

UNDESA (1996). Urban Agglomerations, 1950-2015: The 1996 Revision. United Nations Population Division, New York.

UNDESA (2000). World urbanization prospects: The 1999 revision. New York, United Nations Population Division, 2000. 128 p.

UNDP (2004a). *Human Development Report 2004.* United Nations Development Programme, New York

UNDP (2004b). *Water resources of Kazakhstan in the new millennium.* United Nations Development Programme. http://www.undp.kz/library_of_publications/ center_view.html?id=2496

UNEP (2004a). *North East Asian Dust and Sand Storms growing in scale and intensity.* United Nations Environment Programme/Global Resource Information Database. http://www.unep.org/Documents.Multilingual/Default.asp?DocumentID= 389&ArticleID=4401&l=en

UNEP (2004b). *UNEP and Small Island Developing States: 1994 to 2004 and Future Perspectives.* United Nations Environment Programme, Nairobi

UNEP (2004c). *Clarity brought to Earth's cloud forests.* United Nations Environment Programme/Global Resource Information Database. http://www.unep.org/Documents. Multilingual/Default.asp?ArticleID=4355&DocumentID=383&l=en

UNEP (2005). Atlantic and Indian Oceans Environment Outlook. United Nations Environment Programme, Nairobi *In press*

UNESCAP (2004). *ESCAP Population Data Sheet.* United Nations Economic and Social Commission for Asia and the Pacific. http://www.unescap.org/esid/psis/ population/database/data_sheet/2004/index2.asp

UNEP RRCAP (2004). *Ewaste Background Paper.* Regional Resource Centre for Asia and the Pacific, Pathumthani, Thailand

UNICEF (2004). *Philippines: Struggling to recover after storms.* United Nations Children's Fund, ReliefWeb. http://www.reliefweb.int/w/rwb.nsf/f303799b16d 2074285256830007fb33f/95b42abfb283853bc1256f66002c20ea?OpenDocument

UNOSAT (2004). UN Office for Outer Space Affairs. http://unosat.web.cern.ch/ unosat/asp/charter.asp?id=46

USGS (2001) EarthShots:Satellite Images of Environmental Change. USGS http://edc.usgs.gov/earthshots/slow/Beijing/Beijing

WWF (2004a). *New survey reveals nearly 1 600 giant pandas in the wild.* World Wide Fund for Nature. http://www.panda.org/news_facts/newsroom/news.cfm? uNewsId=13641&uLangId=1

Tandong, Y., Youqing, W., Shiying, L., Jianchen, P., Yongping, S., and Anxin, L. (2004). Recent glacial retreat in High Asia and its impact on water resource in Northwest China. *Science in China* (D), 34, 6, 535–43.

Our Changing Environment

Beijing, China: Rapid urbanization

Beijing, the second largest city in China after Shanghai, is the cultural, political, and intellectual centre of the country, as well as a major industrial and commercial metropolis. By the beginning of 2004 the city's population was over 14 million – three million more than a decade ago. The increase was mainly due to in-migration. Satellite towns have been constructed covering an area of more than 200 km². Extremely rapid industrial and commercial development is putting pressure on the city's historical and cultural landmarks, and causing significant loss of productive agricultural land. Like many other large cities, Beijing has also encountered serious pollution problems.

The Landsat images show the city's growth trends and remarkable changes during the era of economic reforms since 1979. The first image shows the status of Beijing before the new economic reforms of 1979. The blue grey area (centre left) shows Beijing, including the Forbidden City. The green hills west of the city are covered with deciduous forests. A mixture of rice, winter wheat and vegetables, represented in a range of colours depending upon the stage of their development, dominates the agricultural lands.

The second image shows how urban growth expanded from the city centre often along major transportation corridors and toward the airport. The suburbs grew rapidly as new construction of institutional, industrial, and residential buildings covered the landscape and resulted in the conversion of prime agricultural land to urban uses. The agricultural lands closest to the city centre that historically were dominated by vegetable and rice production are among the most threatened by commercial and residential development.

Sources: UNDESA 2000 and 1996, USGS 2001

12 Jun 1978

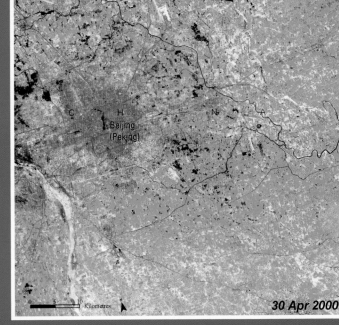

30 Apr 2000

Source: USGS 2001

Europe

With the 2004 European Union expansion from 15 to 25 countries, political and economic integration is increasing in Europe. Recent international environmental agreements for regional seas, mountain areas, and river basins are a further integrating force. Social and economic conditions, however, still vary significantly. Trends in energy, transport, waste, agriculture and tourism all over Europe are expected to have negative impacts on environmental issues such as air, water, climate and biodiversity.

SUSTAINABLE ENERGY: A LONG WAY TO GO

Total energy consumption in Europe has been on the increase again since the mid-1990s and this trend is expected to continue in coming decades. Fossil fuels (especially gas and oil) are expected to remain the largest energy source in Europe for the next 30 years (**Figure 2**). The global warming impacts from this will have widespread social, economic and environmental implications across Europe for a long period to come (**Box 1**).

The Kyoto Protocol is a first step on the road to slowing global warming. It will formally enter into force on 16 February 2005. Current projections show that many Western European countries will not meet their Kyoto targets, while most Central European countries probably will (EEA 2004a). In Eastern European countries, which often have rich energy sources, the link between energy efficiency strategies and environmental issues is not a well-established policy concern as yet (OECD 2004).

In all of Europe, transition to a more sustainable use of energy will require substantial increases in energy savings and energy efficiency, and in use of renewable sources.

The recent steep rise in oil prices and instability in major oil producing regions have improved the prospects for large-scale use of energy conservation techniques and alternative technologies (EPI 2004, Pacala and Socolow 2004). Renewable energy production is increasing rapidly, but because it started from a small base, its proportion of total energy production remains small (**Figure 2**) (EPI 2004). Nuclear energy is

---

Key Facts

- On 1 May 2004, the 15 older European Union (EU) Member States were joined by 10 new Members. This makes the EU the second largest economy after the United States.

- With just over 820 million people (in 2002), Europe has a large and ageing population, which is increasingly healthy and wealthy in much of Western Europe, more and more of Central Europe, but only part of Eastern Europe.

- Almost three-quarters of Europeans live in urban agglomerations, on just 15 per cent of the total land area.

- The EU's ecological footprint is very large and increasing. An area half the size of the new enlarged EU is needed just to cover EU imports of wood and food.

- With economic growth and increased consumption, overall volumes of waste (such as packaging, electronic and hazardous waste) are particularly high in Europe and increasing.

- Energy consumption in Europe is rising, but more slowly than the economy because of rising energy efficiency. Fossil fuels dominate the fuel mix with an 80 per cent share.

- Transport is the largest energy-consuming sector in Europe. In Western Europe it is responsible for around 30 per cent of total energy consumption, compared to around 21 per cent in Central and 19 per cent in Eastern Europe (2002 data).

- Road transport has by far the biggest share of transport energy consumption, being responsible for about 82 per cent in Western Europe, about 86 per cent in Central and 47 per cent in Eastern Europe (2002 data).

- About 41 per cent of the total Western European land area is agricultural land, compared to 54 per cent in Central and only 16 per cent in Eastern Europe. Much of Europe's biodiversity is found on farmland and depends on maintaining certain farming practices.

Sources: EEA 2004a,b and c, FAOSTAT data in GEO Data Portal, IEA 2004, OECD 2004, UNPD data in GEO Data Portal, Van Vuuren and Bouwman 2005

Figure 1: With the 2004 EU expansion and the plans for future enlargements Western and Central Europe are becoming more and more integrated

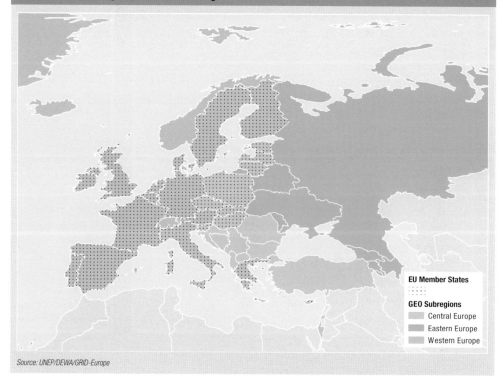

EU Member States

GEO Subregions
- Central Europe
- Eastern Europe
- Western Europe

Source: UNEP/DEWA/GRID-Europe

Windmills old and new, Netherlands.
Source: Frans Lemmens/Still Pictures

Landfill is still the predominant municipal waste treatment option in most countries throughout Europe.
Source: RIVM

projected to decrease slightly, mainly as a result of moratoria and phase-out policies, though some new nuclear power plants are still being connected (IAEA 2004).

Reaching a more sustainable energy system is a task for Europe's society as a whole at regional, national and local levels. It will require changed public attitudes towards consumption, innovative measures by governments and more voluntary action by industry. Policy measures could help by setting long-term targets to provide investment security, supporting innovation and alternative technologies, and adjusting energy prices and subsidies to reflect full environmental costs (EEA 2004a, OECD 2004). In addition, strategies are needed to adapt to unavoidable negative impacts of climate change (EEA 2004d).

MATERIALS AND WASTE

Economic growth and consumption in Europe remain coupled to increased use of materials and generation of wastes (RIVM 2004). Construction and demolition are the leading waste generators in Western Europe, mining and quarrying in Central Europe (EEA 2003). In Eastern Europe, waste generation is on the increase again in most countries: oil industries, mineral extraction and power plants are major waste generators (OECD 2004). Landfill is still the predominant form of municipal waste treatment in all of Europe (RIVM 2004, OECD 2004).

So far, policies to deal with waste have targeted individual waste streams (such as hazardous, packaging or electronic waste), and treatment methods (such as landfill or incineration). In Central and Western Europe, landfill is slowly giving way to incineration. Policies are becoming more comprehensive and integrated, including strategies on waste prevention and recycling and on sustainable use and re-use of resources (RIVM 2004). In Eastern Europe, lack of capacity to monitor and enforce regulation, and of finance to invest in better facilities, results in overloaded, improperly operated municipal waste disposal sites, and in illegal dumping (OECD 2004).

TRANSPORT: FULL-COST PRICING NEEDED

Transport demand continues to grow rapidly in all of Europe and remains a major environmental threat. In Western Europe, freight transport by road continues to grow faster than the overall economy. In Central and Eastern Europe, after the economic stagnation of the 1990s, road transport is increasing again, especially passenger transport (UNEP 2004, EEA 2004c, OECD 2004).

Passenger transport is boosted by increased car use for commuting, leisure and tourism. Freight volumes are increasing due to the EU expansion and the growing internationalization of markets. Other factors boosting freight include new production and delivery structures (outsourcing, low-storage production, decentralization, just-in-time delivery), and new freight services (notably express services).

Figure 2: Total energy consumption for the enlarged European Union, by fuel type

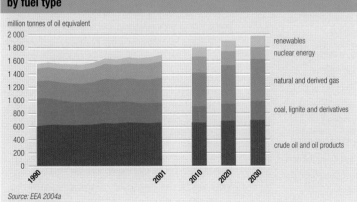

million tonnes of oil equivalent

renewables
nuclear energy
natural and derived gas
coal, lignite and derivatives
crude oil and oil products

Source: EEA 2004a

Box 2: Taxing leaded petrol out of existence

Even at low concentrations lead can cause harmful effects for human health, and can bio-accumulate. In Western Europe, efforts to reduce lead emissions started in the early 1990s, through taxes and regulatory measures. In Central and Eastern Europe, the Sofia Initiative on Local Air Pollution has helped to reduce emissions of lead and sulphur. And the 1999 UNECE/CLRTAP Protocol on Heavy Metals, which deals with controlling emissions, includes lead (UNECE 2004).

Differential taxation of leaded and unleaded petrol is a good example of using market-based instruments to reduce the environmental impact of transport. In Western Europe this has led to a complete phase-out of leaded petrol (EEA 2004b), which is now also absent in nearly all of Eastern Europe (OECD 2004). In Central Europe, the situation varies. Several countries levy higher taxes on leaded than on unleaded petrol, and in some countries leaded petrol is no longer sold (EEA 2004b).

Figure 3: Change in species abundance

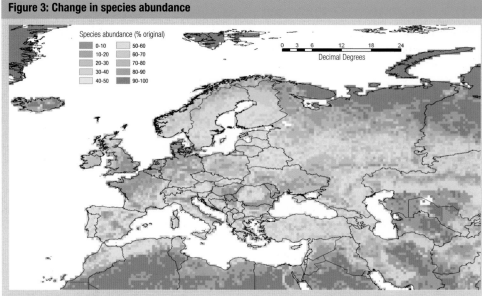

Species abundance (% original)

0-10	50-60
10-20	60-70
20-30	70-80
30-40	80-90
40-50	90-100

Note: The percentages give an indication of the average number of individuals per species still present as compared to the original (undisturbed) number of individuals.

Source: GLOBIO 3

Unsustainable mobility patterns in Europe have increasingly negative impacts on human health, buildings and habitat fragmentation (**Figure 3**). Human health is affected by air pollution problems, as well traffic noise, road accidents, congestion and reduction in physical exercise. Particulate emissions are thought to be responsible for some 120 000 fatalities per year in Western Europe alone (INFRAS/IWW 2004).

Air quality trends in Europe have shown significant improvements, but more reductions are needed (EEA 2004b, OECD 2004). Ground-level ozone still causes serious problems (EEA 2004b, OECD 2004, ESA 2004). Recent monitoring by the European Space Agency (ESA) Earth observing satellite ENVISAT showed large parts of the Netherlands, the German Ruhr area and the Italian Po valley among the areas with the highest NO_2 concentration in the world (ESA 2004).

In reducing the environmental impacts of transport, decoupling transport demand from economic growth is a key challenge all over Europe. Improvements so far can be attributed to voluntary action by the private sector, to EU legislation, and to the 1999 UNECE Convention on Long Range Transboundary Air Pollution. Legislation has stimulated technological innovation to limit emissions, for example, reducing the lead and sulphur content in fuels (**Box 2**).

Most of the measures taken so far have been easy and/or inexpensive. Future innovations should focus on reducing emissions, congestion, noise, road deaths and injuries, and on enhanced mobility opportunities for vulnerable groups in society (WBCSD 2004).

Prices should be adjusted to cover the full external costs caused by transport activities. Improved regulation and financial incentives can promote such price adjustments (EEA 2004a, OECD 2004). In general, financial instruments are more common in Western than in Central or Eastern Europe. Charges and taxes so far mostly concentrate on air pollution in the road sector (**Box 2**) and noise in the aviation sector. Only a few measures have yet been taken to internalize the costs of congestion in urban areas (**Box 3**).

Box 3: Successful road pricing fights congestion in big cities

Concerns over public acceptability and costs to motorists dominate public debate about road pricing across Europe, challenging environmental gains on economic and social grounds. Urban road pricing is nonetheless gaining momentum.

In 2003 the city of London introduced a controversial but eventually very successful congestion charge – a flat-rate charge for daytime travel in central London. After one year's operation this resulted in a 15 per cent reduction in traffic inside the charging zone, and a 30 per cent reduction in traffic delays (TFL 2004). Building on this success, the UK Department for Transport conducted a study to review the feasibility of a national road pricing system. The study concluded that national road pricing is feasible and could meet government objectives (DFT 2004).

Other European cities such as Rome and Oslo have now introduced similar, albeit more modest, initiatives. Copenhagen, Milan and a few smaller cities are likely to follow suit. Recent modelling results for the city of Paris show that, contrary to prevailing wisdom, urban road pricing need not take a greater portion of income from those in lower levels than from those in upper income levels (CERNA 2004).

AGRICULTURE AND BIODIVERSITY IN THE NEW EU

The agricultural sector, is a major source of pressure on Europe's environment. Through trade, European agriculture also has impacts on other regions in the world.

The agricultural scene varies widely in different parts of Europe. In Western Europe, agricultural expenditure is shifting from market support towards subsidies supporting farmers' incomes, and rewarding farmers for being managers of Europe's landscape and environment, rather than just food producers. Furthermore, EU funding for rural development is slowly rising (EEA 2004a).

In Central and Eastern Europe, farming currently involves lower nutrient input, lower productivity, and often land with a higher nature value than in the West (EEA 2004d, EEA/UNEP 2004). With EU enlargement, more stable market returns and new funding will probably induce better-off farmers in Central Europe to expand and intensify (EEA 2004d). At the same time, an ageing population and new economic opportunities in cities may lead to land abandonment (EEA 2004d, OECD 2004). These developments may have impacts on Europe's biodiversity, which is already under high pressure (**Figure 3**).

To reduce the stress on Europe's biodiversity, more agri-environment programmes and support to farmers in less-favoured areas will be needed. In doing so, funds could be better targeted towards high nature value farmland (EEA/UNEP 2004).

CHALLENGES FOR THE FUTURE

Despite the dramatic variations across Europe, the environmental challenges are comparable. Everywhere the goal is to improve management of environmental impacts in all economic sectors, while also taking more responsibility in a global context (EEA 2004a, OECD 2004, RIVM 2004). Central and Western Europe need to build and expand on current policy processes. In Eastern Europe, a key task is to harness the skills and commitment of professionals and citizens more effectively (OECD 2004).

In all of Europe, improvements can be achieved by:
- Increasing use of market-based instruments to manage demand and internalize external environmental costs;
- Switching more extensively to environmentally sound subsidies;
- Promoting innovation; and
- More targeted monitoring of environmental change.

The benefits for the environment and human health will be multi-dimensional, cutting across issues such as climate change, air pollution, biodiversity and air and water quality (EEA 2004a).

Source: NRSC/Still Pictures

Agricultural landscapes in the UK: small and large scale crop cultivation.
Source: P&A MacDonald/Still Pictures

REFERENCES

Alcamo, J., Dronin, N., Endejan, M., Golubev, G., and Kirilenco, A. (2003). *Will Climate Change Affect Food and Water Security in Russia?* Report No. A0302. Centre for Environmental Systems Research. http://www.usf.uni-kassel.de

CERNA (2004). *Equité sociale et péage urbain – une évaluation de huit scénarii pour Paris.* Centre d'Economie Industrielle, Paris

DFT (2004). *Feasibility Study of Road Pricing in the UK.* UK Department for Transport, London

Earth Observatory (2004). Greenhouses of the Campo de Dalías, Spain. NASA. http://earthobservatory.nasa.gov/Newsroom/NewImages/images.php3?img_id=16554

EEA (2003). *Europe's environment: the third assessment.* Environmental assessment report No. 10. European Environment Agency, Copenhagen

EEA (2004a). *EEA Signals 2004.* European Environment Agency, Copenhagen

EEA (2004b). *Air pollution in Europe. 1990-2000.* Topic report No. 4/2003, European Environment Agency, Copenhagen

EEA (2004c). *Impacts of climate change in Europe.* EEA Report No. 2/2004. European Environment Agency, Copenhagen.

EEA (2004d). *Agriculture and the Environment in the EU accession countries.* Environmental issues report No. 37. European Environment Agency, Copenhagen

EEA/UNEP (2004). *High nature value farmland.* United Nations Environment Programme and European Environment Agency, Copenhagen

EPI (2004). *Eco-Economy Indicators.* Earth Policy Institute, Washington D.C. http://www.earth-policy.org/Indicators/index.htm

ESA (2004). *Global air pollution map produced by Envisat's SCIAMACHY.* European Space Agency. http://www.esa.int/esaCP

FAOSTAT data in GEO Data Portal at http://geodata.grid.unep.ch. UNEP/DEWA/GRID-Europe

GLOBIO 3. http://www.globio.info

IAEA (2004). Power Reactor Information System (PRIS). http://www.iaea.org/programmes/a2/index.html

IEA (2004). *IEA Energy Statistics.* International Energy Agency. http://www.iea.org/Textbase/stats/index.asp

INFRAS/IWW (2004) *External Costs of Transport.* INFRAS Consulting Group for Policy Analysis and Implementation. Karlsruhe University, Zurich / Karlsruhe.

OECD (2004). *Taking stock of environmental management challenges in Eastern Europe, Caucasus and Central Asia.* Report for the Conference of EECCA Environment Ministers, Tbilisi, Georgia. Report ENV/EPOC/EAP/MIN(2004)2. OECD, Paris

Pacala, S. and Socolow, R. (2004). Stabilization Wedges. *Science,* 13 August 2004, 305, 968-72.

RIVM (2004). *Outstanding Environmental Issues. A review of the EU's environmental agenda.* National Institute for Public Health and the Environment, Bilthoven

TFL (2004). *Congestion Charging: Update on Scheme Impacts and Operations.* Transport for London, London

UNECE (2004). Information on the UN Economic Commission for Europe Convention on Long Range Trans-boundary Air Pollution. http://www.unece.org/env/

UNEP (2004). *GEO Year Book 2003.* United Nations Environment Programme, Nairobi

UNPD data in GEO Data Portal at http://geodata.grid.unep.ch. UNEP/DEWA/GRID-Europe

Van Vuuren, D. and Bouwman, L. (2005). Exploring past and future changes in the ecological footprint for world regions. In print

WBCSD (2004). *Mobility 2030: Meeting the challenges to sustainability.* World Business Council for Sustainable Development, Geneva

Our Changing Environment

Almeria, Spain: From fields to greenhouses

The sunny south of Spain offers more to the national economy than simply tourism. Over the past 50 years, the small coastal plain of Campo de Dalias, some 30 km southwest of the city of Almería, has been intensively developed for agriculture.

The area has a dry, mild, Mediterranean climate and is further sheltered on the north by the Sierra de Gador mountains. With just slightly more than 200 mm of annual precipitation to support crop growth, the area also relies on groundwater fed by small stream aquifers from the mountains to the north.

Over the past three decades the land-use pattern has changed dramatically. In the image from 24 June 1974, mixed landuse including urban development and agriculture occupy the Campo.

Since then agriculture has shifted from open fields to the greenhouse production of early and out-of-season vegetables – including lettuce, cucumbers, watermelons, beans, squash, cucumbers, peppers, and tomatoes. The greenhouses are mostly unheated.

In the image of 18 July 2004, note the dense, bright pattern of thousands of greenhouses extending from the shoreline right up to the base of the mountains and even into some of the smaller valleys. Salt pan operations can also be seen in the long coastal lagoons (bottom).

There are now an estimated 20 to 40 000 ha of greenhouses in the Campo de Dalías, the largest concentration in the world. Their produce accounts for over US$1.5 billion in economic activity. Over 2.7 million tonnes of produce are grown in the plain each year.

Source: Earth Observatory

24 Jan 1974

18 Jul 2004

Source: Earth Observatory 2004

Images provided courtesy UNEP/GRID – Sioux Falls

Latin America and the Caribbean

The region remains vulnerable to natural hazards. The wider Caribbean Region was hit once more by storms and hurricanes with a higher number of victims than in previous years. There was also the occurrence of the first major scale cyclone in the South Atlantic, and continuation of human-induced fires with strong effects on biodiversity, air quality and climate.

The countries in the region have been implementing important initiatives and investing their resources to tackle these conditions. Brazil, Mexico, and Venezuela have strengthened programmes to combat forest fires in order to reduce environmental and socio-economic impacts of forest fires. The Brazilian government has launched the Action Plan for the Prevention and Control of Deforestation in the Legal Amazon, the largest effort ever undertaken in the country against deforestation (Presidência da República Casa Civil 2004).

FRAGMENTATION: A GROWING THREAT TO BIODIVERSITY

Much of the attention given to biodiversity loss has centred on the threat to wilderness areas. New studies in the region, however, show that fragmentation of ecosystems into smaller patches is a major problem.

Islands of natural vegetation, surrounded by areas that have been deforested, burnt or used for agricultural and livestock production, are more and more common, especially in Central American tropical forests, the Amazon, the Cerrado (Brazilian savannah) and the areas that remain of the 'Mata Atlántica' forest in Brazil. It is estimated that only 43 per cent of the original area of the Cerrado (1.96 million km2) and 8 per cent of the Atlantic forest region (1.10 million km2) in Brazil remain, and much of these areas exist only in remnant patches of various sizes (Lopes 2004).

When large forest blocks are broken into smaller ones, not all species are included in all the remaining patches. Rare species and those requiring large areas of habitat are especially vulnerable. Among tree species, because of differences in seed dispersion, slow growing species are lost, while opportunistic species become more

common. The life span and reproductive capabilities of mature specimens are affected, along with flows of biomass and dead organic matter, mainly plant litter (Tabarelli and others 2004).

These patches also suffer an 'edge effect' from juxtaposition with a contrasting environment, most commonly cropland or grassland. For example, large trees die three times faster in areas less than 300 metres from the edge of the patches (Laurence and others 2000). Species unable to tolerate the altered microclimate in these edge areas, or facing too much competition from other species, are driven back into a reduced area, while species from outside invade and become more common.

Fragmentation also allows more human access to the forests, leading to increased subsistence and industrial logging, hunting and resource gathering. Human-induced fires are also more frequent. All of these contribute to the decline of many species. For example, new estimates show that

35 per cent of the tree species in the remaining areas of the Atlantic forest of northeast Brazil are likely to become extinct if the current rate of fragmentation continues (da Silva and Tabarelli 2000).

Fragmentation creates gaps between forest blocks that reduce the movement of species, so there have also been some local extinctions of vertebrate species that help disperse plant seeds. This has reduced the

Patches of tropical rain forest in Brazil.
Source: Rainer Wirth

Key Facts

- Latin America and the Caribbean is the region with the highest inequalities in the world. The poorest 10 per cent get only 1.6 per cent of the total income, while the wealthiest 10 per cent get 48 per cent.
- The region is now 75 per cent urbanized. There are 409 million people in the cities and 127 million in the rural areas. In rural areas the poor make up almost 40 per cent of the population, considerably higher than in urban areas.
- Some 47 per cent of the regional land area is covered by forests. The future of the forests in the region is hardly promising. Nearly 57 per cent of the Cerrado, a dry forest in Brazil, has disappeared already and if current conditions prevail, it could disappear totally by the year 2030.
- Protected areas constitute a high proportion of the total area: 13 per cent in Mesoamerica, 28 per cent in the Caribbean, and 20 per cent in South America. It is estimated that only 6 per cent of the marine areas in the Caribbean are protected effectively.
- More than 60 per cent of coffee and 50 per cent of soy beans in the global market come from the region. Cultivation of soy has become a key cause of agricultural land encroachment on natural areas in tropical and subtropical regions of South America.
- Organic agriculture has made headway: the region has at least 5.8 million certified hectares – 24 per cent of the world's total. Argentina has the largest certified organic cropland in the region (and the second largest in the world after Australia).
- All the countries in Latin America and the Caribbean, except Grenada, Guyana, and St. Vincent and the Grenadines, have signed and/or ratified the Stockholm Convention on Persistent Organic Pollutants which entered into force on 17 May 2004.

Sources: CEPAL 2003, Chape and others 2003, De Ferranti and others 2003, Dirven 2004, FAO 2004, FAOSTAT 2004, GEO Data Portal, Machado and others 2004, UNDESA 2004, Willer and Yussefi 2004

Box 1: Relaunching the Treaty of Amazon Cooperation

In September 2004, ministers of foreign affairs from the member countries of the Amazon Cooperation Treaty Organization (ACTO) – Bolivia, Brazil, Colombia, Ecuador, Guyana, Peru, Suriname and Venezuela – produced the 'Manaus Declaration'. The treaty aims to coordinate activities for development and conservation of the 7.5 million km^2 of Amazon rainforest.

In the declaration, the states reiterate their responsibilities to promote the economic and social development of the region and the protection of its cultural and environmental patrimony for the benefit of their populations. They aim to establish cooperation programmes and declare a common interest in issues such as defence and internal security, social development, infrastructure and physical integration, trade and integration, science and technology, protection of biodiversity and intellectual property.

The original treaty produced little tangible result since its signing in 1978. But in 2004 the Secretariat of ACTO was established, headquartered in Brazil. It has signed agreements and implemented projects to promote sustainable development in the Amazon. ACTO has also secured approval of a Strategic Plan outlining actions to be undertaken to the year 2012 by the foreign ministers. The plan establishes four strategic themes, six priority areas of action, and the instruments needed to meet these objectives. Other key developments include:

● Approval for agreements with the Andean countries and the countries of the Plata River Basin;

● Launch of a plan to develop sustainable indicators for the Amazon (with FAO help); and

● Agreement with UNCTAD to promote biotrading, which aims to stimulate trade and investment in biological resources and to further sustainable development, with conservation of biological diversity and equitable sharing of the benefits.

Sources: ACTO 2004a and b

Figure 1: Cyclone Catarina in the South Atlantic ocean, nearing the Brazilian coast in March 2004

Source: NASA Satellite Photo

rate of plant reproduction further. Fragments smaller than 100 ha typically lose half of their bird species within 15 years (Ferraz and others 2003). Agoutis, primates and fruit-eating birds such as toucans and aracaris are often affected. Fragmentation reduces the genetic flow between isolated populations of a species. In some cases a population as a whole is replaced by other species – including invasive species transported to the area by humans (Lopes 2004, Tabarelli and others 2004).

This understanding demands new perspectives in forest conservation. One response is to establish ecological corridors to allow the movement of fauna and flora between 'islands'. Others include controlling human activity and the entry of invasive species along the edges, controlling fires, and encouraging sustainable land use and local wildlife-friendly management in the adjacent areas. New studies call for a regional conservation approach, going beyond national environmental policies (Lopes 2004).

Countries in Latin America and the Caribbean (LAC) are trying to develop and implement environmental strategies and initiatives of this type. The Mesoamerican Biological Corridor project, a sub-regional project for biodiversity conservation, is being implemented by the Central American Commission for Environment and Development, comprised of ministries of environment and natural resources. Ministers of foreign affairs from the member countries of the Amazon Cooperation Treaty Organization (ACTO) coordinate activities for development and conservation of the Amazon rainforest (**Box 1**).

STORMS AND HURRICANES RETURN WITH MORE FORCE

In 2004, a succession of tropical storms and hurricanes occurred in the Caribbean, the Gulf of Mexico and south eastern United States. In addition, the first ever cyclone in the South Atlantic was recorded.

The tropical hurricane season in the North Atlantic normally begins in early June and lasts until the end of November. During the 2004 season, there were at least 15 events of importance (nine hurricanes and six tropical storms). The most severe of them was Ivan (a category 5 hurricane) with wind speeds of up to 250 km/h causing the death of at least 90 people. In August alone, eight cyclones were recorded, which set a new record for the month (the previous record was seven, in both 1933 and in 1995). This was twice the number predicted for 2004.

The environmental, social and economic impact has been severe, especially in the Bahamas, the Cayman Islands, Cuba, Granada, Jamaica, and Hispaniola. The estimated damage totals at least US$30 billion (US NHC 2004). The human impact was especially serious. When Hurricane Jeanne hit the Dominican Republic and Haiti, more than 2 000 people died due to flooding and other side effects. The direct and indirect impact of Hurricane Ivan on Grenada was estimated at almost US$900 million and the disaster caused a decline in the GNP by an estimated 1.4 per cent compared to 2003 (OECS 2004). Existing vegetation – already weakened by deforestation – was removed from around 90 per cent of wooded areas and river basins. The effects of the hurricane were intensified by housing built in unsuitable sites, poorly built infrastructure and ineffective disaster impact reduction and mitigation measures.

In late March, the South Atlantic experienced the first hurricane observed in 40 years of satellite meteorological surveillance (US NHC 2004). 'Catarina' formed more than 400 km from the South Atlantic Brazilian coast (at about latitude 28° S) and proceeded to the states of Santa Catarina and Rio Grande do Sul with wind speeds of up to 120 km/h. It caused the death of 12 people and damaged or destroyed some 37 400 homes. More than 31 000 people were affected and more than 700 evacuated. Losses in infrastructure were estimated at more than US$340 million, with crop losses estimated at US$34 million (Phillips 2004).

Previously, hurricanes or cyclones of this strength did not occur in the South Atlantic, since the necessary combination of wind and temperature conditions needed to create them were absent. This new event has stimulated research, as some assessments of climate change predict an increased probability of hurricanes. A regional coordination mechanism for forecasting, early warning and tracking is becoming increasingly important, along with capacity building on meteorological and hydrological issues, linked to disaster preparedness and prevention.

FIRE DEVOURS THE FORESTS

Human induced forest fires have become one of the most serious environmental problems in Latin America and the Caribbean, especially in Central America and tropical South America. The fires are started to clear land for agriculture, and promote the growth of new grass for livestock.

Between June and September 2004, more than 137 000 fire hotspots were recorded in Brazil, especially in the Amazon and the Cerrados, gradually moving northeast (PROARCO 2004). In Bolivia at least 25 000 fires were recorded between June and September. At one point, smoke covered an area of about 648 000 km^2 – 59 per cent of

Box 2: Coasts, mangrove forests and coral reefs in the wider Caribbean

The Caribbean's coral reefs have more than 500 species of coral spread over around 26 000 km^2 of Caribbean water. About two-thirds of the reefs are at risk, especially in the eastern and southern Caribbean, the Greater Antilles and Yucatan, where the diversity of species is decreasing and ranges are diminishing. The principal impacts are caused by coastal development, effluents (especially from agricultural activities), overfishing and tourism.

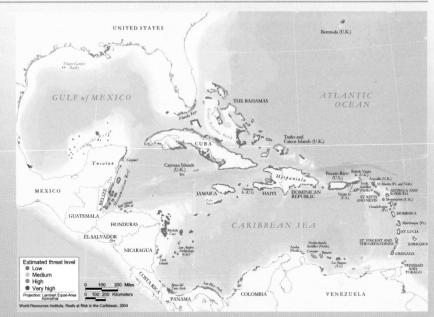

Reefs at Risk Threat Index in the Caribbean.

Source: Burke and Maidens 2004

Coral reefs provide net annual revenues in the Caribbean valued at US$310 million from fishing, more than US$2 billion from dive tourism, and various ecological services such as shoreline protection. However, only 20 per cent of the reefs are within marine protected areas, and only four per cent of them are rated as effectively managed (Burke and Maidens 2004). Mangrove deforestation has adverse effects on coral reefs and reef fish communities, including some species that are commercially important, such as the rainbow parrotfish (*Scarus guacamaia*).

The Mesoamerican Barrier Reef System (MBRS), endorsed by the Central American Environment and Development Commission, aims to improve protection of the unique and vulnerable ecosystems that make up the MBRS. It has four components:

● Protection of marine areas;

● Regional environmental monitoring, and an environmental information system;

● Sustainable use of the MBRS (including sustainable fisheries management and sustainable coastal and marine tourism); and

● Environmental education and public awareness.

Belize, Guatemala, Honduras, and Mexico are involved in this project, supported by the World Bank and the Global Environment Facility.

Thirteen Caribbean nations have also established a joint strategy to reduce the amount of pollutants in waterways that flow into the ocean, in the framework of a GEF project on Integrating Watershed and Coastal Area Management in Small Island Developing States of the Caribbean (IWCAM).

Sources: Burke and Maidens 2004, Mumby and others 2004, UNEP 2005

Bolivia's territory. All the countries in Central America also experience this problem. It is especially serious in Guatemala, where it is estimated that fires affected 300 000 ha during 2004, especially in the Peten rainforest (López 2004). In absolute terms, Honduras follows (with 53 000 ha of affected forestland) and Costa Rica (40 000 ha). However, in relative terms, fires are also a serious problem in El Salvador and Belize.

Although fires occur naturally and in some ecosystems are an essential part of the cycle

Figure 2: Fires in the rainforest areas of Brazil, Bolivia, southern Peru and northern Paraguay on 7 October 2004

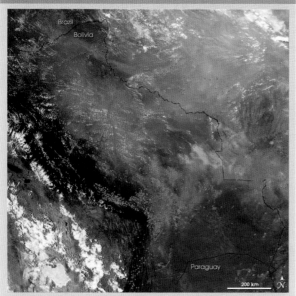

Source: NASA Satellite Photo

of diversity and renewal, excessive fires reduce biodiversity by killing animals and destroying their breeding and nesting sites, their food sources and ultimately – if conversion is permanent – their habitat (SCBD/UNEP 2001).

Fire may have negative effects on regional, continental and global climates. In the case of the Amazon, fires, the loss of forestland and spreading pastures lead to an increase in wind and average temperatures, while evapotranspiration decreases, leading to local climate changes, such as changes in rainfall (Andreae and others 2004). In Brazil, it is estimated that 74.5 per cent of CO_2 emissions and 14 per cent of CH_4 emissions are due to land-use change and forestry. Almost 60 per cent of the net annual CO_2 emissions due to land use change and forestry (1988–94) were from the Amazon (Ministry of Science and Technology 2004). Finally, particulates from fires cause air pollution over thousands of kilometres. For instance, smoke from the Amazon fires reaches the South Atlantic coast and southeast Brazil (Escobar 2004).

Attempts at fire fighting and the introduction of practices that prohibit or regulate field burning have revealed several problems: farmers resist changing their farming practices; there are shortcomings in monitoring and inspection due to limited financial and human resources in environmental and farming agencies; and enforcement by the justice system is lax (Cochrane 2002).

CHALLENGES FOR THE FUTURE

Progress has been made in biodiversity conservation, but the strain on natural resources is still high. Fragmentation of habitat in particular demands new approaches for conservation from a bioregional perspective, and on a continental scale compatible with new economic strategies.

Countries are trying to strengthen their economies by increasing bilateral trade agreements and promoting sub-regional market blocks. This will affect the pace and patterns of natural resources consumption. However, these same efforts of collaboration can help to develop and implement environmental policies and initiatives that cross over national boundaries, such as watershed management and adaptation to climate change impacts.

REFERENCES

ACTO (2004a). *In the pursuit of the Continental Amazon: Country-members join efforts to strengthen ACTO and face the challenges posed by the regional sustainable development.* Amazonian Cooperation Treaty Organization, 1, 1 – June/August, Brasilia, Brazil

ACTO (2004b). *Agreements and Programs.* Amazonian Cooperation Treaty Organization. http://www.otca.info/en/programs-projects/index.php

ANAM (2004) Informe del Estado del Ambiente, Geo Panamá. Autoridad Nacional del Ambiente, Panama City, Panama

Andreae, M. O., Rosenfeld, D., Artaxo, P., Costa, A. A., Frank, G. P., Longo, K. M., and Silva-Dias, M. A. F. (2004). Smoking rain clouds over the Amazon. *Science*, 303, 1337-42.

Burke, L. and Maidens, J. (2004). *Reefs at risk in the Caribbean.* World Resource Institute, Washington, USA

CEPAL (2003). *Panorama social de América Latina 2002-2003.* Comisión Económica para America Latina y el Caribe, Santiago, Chile

Chape, S., Fish, L., Fox, P. and Spalding, M. (2003). *United Nations list of protected areas 2003.* World Conservation Union, United Nations Environment Programme and World Conservation Monitoring Centre, Cambridge, UK

Cochrane, M.A. (2002). *Spreading like wildfire. Tropical forest fires in Latin America and the Caribbean: prevention, assessment and early warning.* United Nations Environment Programme Regional Office for Latin America and the Caribbean, Mexico City

da Silva, J.M.C. and Tabarelli, M. (2000). Tree species impoverishment and the future flora of the Atlantic forest of northeast Brazil. *Nature*, 404, 72-4

De Ferranti (2003). *Desigualdad en América Latina y el Caribe: ¿ruptura con la historia?* World Bank, Washington

Dirven, M. (2004). *La pobreza rural: una situación que perdura*, Notas CEPAL No 33. Comisión Económica para America Latina y el Caribe, Santiago

Escobar, H. (2004). *Os viloes brasileiros do efeito estufa. Estado S Paulo*, Sao Paulo

FAO (2004). *State of Food and Agriculture.* Food and Agriculture Organization of the United Nations, Rome

FAOSTAT (2004a). *Land Use.* Food and Agriculture Organization of the United Nations. http://faostat.fao.org/faostat/collections?subset=agriculture

FAOSTAT (2004b). *Agricultural Data.* Food and Agriculture Organization of the United Nations. http://faostat.fao.org/faostat/collections?subset=agriculture

Ferraz, G., Russell, G.J., Stouffer, P.C., Bierregaard, R.O. Jr, Pimm, S.L and Lovejoy T.E. (2003). Rates of species loss from Amazonian forest fragments. *Proceedings of the National Academy of Sciences*, 100, 24, 14069-73.

GEO Data Portal (2004). http://geodata.grid.unep.ch

Gudynas, E. (2003). Producción orgánica en América Latina, Observatorio del Desarrollo, Centro Latino Americano de Ecología Social, Montevideo

Laurence, W.F., Delamónica, P., Laurence, S.G., Vasconcelos, H.L. and Lovejoy T.E. (2000). Rainforest fragmentation kills big tress. *Nature*, 404, 836

Lopes, R.J. (2004). Diversidade aos pedaços. *Scientific American Brasil*, 3(28): 70-7.

López, M.A. (2004). *Diagnóstico Regional de América Central y México sobre la cooperación internacional en el manejo de incendios forestales. Conferencia Panamericana sobre incendios forestales*, Costa Rica

Machado, R.B. (2004). *Estimativas de perda da área do Cerrado brasileiro.* Conservaçao Internacional, Brasilia

MARN (2003). *Geo Guatemala 2003.* Ministerios de Ambiente y Recursos Naturales, Guatemala

Ministry of Science and Technology (2004). *Brazil's Initial National Communication to the United Nations Framework Convention on Climate Change.* Secretariat of Research and Development Policies and Programs, Brasilia

Mumby, P.J., Edwards, A.J., Arias-González, J.E., Lindeman, K.C., Blackwell, P.G., Gall, A., Gorczynska, M.I., Harborne, A.R., Pescod, C.L., Renken, H., Wabnitz, C.C.C., and Llewellyn, G. (2004). Mangroves enhance the biomass of coral reef fish communities in the Caribbean. *Nature*, 427, 533-6

OECS (2004). *Grenada: Macro-Socio-Economic Assessment of the damages caused by Hurricane Ivan.* Organization of Eastern Caribbean Status, Castries, St. Lucia

Phillips, T. (2004). *Un huracán sin nombre.* Centro Marshall, NASA http://ciencia.nasa.gov/headlines/y2004/02apr_hurricane.htm

Presidência da República Casa Civil (2004). Plano de Ação para a Prevenção e Controle do Desmatamento na Amazônia Legal, Brasilia http://www.presidencia.gov.br/casacivil/desmat.pdf

PROARCO (2004). *Banco de Dados de Queimadas.* Programa de Prevenção e Controle de Queimadas e Incêndios Florestais na Amazônia Legal, Instituto Brasileiro Meio Ambiente. http://www.dpi.inpe.br/proarco/bdqueimadas/

SCBD/UNEP (2001). *Impacts of human-caused fires on biodiversity and ecosystem functioning, and their causes in tropical, temperate and boreal forest biomes.* CBD Technical Series no 5. United Nations Environment Programme and Secretariat of the Convention on Biological Diversity, Quebec

Tabarelli, M., Cardoso da Silva, J.M., and Gascon, C. (2004). Forest fragmentation, synergisms and the impoverishment of neotropical forests. *Biodiversity and Conservation*, 13, 1419-25

UNCTAD (2004). *The Biotrade Initiative.* United Nations Conference on Trade and Development. http://www.biotrade.org/

UNDESA (2004). *World Population Prospects: The 2002 Revision and World Urbanization Prospects: The 2001 Revision.* Population Division of the Department of Economic and Social Affairs of the United Nations Secretariat. http://esa.un.org/unpp

UNEP (2005). *Caribbean Environment Outlook.* Special Edition for the Mauritius International Meeting for the 10-year Review of the Barbados Programme of Action for the Sustainable Development of Small Island Developing States. UNEP, Nairobi

US NHC (2004). *Monthly tropical weather summaries.* July, August, September and October reports. National Hurricane Center. http://www.nhc.noaa.gov/

Willer, H. and Yussefi M. (eds). (2004). *The world of organic agriculture.* International Federation of Organic Agriculture Movements, Bonn

Our Changing Environment

Lake Maracaibo, Venezuela: Invasive species

Lake Maracaibo in northwestern Venezuela is the largest natural lake in South America at 13 330 km². At its widest point, it is more than 125 km wide. It has been suffering from a serious problem of invasive duckweed, a tiny aquatic plant that grows in freshwater. The first image (right), from the Aqua MODIS satellite on 17 December 2003, shows the lake during the winter months, when duckweed is absent from the lake's waters, and the silvery sunglint is absent.

In summer the weed blooms. The true-colour image from 26 June 2004 (bottom left) shows strands of duckweed curling through the lake, floating at the surface or slightly submerged in the brackish water. The lake itself lies in the Maracaibo basin, which is semi-arid in the north, but averages over 1 200 mm of annual rainfall in the south.

A closer look in August 2004 (bottom right) reveals the stranglehold the duckweed has on port areas, especially along the important oil shipping routes in the neck of Lake Maracaibo. Fish and the fishing industry suffer: thick green mats block photosynthesis and alter fish habitats. The weed also adheres to boats, affects cooling systems and obstructs travel.

In September 2004 Venezuela's Ministry of Environment and Natural Resources reported that it had reduced the duckweed area by 75 per cent, using duckweed harvesting machines from the United States. The ministry is investigating using the harvested weed as fodder.

Source: Jeff Schmaltz MODIS Land Rapid Response Team, NASA GSFC http://modis.gsfc.nasa.gov/gallery/individual. php?db_date=2004-07-09#

September update: http://www.vheadline.com/ readnews.asp?id=22759

Source: LPDAAC – USGS EROS Data Centre MODIS imagery

17 Dec 2003

26 Jun 2004

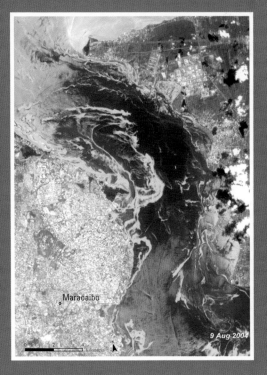

9 Aug 2004

North America

Worrying trends in coastal ecosystems and fisheries were counterbalanced by promising new air quality regulations and a decline in mercury air emissions. The reintroduction of grey wolves to Yellowstone National Park is a symbol of hope and a success story in ecosystem restoration.

OCEAN STRATEGIES

Both Canada and the United States addressed ocean-related issues in 2004.

The last comprehensive US report on oceans, in 1969, noted a wealth of marine resources and suggested increasing their exploitation (Stratton Commission 1969). Since then, poorly coordinated ocean management has led to an alarming deterioration of conditions. Between 2001 and 2004, there were only slight improvements in the country's six coastal regions (**Figure 1**). In a new report released in April 2004 by the US Commission on Ocean Policy, the Commission's chairman noted that "In the United States, we have already depleted some of our major fishery resources, lost treasured recreational areas, and damaged wetlands that help keep our water clean. In many cases we have paid dearly with lost jobs, degraded water quality, increased health care costs, and decreased revenue" (Watkins 2004).

The Commission recommended changes in three major areas:
- Creating a new national ocean policy framework to improve decision-making;
- Strengthening science and generating high quality, accessible information to inform decision makers; and
- Enhancing ocean education to promote a stewardship ethic (US Commission on Ocean Policy 2004).

In response to this report, the US President created a new committee on Ocean Policy in December.

Coastal waters in the US are increasingly subject to low oxygen conditions called 'dead zones' where most marine life cannot survive and reproduce. The Gulf of Mexico, which provides about 18 per cent of the US annual fish catch, is subject to an expanding dead

Key Facts

- Enforcement action by the United States Environmental Protection Agency (EPA) cut pollution by 455 million kg in 2004. This represents a 40 per cent improvement over the reduction in 2000 of 325 million kg.

- According to a nationwide study in 95 large urban communities, changes in ground-level ozone were significantly associated with an increase in deaths in many cities in the United States. The increase in deaths occurred even at ozone levels below the EPA clean air standards.

- The United States and other countries signed the Methane to Markets partnership – an initiative that aims to reduce global methane emissions, to promote energy security, improve the environment, and reduce greenhouse gases. The partnership has the potential to reduce net methane emissions by up to 50 million tonnes of carbon equivalent annually by 2015.

- Canada's new environment minister stressed the need for a business-oriented approach to environment and sustainable development and urged Canadians to build business interests that tie environmental issues to economic development.

- The results of a 10-year study on warming in the Arctic, from an intergovernmental forum of eight governments including Canada and the United States, reveal that the Arctic is warming much more rapidly than previously known, at nearly twice the rate as the rest of the globe.

Sources: EPA 2004f, Bell and others 2004, EPA 2004g, Dion 2004, ACIA 2004

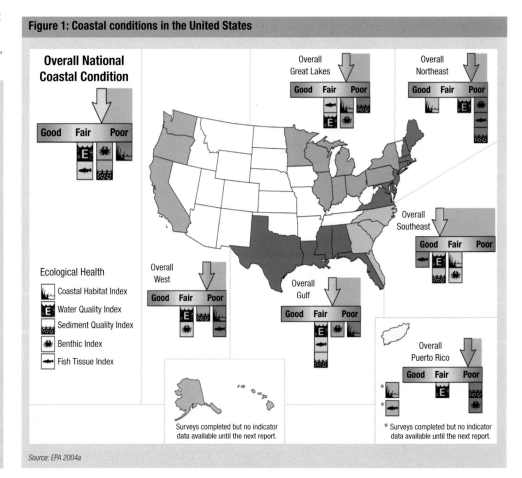

Figure 1: Coastal conditions in the United States

Overall National Coastal Condition — Good Fair Poor

Overall Great Lakes — Good Fair Poor

Overall Northeast — Good Fair Poor

Overall Southeast — Good Fair Poor

Overall West — Good Fair Poor

Overall Gulf — Good Fair Poor

Overall Puerto Rico — Good Fair Poor

Ecological Health
- Coastal Habitat Index
- E Water Quality Index
- Sediment Quality Index
- Benthic Index
- Fish Tissue Index

Surveys completed but no indicator data available until the next report.

* Surveys completed but no indicator data available until the next report.

Source: EPA 2004a

zone that is larger than the state of New Jersey. The main cause is thought to be excess nutrients from fertilizer runoff transported by the Mississippi River, mainly from the Corn Belt (Larsen 2004). A new dead zone off the central Oregon Coast appeared in 2004 for the second time in three years, leading scientists to suspect that a fundamental change in ocean conditions is occurring in the North Pacific Ocean (Stauth 2004).

Innovative programmes are helping to reduce excess fertilizer use and runoff into the ocean. Test programmes run by the American Farmland Trust's 'Nutrient Best Management Practices' achieved declines in fertilizer use of up to 25 per cent (Larsen 2004).

Canada established its own Ocean Strategy in 2002 to overcome governance problems similar to those in the United States. A complex web of laws, regulations and different levels of government had led to deteriorating conditions (Government of Canada 2002). Canada continues to protect cod stocks since their collapse a decade ago. Three more cod fisheries were closed in April 2004, following a decline in stock abundance and numbers of spawning adults, as well as high mortality and low production of juveniles.

In May, officials reported that the entire cod fishery could be eliminated within three to five years if foreign trawlers continue to exploit areas of the Grand Banks off Newfoundland in defiance of an international moratorium (DFO 2004a). After Canada increased inspections, the number of foreign boats fishing off the Grand Banks decreased to 66 between May and August 2004, compared to 93 during the same months in 2003. The action is part of a new federal strategy against overfishing (DFO 2004b).

Fisheries and Oceans Canada announced several policy measures in April. These included:
- An investment of circa US$37 million over two years in community-based economic development assistance;
- Increased conservation measures, including seal exclusion zones and no-trawling zones; and
- A two-year programme of about US$5 million to expand scientific research to evaluate and assess the impact of seals on fish stocks (CNLBSC 2004).

TOXIC RELEASES

Air pollution from power plants was the focus of a 2004 report by the North American Commission for Environmental Cooperation (CEC). Power plants accounted for 46 of the top 50 stationary sources of air pollution in North America in 2001, and they generated 45 per cent of the 755 502 tonnes of toxic air releases (CEC 2004a).

The release of chemicals to the air is the most common type of emission in North America. The largest air release was of hydrochloric acid, primarily from electric utilities burning coal and oil.

There was an encouraging 20 per cent decline in on-site air releases in the United States between 1998 and 2001 (**Figure 2**). The electric utilities industry, the largest source of toxic air releases of any industry sector, reported a decrease of 10 per cent during the period.

In Canada, by contrast, on-site air releases increased by 2.6 per cent over this period.

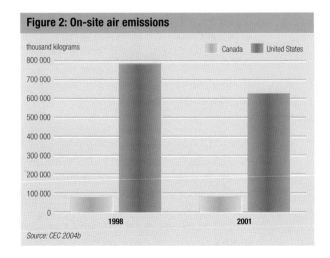

Figure 2: On-site air emissions

thousand kilograms
Canada | United States

Source: CEC 2004b

The paper products industry reported a 5 per cent increase. Factors contributing to the increase included changes in estimation methods, increased production, and new facilities reporting in 2001 (CEC 2004a).

Persistent bio-accumulative toxic chemicals are another significant class of toxic release –

Box 1: Fine particulates – new evidence and new regulations

New policies are being put in place in the United States to reduce emissions of fine particulates, following strong evidence of the threat that they pose to human health.

In 2004, the EPA released the findings of a 5-year intensive research programme on the effect of fine particulate matter ($PM_{2.5}$) on human health in the US. Exposure to ambient particulate matter was associated with increases in respiratory health problems, hospitalizations, and premature deaths. The research also found that fine particles move indoors, that people already suffering from lung disease collect more particles in their lungs, and that $PM_{2.5}$ also affects the heart. The EPA report pointed out that there is a need for improved air quality standards to reduce fine particulates in the air (EPA 2004c).

Three new regulations will soon be in place to help prevent particulates from entering the air:

- Finalization of the United States Clean Air Interstate Rule would reduce emissions of sulphur dioxide (SO_2) and nitrogen oxides (NO_X), the two most important precursors to $PM_{2.5}$. The proposed rule focuses on states whose air pollution causes problems in other downwind states. It requires them to meet specific emission reductions. It covers 29 eastern states and the District of Columbia (EPA 2004d). It was not clear at the time of going to press whether this rule would be enacted;

- By December 2004, the EPA will make final designations identifying places with air quality levels that exceed national standards. The EPA designates an area as 'nonattainment' if it has violated the fine particle standards over a three-year period, or if relevant information indicates that it contributes to violations in a nearby area. In mid-2004, the EPA identified 243 counties, with 99 million inhabitants, where the national air quality standard for fine particulate matter was violated. Within three years, states and local governments must develop implementation plans showing how they will meet the $PM_{2.5}$ standards (EPA 2004e). Environmentalists are pressing for more comprehensive protection, including strengthening the control of power plant emissions, which they say cut short the lives of nearly 24 000 people each year (Schneider 2004); and

- The Clean Air Nonroad Diesel Rule will also help to reduce $PM_{2.5}$. It requires stringent pollution controls on diesel engines used in industries (EPA 2004b).

principally mercury and its compounds (CEC 2004b). Coal and oil-fired power plants accounted for almost two thirds of the 43 384 kg of mercury air emissions from North American industrial facilities. Total releases of mercury fell 48 per cent from 2000 to 2001 (CEC 2004b). In Canada, most mercury emissions come from zinc smelting and garbage incineration (CEC 2004a). Governments in both countries are examining ways to further reduce mercury emissions from coal-fired electrical generation facilities (IJC 2004).

Despite the decrease in emissions, mercury is still building up in the food chain. Micro-organisms in water help convert it to methyl mercury, which travels up the food chain, accumulating in fish and animal tissues. At sufficient levels, it has highly toxic effects for birds and mammals, including brain and nerve tissue damage, cardiovascular effects and kidney damage (IJC 2004). Children exposed to methyl mercury in the womb can have problems later with language, memory, fine motor function, and other neurobehavioral tasks (EPA 2004b).

In March 2004, the EPA and the US Food and Drug Administration issued a joint consumer advisory about the levels of mercury in fish and shellfish, and the quantities and frequency with which they can be eaten safely (FDA and EPA 2004). The goal is to reduce exposure to mercury in women who are, or may become, pregnant, nursing mothers, and young children (IJC 2004).

CANADA'S ONE-TONNE CHALLENGE

In 2004, Canada ranked 12th out of 24 OECD countries in both carbon dioxide emissions per capita and emissions per unit of GDP (Conference Board of Canada 2004). Given its

Box 2: Canada led world growth in forest certification

Worldwide, certified forest areas grew by 31 per cent in 2003 to reach 173 million ha. The increase was mainly due to a doubling of certified lands in Canada, where they totalled 56 million ha (Forest Certification Watch 2004).

North America produced a new wave of policy developments in 2004 aimed at forest certification and responsible procurement.

In the US there were some encouraging major corporate commitments to purchase from sustainably managed sources. Time Inc. announced a paper purchasing policy by which it expects 80 per cent of its fibre purchases to come from certified lands. Office stationery and equipment supplier, Office Depot, announced a paper procurement policy giving preference to third-party certified wood products. Copying and stationery company, Kinko's, issued requirements for forest product suppliers and targets for recycled content (Forest Certification Watch 2004).

Box 3: Wolves improve ecological balance in Yellowstone

The reintroduction of grey wolves (*Canis lupus*) to Yellowstone National Park is stimulating intensive scientific research and heated public debate.

Wolves were once the region's top predator, but in the 1920s they were eliminated because of the danger they allegedly posed to livestock and humans. The results were dramatic: the elk population exploded, preventing regeneration of some tree species, with a cascade effect on the abundance of other animal species such as beaver, trout, and grizzly bear.

To restore the situation, 41 grey wolves from Canada and the state of Montana were moved to the park in 1995–96. Today, there are 306 grey wolves in the Yellowstone region (Smith 2004), and their presence has sparked a dramatic regeneration throughout the ecosystem. For the most part, the wolves are preying on elk and deer. Elk numbers have declined, reducing the grazing pressure on tree seedlings. As a result, there are more trees for beavers, whose dams slow water flows and create pools. This has sparked trout regeneration, helped along by cooler waters due to shade from newly grown trees. Since elk carcasses become food for many scavengers, the wolves' presence has also led to an increase in the numbers of grizzly bears, magpies, ravens, and eagles (Robbins 2004).

Grey wolf (*Canis lupus*).
Source: Gary Kramer courtesy Fish and Wildlife Service

Most conservationists and scientists see this as a unique opportunity to study and document the dramatic effects that reintroduction of a key predator species can have upon an entire ecosystem. But the scheme has faced opposition. Local ranchers are concerned about wolf predation of livestock, while the hunting industry fears a significant decrease in the number of game (Robbins 2004). Interest conflicts have led to protracted legal battles, more than a hundred public hearings, and years of costly scientific studies. On the other hand, early evidence strongly suggests that this is a success story in ecological restoration and scientists and conservationists are keen to continue monitoring the experiment.

commitments under the Kyoto Protocol, Canada is stepping up efforts to curb greenhouse gases (GHGs).

In April 2004, the Canadian government launched a new initiative to increase public participation in combating climate change. The 'One-Tonne Challenge' calls on individual Canadians to cut their annual greenhouse gas emissions by one tonne of CO_2 – 20 per cent of the current average. It makes a range of straightforward suggestions that can help Canadians use less energy, conserve water and resources, and reduce waste. Examples include using public transport more often, draught-proofing homes, using compact fluorescent light bulbs, and composting.

Citizens who sign up to the challenge on the Internet can use an interactive calculator to find out what emissions they produce now, and to plan new actions to reach the one-tonne goal (Government of Canada 2004).

A number of environmental NGOs in North America also have Internet campaigns challenging people to take simple steps with measurable, positive impacts. The Center for a New American Dream suggests that for every participant who signs up and acts on their campaign, there is a reduction of about 1.8 tonnes of carbon dioxide emissions per year (Center for a New American Dream 2004).

CHALLENGES FOR THE FUTURE

New policies and regulations were put in place this year to protect coastal and ocean resources, and to prevent emissions of mercury and particulates that threaten human health. North America needs to act quickly to implement these.

Cooperative efforts to protect and monitor environmental issues and ecosystems shared between Canada and the United States could be stepped up, such as those fostered by the CEC. Canada's progress in forest certification should be emulated by other regions.

REFERENCES

ACIA (2004). *Impacts of a Warming Arctic*. Artic Climate Impact Assessment. Cambridge University Press. Cambridge, UK. http://amap.no/acia/

Bell, M.L, McDermott, A., Zeger, S.L., Samet, J., M, and Dominici, F. (2004). Ozone Levels and Short term Mortality. *Journal of the American Medical Association*, 292 (19), 17

CCRS (2004) Canada Center for Remote Sensing and Natural Resources Canada http://www.ccrs.nrcan.gc.ca/ccrs/learn/tour/36/36que_e.html

CEC (2004a). *Pollutants Backgrounder*. North American Commission for Environmental Cooperation. http://www.cec.org/files/PDF/POLLUTANTS/TS01-backgrounder_en.pdf

CEC (2004b). *Taking Stock 2001: Executive Summary*. North American Commission for Environmental Cooperation. http://www.cec.org/files/PDF/POLLUTANTS/TS2001-Executive-Summary_en.pdf

Center for a New American Dream (2004). *Turn the Tide Campaign*. http://www.newdream.org/tttoffline/index.php

Conference Board of Canada (2004). *Performance and Potential 2004–05: How Can Canada Prosper in Tomorrow's World?* Conference Board of Canada. http://www.conferenceboard.ca/boardwiseii/LayoutRecentPublications.asp

CNLBSC (2004). *Closure of the Cod Fisheries – Action Plan*, Document No. 6145. Canada/Newfoundland & Labrador Business Service Centre. http://www.cbsc.org/nf/search/display.cfm?Code=6145&coll=NF_PROVBIS_E

DFO (2004a). *Government of Canada Announces New Measures to Combat Foreign Overfishing*. Fisheries and Oceans Canada. http://www.nafo.ca/Info/News/Others/goverofCanada.html

DFO (2004b). *Enforcement and Surveillance Measures Changing Fishing Behaviour*. Fisheries and Oceans Canada. http://www.dfo-mpo.gc.ca/media/backgrou/2004/enforcement_e.htm

Dion, Stéphane (2004). *Environmental action for economic competitiveness: Will Canada lead the new Industrial Revolution?* Environment Canada. http://www.ec.gc.ca/minister/speeches/2004/040910_s_e.htm

EPA (2004a). *Draft National Coastal Condition Report II*. US Environmental Protection Agency, Office of Wetlands, Oceans, and Watersheds. http://www.epa.gov/owow/oceans/nccr2/

EPA (2004b). *Fact Sheet: National Listing of Fish Advisories*. EPA-823-F-04-016. US Environmental Protection Agency, Office of Water. http://www.epa.gov/waterscience/fish/advisories/factsheet.pdf

EPA (2004c). *Particulate Matter Research Programme: Five Years of Progress*. US Environmental Protection Agency, Office of Research and Development. http://www.epa.gov/pmresearch/pm_research_accomplishments/pdf/pm_research_programme_five_years_of_progress.pdf

EPA (2004d). *Interstate Air Quality Rule; Basic Information*. US Environmental Protection Agency, Office of Air and Radiation. http://www.epa.gov/air/interstateairquality/basic.html

EPA (2004e). *Fine Particle (PM 2.5) Designations*. US Environmental Protection Agency, Office of Air Quality Planning and Standards. http://www.epa.gov/pmdesignations/documents/120/statusMap.htm

EPA (2004f). *FY 2004 End of Year Enforcement and Compliance Assurance Results Summary*. US Environmental Protection Agency, Office of Enforcement and Compliance Assurance. http://www.epa.gov/compliance/resources/reports/endofyear/eoy2004/fy04results.pdf

EPA (2004g). *Methane to Market Partnership*. US Environmental Protection Agency, http://www.epa.gov/methanetomarkets/basicinfo.htm

FDA and EPA (2004). *FDA and EPA Announce the Revised Consumer Advisory on Methylmercury in Fish*. US Department of Health and Human Services, Food and Drug Administration (FDA) and the US Environmental Protection Agency http://www.fda.gov/bbs/topics/news/2004/new01038.html

Forest Certification Watch (2004). *Forest Certification: 2003 Year in Review*. http://certificationwatch.org/article.php3?id_article=1252

Government of Canada (2002). *Canada's Oceans Strategy: Our Oceans, Our Future*. http://www.cos-soc.gc.ca/doc/pdf/COS_e.pdf

Government of Canada (2004). *One-Tonne Challenge*. http://www.climatechange.gc.ca/onetonne/english/index.asp

IJC (2004). *12th Biennial Report on Great Lakes Water Quality*. International Joint Commission. http://www.ijc.org/php/publications/html/12br/english/report/contents.html

Larsen, J. (2004). *Dead Zones Increasing in World's Coastal Waters*. Earth Policy Institute. http://www.earth-policy.org/Updates/Update41.htm

Robbins, J. (2004). Lessons from the Wolf. *Scientific American*, June 8 2004. http://www.sciam.com/article.cfm?chanID=sa006&articleID=00076914-0667-10AA-84B183414B7F0000&pageNumber=1&catID=2

Schneider, C. G. (2004). *Dirty Air, Dirty Power*. Clean Air Task Force. http://www.cleartheair.org/dirtypower

Smith, D. (2004). Head of the wolf reintroduction project in the Yellowstone. Personal Communication. July 30, 2004

Stauth, D. (2004). *New hypoxic event found off Oregon coast*. Oregon State University News and Communication Services. http://oregonstate.edu/dept/ncs/newsarch/2004/Aug04/hypoxic.htm.

Stratton Commission (1969). *Our Nation and the Sea. A Plan for National Action*, Report of the Commission on Marine Science, Engineering and Resources. United States Government Printing Office, Washington, D.C.

US Commission on Ocean Policy (2004). *Preliminary Report of the US Commission on Ocean Policy – Governors' Draft*. http://oceancommission.gov/documents/prelimreport/welcome.html

Watkins, J. D. (2004). An ocean blueprint for the 21st Century. *Shared Oceans, Shared Future* 9 (1). http://usinfo.state.gov/journals/itgic/0404/ijge/ijge0404.htm

Our Changing Environment

Gaspé Peninsula, Quebec, Canada: Clearcut logging

These images show the impact of clearcut logging in the Gaspé peninsula, Quebec, the Canadian province with the highest total logged area. Historically, forest covered about 95 per cent of the Gaspé Peninsula. Typical tree species include fir, birch and maple.

The left image shows natural forest with some clearcutting, in September 1993. The second image from August 2004 shows clearcutting in the same area, with recent cuts shown in brighter tones. Saplings and ground vegetation emanate brighter greens in less recent cut areas. The uncut, standing forest is a dark green colour. Bright white areas are clouds and black areas are their shadows. More than 40 000 ha have been cleared in the area represented here.

Forests are crucial to Canada's economy and natural patrimony. Canada has about 10 per cent of all the world's forests, and of the country's 909 million ha of land area, 402 million ha are forest and woodland. Of the 145 million ha considered accessible, about one million ha are harvested each year. The forest industry is worth about US$82 billion annually and exports almost US$40 billion. Direct employment in the forest sector in 2003 was some 376 300 person-years.

The practice of clearcutting has serious environmental effects. It can have a major impact on plant and animal biodiversity, soil erosion, and microclimates. By increasing sediment in rivers and increasing water temperatures it can also seriously affect fish such as salmon.

Source: UNEP/GRID – Sioux Falls

2 Sep 1993

15 Aug 2004

Sources: CCRS/NRC 2004, UNEP/GRID – Sioux Falls

West Asia

Two environmental issues dominated in West Asia in 2004: water scarcity in cities and the impact of conflict on the environment. Despite these difficulties, the year also saw increased commitment to biodiversity conservation in the region, highlighted by the re-flooding of the Mesopotamian Marshlands.

Box 1: MDGs in urban areas and integrated water resources management

A comparatively high percentage of people in West Asia has access to water supply and basic sanitation and the region is favourably placed to achieve the Millennium Development Goals (MDGs) for these sectors. These goals aim to halve the proportion of people without sustainable access to safe drinking water and basic sanitation by 2015.

However, the development of integrated water resources management and water efficiency plans between 2000 and 2004 has been slow. They will require effective national institutional frameworks; adoption of national water plans; improvement of irrigation systems; and cooperation in shared river basins. Sound water resources assessment in several countries requires monitoring networks and databases.

Poor water resources management threatens aquatic ecosystems in the region. To protect them, the issues of pollution and increased salinity, recycling of wastewater through treatment and reuse, and water harvesting must be addressed.

An Economic and Social Commission for West Asia report submitted to the 13th Session of the Commission on Sustainable Development underscored the need for sufficient funds, training and credible information. Among its recommendations were the:

● Establishment of an Arab fund to finance preparation and implementation of water development projects;

● Development of a regional programme for education, training and awareness raising; and

● Creation of regional water monitoring and information networks.

WATER SCARCITY AND THIRSTY CITIES

While water scarcity is a chronic problem in West Asia, accentuated water shortage in urban areas in 2004 highlighted how growing demand is pressing on finite supplies. The main pressures boosting demand are rapid population growth, expansion of irrigated agriculture and the fast pace of industrialization (Abu-Zeid and others 2004).

Water shortage means increasing competition for water among the various sectors. Agriculture accounts for 85 per cent of water use in West Asia, domestic use for 10 per cent and industry five per cent. The agricultural share is well above the world average of 70 per cent (ESCWA 2003a, GEO Data Portal 2004).

High population growth (2.6 per cent) and rapid urbanization (ESCWA 2003b) present major challenges in the struggle to meet increasing domestic water demand (**Figure 1**) with scarce public funds (ESCWA 2003a). Although most people have access to clean drinking water and sanitation services (**Box 1**), services are not always reliable – especially in lower-income areas.

Water shortage for domestic use is a problem in key cities in the region, especially Sana'a, Amman and Damascus (Elhadj 2004, ESCWA 2003b). In Yemen, annual water abstraction is running at about one and a half times the rate of recharge, with even higher rates in the Sana'a Basin (World Bank 2003). Rapid population growth (3.6 per cent a year) is outpacing new water supply schemes. Although the city of Sana'a faces severe water shortage, water resources have been increasingly diverted to grow Qat. This narcotic plant consumes about 40 per cent

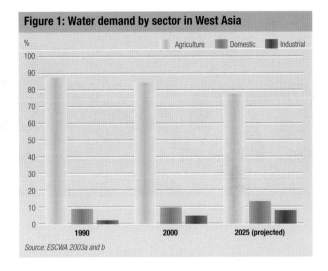

Figure 1: Water demand by sector in West Asia

Source: ESCWA 2003a and b

Key Facts

● Some 80 per cent of the land area of West Asia is classified as semi-desert or desert.
● Five of the 12 countries of West Asia have a per capita water use of less than 500 m³ a year, indicating chronic water scarcity.
● The annual per capita availability of water resources in West Asia is decreasing at an alarming rate. If these resources are developed on a business-as-usual basis, the region will suffer serious water shortages. In the Arabian Peninsula the annual water deficit could increase to as much as 67 per cent of demand by 2015.
● Forest areas cover only 52.6 million ha in West Asia, representing 3.9 per cent of the total land area of 1 352 million ha.
● The total irrigated agricultural area in West Asia is about 7 345 thousand ha, of which 48 per cent is in Iraq.
● There are 293 critically endangered and vulnerable species in West Asia with the highest number in Yemen.
● The population of the region in 2005 is 116 million. By 2020 it is projected to reach 167 million – a 69 per cent increase.
● The average population density in the region is 29 inhabitants per km². The Kingdom of Bahrain has the highest population density of 1 066 inhabitants/km², while Oman has the lowest, at 10 inhabitants/km².

Sources: ACSAD 1997, AOAD 1995 and 2003, IUCN 2004, UNDP 2004a, UNEP 2000, UNDESA 2004, WRI and others 1996

Ship wrecks contribute to water quality problems.
Source: UNDP

of groundwater extraction for agriculture in the basin – more than the water consumption of the city itself (WEC 2001). Another problem is the uncontrolled spread of private agricultural wells now numbering 13 400, which have been lowering groundwater levels in the Sana'a basin by 3–6 metres a year (WEC 2004).

In Amman, Jordan, shortages have reached the point where many residents receive water only one day a week. The government is undertaking a series of initiatives to address this problem, including piping water to the city from the Disi aquifer some 325 km away. The sustainability of supply remains a concern. The aquifer holds fossil water, and is already showing signs of depletion and increasing salinity (Water Industry 2004, World Bank 2004a).

The Gulf Cooperation Council (GCC) countries face even greater water scarcity. Demands are being satisfied overwhelmingly by groundwater mining (91 per cent), though there is rapid growth in desalination (seven per cent) and expansion in wastewater treatment and reuse (two per cent), along with harvesting of surface runoff water. If present trends in population growth and water consumption prevail, the water shortage problem will soon reach crisis level (Al-Zubari 2004).

While the GCC countries have adequate financial resources to meet urban water needs, rising demand for domestic water will require additional desalination plants and wastewater treatment facilities, demanding heavy capital investment (ESCWA 2003a). Desalination also raises environmental concerns, especially over brine disposal and air pollution. Dealing with these would raise investment costs even higher (ESCWA 2001).

All the GCC countries have realized that efficient development and management of water resources require water policy reforms, with emphasis on supply and demand management measures and improvement of legal and institutional provisions (Al-Zubari 2004).

THE ENVIRONMENTAL TOLL OF CONFLICT

Political instability and escalating violence continued to dominate the scene in 2004, especially in Iraq and the Occupied Palestinian Territories, depriving the region of the stability needed to achieve sustainable development.

In Iraq, wars, sanctions, and limited regional cooperation have left the environment badly damaged. Land, air, and water are contaminated. Poor waste and sanitation infrastructure have led to increasingly polluted soils, rivers and groundwater resources, posing major health risks (Iraqi Ministry of Environment 2004, UNEP 2003a and b).

There is concern over radioactive contamination. Depleted uranium, used in the wars of 1991 and 2003, is a concern for its potential effects on human health (Iraqi Ministry of Environment 2004).

Repeated attacks on oil facilities are depriving Iraq of funding for reconstruction, and at the same time causing degradation of land, air and water resources. Wreckage of some 282 ships in Iraq's and neighbouring territorial waters also became a problem in 2004. The wrecks block navigation waterways, and raise concerns for tourism, quality of waters used for desalination, and health of fish stocks (UNDP 2004b).

A joint UNEP/Ministry of the Environment team identified more than 300 sites from the United Nations Monitoring, Verification and Inspection Commission (UNMOVIC) database as contaminated at various levels by a range of pollutants. The team highlighted ten sites of particular concern for assessment and prioritization. Five of these have been chosen as pilot assessment projects (UNEP 2004a).

Environmental problems have intensified in the Occupied Palestinian Territories. Infrastructure services such as water, power and sewerage networks are frequently damaged in conflicts (UN-OCHA 2004). Continued restrictions of movement of people and goods, through closures, checkpoints, curfews and so on, are deepening the economic crisis (World Bank 2004b) and affecting the environment. Restricted access to agricultural land has reduced land productivity, while closures have hindered solid waste collection (UNEP 2003c).

PRESERVING BIODIVERSITY

Human activities are the main factors triggering biodiversity loss in West Asia. Habitat destruction and fragmentation due to urban expansion, tourism developments, dredging and reclamation of coastal areas are serious problems in the region, especially along the coasts.

Multilateral agreements to minimize these threats are gaining ground in the region. In 2004, Lebanon, Oman and United Arab Emirates joined the International Treaty on Plant Genetic Resources for Food and Agriculture, which entered into force on 29 June 2004. Jordan, Kuwait and Syria had joined previously (FAO 2004).

Box 2: Re-flooding of the Mesopotamian marshlands

The Mesopotamian marshes, devastated by dams and diversions under the previous regime, saw an encouraging recovery in 2004 as these NASA satellite images reveal. The left image, from 26 March 2000, shows the marshlands devastated by a policy of drainage and diversion. Inundated expanses appear as blueblack. By early 2003, only about seven per cent of the Mesopotamian Marshlands remained (UNEP 2003a). Good rainfall in 2003–04 in the headwaters of the Tigris-Euphrates marked an end to a four-year drought (1999–2002). Following the spring flood in 2004, about 20 per cent of the marshlands were inundated (UNEP 2004b) and at least 40 000 former residents went back to the marsh areas (Eden Again Project 2004). The re-flooding of the marshes, including breaching of dikes and drainage canals, was spearheaded by direct actions of the local population, sanctioned by the Ministry of Water Resources.

The right image, taken on 21 March 2004, captures the on-going reflooding. Preliminary analysis indicates that the area under water has increased by nearly fourfold, from 759 km^2 in 2002 to 2 928 km^2 in early 2004, though it is still only around 20 per cent of the original size of the permanent marshes (UNEP/PCAU 2004). The recovery of vegetation in some re-flooded areas has been remarkable. Many former natural features are returning, including fish stocks, migratory birds, aquatic flora, and water buffaloes. In some areas vegetation has not re-grown, however, indicating serious environmental degradation (Iraqi Ministry of Environment 2004).

The restoration of the marshes remains a major challenge. It requires intensified national and international efforts, in a strategic programme that must integrate social, economic and environmental aspects. It is essential that the local community should be engaged by providing safe drinking water, sanitation, education, job opportunities, energy, and transportation. The water needed to restore and maintain the marshes must also be secured through negotiation among riparian countries of the Tigris and Euphrates (Iraqi Ministry of Environment 2004). A coalition of donors, international organizations and key ministries in Iraq is now developing a comprehensive plan to restore the marshes and to help repatriate marsh dwellers (UNEP 2004c, Eden Again Project 2004, USAID 2004).

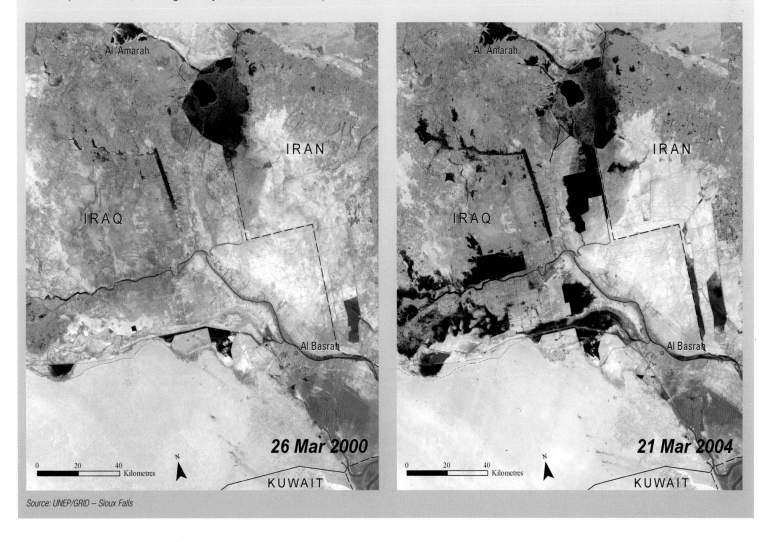

Source: UNEP/GRID – Sioux Falls

Jordan and Syria also became parties to the Cartagena Protocol on Biosafety in 2004 (SCBD 2004a). The West Asian countries face challenges in complying with the provisions of the protocol. For example, they lack expertise in the safe transfer and handling of genetically modified organisms and their products (SCBD 2004b). The capacity of national institutions in the region must be strengthened and national biosafety frameworks developed. Efforts must be made to avoid contamination of local crop varieties and wild relatives with genetically modified strains.

CHALLENGES FOR THE FUTURE

Water scarcity continues to be a pressing issue in West Asia, and water shortage in urban areas is emerging as a priority. The continued conflicts in the region make it very difficult to pursue a sustainable development track. Biodiversity conservation is gaining momentum, but many challenges remain if the region is to achieve the 'significant reduction in biodiversity loss' by 2010 targeted by the 2002 World Summit on Sustainable Development.

Box 3: Putting agrobiodiversity into practice

The UNDP/Global Environment Facility project on the Conservation and Sustainable Use of Dryland Agrobiodiversity in West Asia aims to halt and reverse the loss of biodiversity in ten major crops and their wild relatives (Valkoun and others 2004, UNDP 2003b).

For example 'Hourani,' a wheat variety planted in Syria and Jordan for 1 000 years, nearly became extinct, replaced by highly productive Italian and Mexican wheat varieties in the 1970s. Now, genetic erosion has been slowed by promoting the reintroduction of local wheat varieties into farming systems (Charkasi 2000). Other species targeted by the project have been incorporated in reforestation programmes (ICARDA 2002 and 2004).

Poverty alleviation through income-generating micro-projects is another significant result. Bee keeping and production of organic products are becoming popular on project pilot sites.

REFERENCES

Abu-Zeid, K., Abdel-Megeed, A. and Elbadawy, O. (2004). Potential for Water Demand Management in the Arab Region. *Proceedings of International Water Demand Management Conference.* Dead Sea, Jordan

ACSAD (1997). *Water Resources and their Utilization in the Arab World.* 2nd Water Resources Seminar, Kuwait

Al-Zubari, W. (2004). GCC Water Resources Perspective. *In Proceedings of Water Middle East 2004:* 2nd International Exhibition and Conference for Water and Technology, Manama, Kingdom of Bahrain

AOAD (1995). *Water Use Policies in Arab Agriculture.* Arab Organization for Agricultural Development, AOAD/95/RG, Sudan

AOAD (2003). *A Study on Criteria and Indicators for Monitoring Desertification in Arab Countries.* Arab Organization for Agricultural Development, Khartoum

Charkasi, D. (2000). *Balancing the Use of Old and New Agricultural Varieties to Sustain Agrobiodiversity.* http://www.icarda.org/get/newsLetter34.html

Eden Again Project (2004). *The Eden Again Project: Restoration of the Mesopotamian Marshlands.* The Iraq foundation. http://www.edenagain.org/projects.html

Elhadj, E. (2004). *The Household Water Crisis in Syria's Greater Damascus Region.* SOAS Water Research Group Occasional Paper 47. School of Oriental and African Studies, London

ESCWA (1999). *Survey of Economic and Social Developments in the ESCWA Region.* United Nations, New York

ESCWA (2001). *The Role of Desalinated Water in Augmentation of the Water Supply in Selected ESCWA Member Countries.* E/ESCWA/ENR/2001/19. United Nations, New York

ESCWA (2003a). *Assessment of the Role of the Private Sector in the Development and Management of Water Supply in Selected ESCWA Member Countries,* E/ESCWA/SDPD/2003/14. Economic and Social Commission for Western Asia, United Nations, New York

ESCWA (2003b). *Updating the Assessment of Water Resources in ESCWA Member Countries,* E/ESCWA/ENR/1999/13. Economic and Social Commission for Western Asia, United Nations, New York

ESCWA (2004). *Report on the State of Implementation of Goals and Commitments on Water.* Regional Implementation Forum of the Economic and Social Commission for Western Asia. Commission on Sustainable Development Twelfth Session, e/CN.17/2004/7/Add.5. United Nations, New York

FAO (2004). *International Treaty on Plant Genetic Resources for Food and Agriculture.* Food and Agriculture Organisation. http://www.fao.org/Legal/TREATIES/033s-e.htm

GEO Data Portal. (2004). http://geodata.grid.unep.ch/

ICARDA (2002). *Conservation and Sustainable Use of Dryland Agrobiodiversity,* International Center for Agricultural Research in the Dry Areas. http://www.icarda.cgiar.org/Gef/Agro10_11.pdf

ICARDA (2004). *Women Trained in Producing Dehydrated Fruits.* ICARDA News, International Center for Agricultural Research in the Dry Areas. http://www.icarda.cgiar.org/News/2004News/30Sep04.htm

Iraqi Ministry of Environment (2004). *The Iraqi Environment: Problems and Horizons.* Ministry of Environment, Baghdad

IUCN (2004). *IUCN Red List of Threatened Species.* World Conservation Union. http://www.redlist.org/info/tables/table5.html

SaudiCities (1999) http://saudicities.com/country2.htm [6 January 2003]

SCBD (2004a). *Parties to the Convention on Biological Diversity / Cartagena Protocol on Biosafety.* Secretariat of the Convention on Biological Diversity. http://www.biodiv.org/world/parties.asp

SCBD (2004b). *UNEP-GEF Project for Building Capacity for Effective Participation in the Biosafety Clearing House (BCH).* Biosafety Clearing-House: Capacity Building Project. http://bch.biodiv.org/database/record.aspx?recordid=10922

UNDP (2003a). *The Millennium Development Goals in Arab Countries.* United Nations Development Programme. http//www.undp.org/mdg

UNDP (2003b). *Agrobiodiversity Project Fact Sheet.* United Nations Development Programme. http://www.undp.org.lb/programme/environment/factsheets/word/LEB97G34.doc

UNDP (2004a). *Human Development Report: Cultural Liberty in Today's Diverse World.* United Nations Development Programme. http://hdr.undp.org/statistics/data/indic/indic_8_1_1.html

UNDP (2004b). *Iraqi Waterway Project Wreck Removal Environmental Damage Limitation Survey.* United Nations Development Programme. http://www.undp.org/events/2004/Iraq/WreckRemovalIraqPortsSept04.pdf

UNEP (2000). *Alternative Policy Study: Water Resource Management in West Asia.* GEO-2000. United Nations Environment Programme. http://www.grida.no/geo2000/aps-wasia/

UNEP (2003a). *Environment in Iraq: Progress Report.* Post Conflict Assessment Unit, United Nations Environment Programme, Geneva

UNEP (2003b). *Desk Study on the Environment in Iraq.* Post Conflict Assessment Unit, United Nations Environment Programme, Geneva

UNEP (2003c). *Desk Study on the Environment in the Occupied Palestinian Territories.* Post Conflict Assessment Unit, United Nations Environment Programme, Geneva

UNEP (2004a). *Improving Environmental Governance in Iraq through Environmental Assessment and Capacity Building.* United Nations Environment Programme, Nairobi

UNEP (2004b). A report in preparation by UNEP / Post Conflict Assessment Unit

UNEP (2004c). *UNEP and Its Post Conflict Work in Iraq.* United Nations Environment Programme, Nairobi

UNEP/PCAU (2004) Partow, H. United Nations Environment Programme, Post Conflict Assessment Unit, 2004 http://postconflict.unep.ch/

UN-OCHA (2004). *Preliminary Humanitarian Situation Report: Operation "Forward Shield."* United Nations Office for the Coordination of Humanitarian Affairs – occupied Palestinian territory. http://www.reliefweb.int/hic-opt/docs/UN/OCHA/Beit Hanounassessment_20august2004.pdf

UNPD (2004). *World Population Prospects: The 2002 Revision.* United Nations Population Division. http://www.un.org/esa/population/publications/wpp2002/wpp2002annextables.pdf

USAID (2004). *The Iraq Marshlands Restoration Program.* US Agency for International Development. http://www.usaid.gov/iraq/pdf/iraq_marshlands.pdf

USGS (1998) Overview of Middle East Water Resources. http://exact-me.org/overview/p15.pdf

Valkoun, J., Amri, A., Konopka, J., Street, K., and De Pau, E. (2004). *Collection and conservation of genetic resources for dryland farming systems.* 4th International Crop Science Congress. http://www.regional.org.au/au/cs/2004/poster/1/1/957_valkounj.htm

Water Industry (2004). *Greater Amman Water Supply Project, Jordan,* http://www.water-technology.net/projects/greater_amman/

WEC (2001). *Satellite data analysis of cropping and irrigation water use in the Sana'a basin.* Water and Environment Center at Sana'a University, Sana'a, Yemen

WEC (2004). *Well Inventory in the Sana'a Basin.* Water and Environment Center at Sana'a University, Sana'a, Yemen

World Bank (2004a). *Environmental and Social Assessment Disi-Mudawarra to Amman Water Conveyance System.* World Bank. http://www-wds.worldbank.org/servlet/WDS_IBank_Servlet?pcont=details&eid=000160016_20040824132348

World Bank (2003). *Sana'a Basin Water Management Project.* World Bank, http://web.worldbank.org/external/default/main?pagePK=64027221&piPK=6402720&theSitePK=310165&menuPK=310196&Projectid=P064981

World Bank (2004b). *West Bank and Gaza Update.* World Bank. http://lnweb18.worldbank.org/MNA/mena.nsf/Attachments/West+Bank+and+Gaza+Update+July+2004/$File/Aug+2004.pdf

WRI (1996). *World Resources 1996-97: The Urban Environment.* World Resources Institute. http://pubs.wri.org/pubs_description.cfm?PubI D=2872

Our Changing Environment

Saudi Arabia: Irrigation from fossil water

Saudi Arabia, although rich with oil, is short of a vital natural resource: water. The country's annual groundwater withdrawals in 2000 were 15 times higher than the recharge. However, Saudi Arabia has the highest production of potable desalinated seawater in the world.

Some 90 per cent of water usage is for agriculture. The kingdom has decided to diversify its economy and modernize its agricultural sector in order to become more self-sufficient in meeting the country's growing demand for wheat. As Saudi Arabia has severely limited water resources, the government decided to use the revenues from the oil industry to support the most modern technologies available for farming in arid and semi-arid environments. However, the Saudi government has cut subsidies for wheat production for environmental and budgetary reasons, and as part of a general policy of diversifying agricultural produce and saving water.

The images show Wadi as Sirhan, a large alluvium-filled depression up to 300 metres below the surrounding plateau. Located in the extreme north along the border with Jordan, Wadi as Sirhan is a remnant of an ancient inland sea and is underlain by four aquifers, two of which contain fossil water more than 20 000 years old.

The satellite images reveal the dramatic changes between 1986 and 2004 as a result of the transformation of the desert to agricultural land.

The 1986 image shows Wadi as Sirhan near the village of Al Isawiyah. The 2004 image shows the result of introducing centre pivot irrigation, drawing on fossil water. Once established, centre pivot irrigation quickly spread throughout the surrounding area.

Sources: SaudiCities 1999, USGS 1998

2 Feb 1986

12 Feb 2004

Source: UNEP/GRID – Sioux Falls

Polar

Predicted climate changes in the Arctic could have serious economic, cultural, environmental and health impacts. Runoff from melting glaciers and the Greenland icecap could raise global sea levels and disrupt ocean circulation. Arctic animal species' diversity, ranges and distributions will change. In the Antarctic, bioprospecting and tourism are issues of increasing concern.

CLIMATE CHANGE IN THE ARCTIC HAS GLOBAL IMPACTS

The findings of a major assessment of the impacts of climate change in the Arctic were announced in November 2004. These were the result of four years of research by an international team of 300 scientists, and are unique in combining science-based observations with Arctic traditional knowledge (ACIA 2004). The full scientific report will be launched in 2005.

Among the major findings of the assessment are that:

- The Arctic is warming much more rapidly than previously known, at nearly twice the rate of the global average. In Alaska and western Canada, winter temperatures have increased as much as 3–4° C in the past 50 years. The region is projected to warm an additional 4–7° C by 2100.

- At least half of the current area of summer ice in the Arctic is projected to melt by the end of this century, along with a significant portion of the Greenland Ice Sheet (**Figure 1**). The Greenland melting will contribute to global sea-level rise – although the melting of ice already at sea will not.

- If the Arctic Ocean becomes ice-free in summer, polar bears and some seal species will be at high risk of extinction in the wild.

- Arctic Indigenous Peoples will face major economic and cultural impacts from climate change. Many of their cultures depend on hunting whales, walruses, seals and caribou not only for food, but also as the basis for their cultural and social identity. Changes in species ranges, numbers and accessibility, safety when travelling across ice, and a growing unpredictability of weather could all present unique challenges.

- Thawing could reduce sea ice and open short-cut shipping routes between the Atlantic and Pacific Oceans, stimulating an increase in marine transport and access to resources.

- On land, buildings, oil pipelines, industrial facilities, roads and airports could require substantial rebuilding if permafrost thaws.

NEW CHEMICALS FOUND IN ARCTIC WILDLIFE AND PEOPLES

New research on persistent organic pollutants (POPs) in the Arctic has endorsed previous findings of worrying levels of hazardous substances in animals and human beings (AMAP 2004).

Most of these substances come from sources far outside the Arctic. POPs are chemicals that remain intact in the environment for long periods of time and are spread by air streams and ocean currents over wide areas. Some compounds may last even longer in the cold and dark Arctic environment than they would in temperate climates.

POPs accumulate in the fatty tissue of living organisms, and are toxic to humans and wildlife (**Box 1**). Animals such as polar bears, seals and seabirds, are at the top of the Arctic food chain, and therefore accumulate the highest concentrations of pollutants. Female mammals excrete some types of POPs via placental transfer to the foetus and in breast milk. Due to their lifestyle and diet, indigenous peoples in parts of the Arctic are among the most exposed to POPs in the world.

Brominated flame retardants (such as polybrominated diphenyl ethers or PBDEs) are one of the types of substances whose levels are increasing (AMAP 2004a). This term covers a group of chemicals used in products such as fabrics, TV sets, computers and other equipment, to make them less flammable. They may also be classified as POPs in the future (AMAP 2004).

The discovery and analysis of these flame retardants in the environment is relatively new. Data from Arctic Canada show that levels of brominated flame retardants in male ringed seals from Holman, aged 0–15 years, increased nine-fold in the period 1981 to 2000. Further data from Baffin Island (also Arctic Canada) show that levels of the most predominant brominated flame retardant (BDE47) increased 6.5 times in beluga whales in the period 1982 to 1997 (AMAP 2004). Some studies have shown that the chemicals could be toxic to the immune system and could affect neurobehavioural development (AMAP 2004).

Key Facts

- Antarctica has a land area of 14 million km². It is the coldest place on Earth and is almost entirely covered by ice. Only approximately 2 per cent of the land is barren rock. Antarctica's flora consist mainly of lichens, mosses and algal species.

- There are both permanent and summer-only research stations on the continent, so the population in Antarctica varies from some 1 000 people during winter to 4 000 people during summer.

- The Antarctic Treaty, which entered into force on 23 June 1961, establishes the legal framework for the management of the continent. The objectives of the Treaty are: the use of Antarctica for peaceful purposes only; to promote international scientific cooperation; and to avoid disputes over territorial sovereignty.

- The Arctic region is composed of eight nations surrounding the Arctic Ocean: Canada, Denmark (Greenland and the Faeroe Islands), Iceland, Norway, Sweden, Finland, the Russian Federation and the United States of America.

- The Arctic encompasses about 13.4 million km² with a population of only 3.5 million people, a density of 0.26 people per km².

- The indigenous peoples of the Arctic are estimated to comprise nearly 650 000 individuals, most of whom live in northern Russia.

- Estimates suggest that 25 per cent of the world's undiscovered oil and gas reserves are in the Arctic.

Sources: AMAP 2003, CIA 2004, Midttun 2004, Nation Master 2004, NERC 2004, UNEP 2002

In July 2004 Norway passed a ban on the use and sale of the two most dangerous brominated flame retardants (penta- and octa-bromodiphenyl ether). The European Union (EU) passed a similar ban which became effective August 2004 (EU 2003). Another type, deca-BDE, is at present being discussed in the EU's programme for risk assessment. A Norwegian and Swedish ban is under consideration (Hardeng 2004).

BIOPROSPECTING IN THE ANTARCTIC

Biological prospecting, or bioprospecting, is generally defined as the search for chemical and genetic materials from living resources, including plants, animals and microorganisms, which may be commercially promising.

The Antarctic constitutes almost nine per cent of the world's land area. The organisms which survive here and in the Southern Ocean are among the most highly adapted animals on Earth, making it an important location for bioprospectors. Chemicals derived from Antarctic living resources are already the basis of patents for pharmaceutical products and food products – for example, a compound that makes ice cream smoother.

Although bioprospecting has occurred in the Antarctic for many years, none of the Antarctic Treaty System legal instruments specifically mention bioprospecting. Even the Environmental Protocol to the treaty, adopted as recently as 1991, does not mention the activity. However, the Protocol applies to *all* human activity in the Antarctic region and so it provides some level of protection to the environment from any bioprospecting activities.

The Scientific Committee for Antarctic Research (SCAR) noted as early as 1999 that there had already been collections of microorganisms in Antarctica for pharmaceutical purposes and that a biological prospecting interest was 'developing rapidly' (SCAR 1999). But it was not until the XXV Antarctic Treaty Consultative Meeting (ATCM) in Warsaw, Poland, in September 2002, that bioprospecting appeared as an issue for discussion and as the subject of specific papers (ATCM 2004a and b).

While no substantive discussions on bioprospecting took place at ATCM 2004 held in South Africa in May, one UNEP information paper examined industrial

Box 1: Stockholm Convention on POPs enters into force

The 2001 Stockholm Convention on Persistent Organic Pollutants (POPs) became legally binding on 17 May 2004. The treaty bans or severely restricts 12 extremely harmful chemicals, including polychlorinated biphenyls (PCBs), dioxins, and several pesticides, with provisions for adding further chemicals in the future.

For decades these highly toxic chemicals have affected people and wildlife by inducing cancer, damaging nervous, reproductive and immune systems, and causing birth defects.

By committing governments to eliminating the production, use and environmental release of these chemicals, the Stockholm Convention will greatly benefit human health and the environment. The convention will also strengthen the overall scope and effectiveness of international environmental law. In addition, the treaty has provisions for cleaning up the growing accumulation of unwanted stockpiles of pesticides and toxic chemicals.

Source: POPs Secretariat 2004

involvement in Antarctic bioprospecting (ATCM 2004a). Bioprospecting is on the Agenda for the upcoming 2005 ATCM.

Interest in bioprospecting is putting pressure on the Antarctic Treaty System to develop robust policy and guidelines on the

Figure 1: Projections of the September Arctic sea ice extent over this century

The images show the average of the projections from five climatic models.

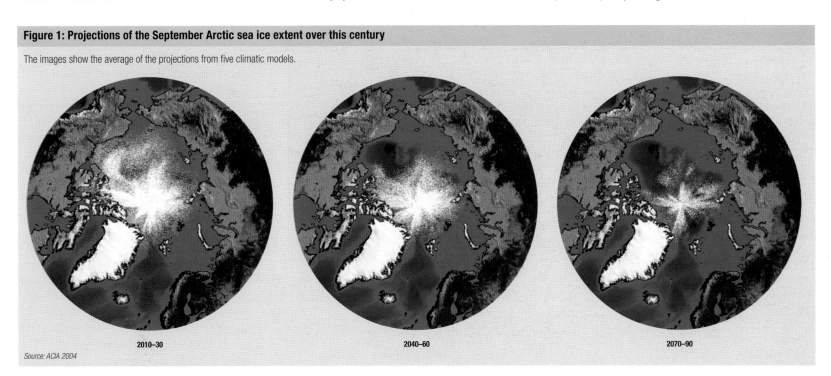

2010–30   2040–60   2070–90

Source: ACIA 2004

Box 2: First Antarctic Specially Managed Area approved

The Protocol on Environmental Protection to the Antarctic Treaty, often referred to as the Environmental Protocol (or Madrid Protocol), came into force in January 1998. This Protocol allows for the creation of Antarctic Specially Managed Areas (ASMA) under its Annex V which came into force in May 2002. In 2004, at the Antarctic Treaty Consultative Meeting XXVII in Cape Town, South Africa, a vast tract of land called the Dry Valleys became the first ASMA after approval by the 27 consultative state parties to the treaty of a joint proposal presented by New Zealand and the United States.

The Dry Valleys area covers approximately 15 000 km² and contains the largest expanse of ice-free ground in Antarctica. It is a cold desert environment which encompasses soils millions of years old, communities of unique plants and micro-organisms and special geological features that have remained relatively pristine because of their remoteness. This area is particularly sensitive to human disturbance, and has extremely slow recovery rates. For example human footprints made in the 1950s in areas of low wind disturbance are still clearly visible today.

The ASMA plan will ensure that the scientific, wilderness, ecological and aesthetic values of the Dry Valleys are protected and that cumulative impacts including tourism are minimized by managing all human activities in the ASMA.

Source: Committee for Environmental Protection 2004

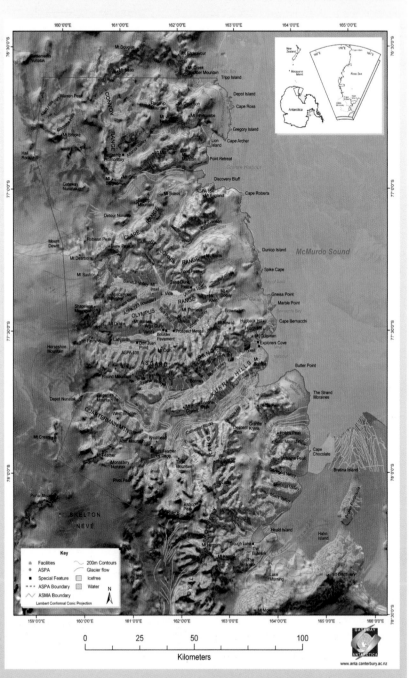

Source: University of Canterbury

activity. These may include issues such as access to Antarctic living resources and benefit-sharing from any product or process deriving from living resources. If the level of bioprospecting increases significantly, then continuing protection of Antarctic and Southern Ocean ecosystems may provide a challenge to the strict provisions of the Environmental Protocol.

INCREASE IN TOURISTS TO ANTARCTICA

There was a significant rise in Antarctic tourist numbers during the 2003–04 austral summer season, according to data presented at the 2004 International Association of Antarctica Tour Operators (IAATO) Annual General Meeting. IAATO was founded by seven companies in 1991 to advocate, promote and practice safe and environmentally responsible private-sector travel to the Antarctic. By 2004 IAATO had grown to include 70 member companies from 14 countries (IAATO 2004).

Antarctic tourism is generally considered to have begun in the late 1950s, and there have been tourist expeditions every year since 1966. They are carried out primarily by around 20 ice-strengthened ships carrying 45 to 280 passengers each. Most of the visits are to the Antarctic Peninsula region. Tourist numbers rose from 6 704 in 1992–93 to 13 571 in 2002–03, but then surged to 19 722 in 2003–04 (**Figure 2**) (IAATO 2004).

Private sector tourism still accounts for a relatively small portion of human activity on the continent, but the sharp rise in visitor numbers is alarming for three reasons.

First, the Environmental Protocol to the Antarctic Treaty requires impact assessment and monitoring of all human activity in the Antarctic region. Both governmental and non-governmental organizations such as IAATO provide impact assessments to their government authorities. However, the Environmental Protocol does not provide an easy mechanism to manage cumulative impacts across the number of countries operating in the region. Thus, accurate monitoring and environmental impact assessment are problematic.

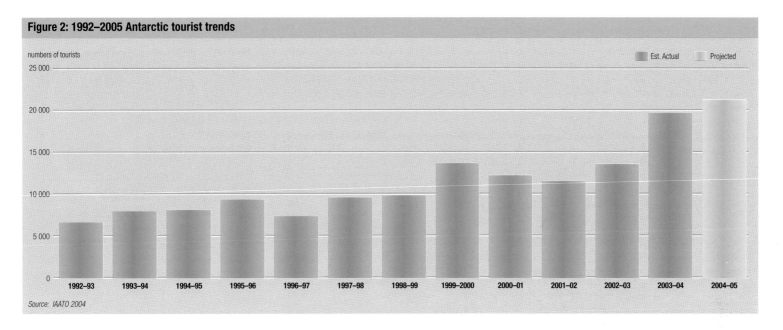

Figure 2: 1992–2005 Antarctic tourist trends

numbers of tourists

Est. Actual   Projected

25 000

20 000

15 000

10 000

5 000

0

1992–93 | 1993–94 | 1994–95 | 1995–96 | 1996–97 | 1997–98 | 1998–99 | 1999–2000 | 2000–01 | 2001–02 | 2002–03 | 2003–04 | 2004–05

Source: IAATO 2004

Second, there is a risk that alien species will be introduced into the pristine Antarctic environment, especially in the biodiverse regions of the Southern Ocean and Antarctic Peninsula. Tourism operators and government programmes alike take precautions to prevent such events from occurring, but any increase in human activity in the region has the potential to increase the danger. An Annex to the Environmental Protocol for liability for damage to the Antarctic environment has yet to be successfully negotiated by Antarctic Treaty parties.

Finally, there are concerns that any increase in Antarctic tourism may lead to greater risks of accident and emergency. Currently there are no adequate emergency response capabilities for the entire region.

An accreditation scheme for Antarctic tourism operators has been proposed within the Antarctic Treaty System. While there was no formal decision as to who would develop and coordinate such a scheme, at the 2004 IAATO AGM, member companies agreed to move ahead themselves with the development of a formal Accreditation Scheme and Audit Procedure (ATCM 2004b). This would formalize IAATO's guidelines and operational standards, and establish mechanisms to audit compliance with them.

CHALLENGES FOR THE FUTURE

The polar regions are unique in their biodiversity and wilderness values. Yet these are increasingly under threat from direct and indirect human impacts, especially global warming, tourism and long-range pollution.

There is a political will to address these and other polar issues and steps are being taken towards regulation and controls. The challenges of global warming and long-range pollution are much broader in their origins, but these too must be addressed if the polar environments are to remain stable.

REFERENCES

ACIA (2004). *Impacts of a Warming Arctic*. Arctic Monitoring and Assessment Programme. Cambridge University Press, Cambridge

AMAP (2003). *AMAP Assessment 2002: Human Health in the Arctic*. Arctic Monitoring and Assessment Programme, Oslo

AMAP (2004). *AMAP Assessment 2002: Persistent Organic Pollutants in the Arctic*. Arctic Monitoring and Assessment Programme, Oslo

ATCM (2004a). *Industry Involvement in Antarctic Bioprospecting*, IP-106. Antarctic Treaty Consultative Meeting XXVII, South Africa

ATCM (2004b). *IAATO's Formalization of an Accreditation Scheme and Internal Audit Process and the Association's Views on an ATCM Accreditation Scheme*, IP-69. Antarctic Treaty Consultative Meeting XXVII, South Africa

Central Intelligence Agency (2004). *World Fact Book*. http://www.cia.gov/cia/publications/factbook/geos/ay.html

Committee for Environmental Protection (2004). Report of the Committee for Environmental Protection (CEP VII), Cape Town, 24 – 28 May 2004

Dixon, K.W., Delworth, T.L., Knutson, T.R., Spelman, M. J. and Stouffer, R.J. (2003): A comparison of climate change simulations produced by two GFDL coupled climate models. *Global & Planetary Change*, 37,1-2, 81-102

EU (2003). *Directive 2003/11/EC of the European Parliament and of the Coucil of 6 February 2003 amending for the 24th time Council Directive 76/769/EEC relating to restrictions on the marketing and use of certain dangerous substances and preparations (pentabromodiphenyl ether, octabromodiphenyl ether)*. Official Journal of the European Union, 15 February 2003

Hardeng, Solvår; Senior Advisor The Norwegian Pollution Control Authority. Personal communication, 15th November 2004

IAATO (2004). Overview of Antarctic Tourism: 2003-2004 Antarctic Season. International Association of Antarctica Tour Operators http://www.iaato.org/tourism_stats.html

Midttun, Øyvind (2004). Cold opportunities. *Norwegian Continental Shelf*, 1-2004, 12-7

Nation Master (2004). *Encyclopedia: Ecology of Antarctica*. http://www.nationmaster.com/encyclopedia/Ecology-of-Antarctica

NOAA (2004). *Arctic sea ice changes in GFDL R30 greenhouse scenario experiments*.

POPS (2004). Stockholm Convention on Persistent Organic Pollutants. http://www.pops.int/

SCAR (1999). *Information Paper 123*. Scientific Committee for Antarctic Research. XXIII Antarctic Treaty Consultative Meeting, Lima

Our Changing Environment

Arctic Seas: Shrinking ice cover

The extent of Arctic sea ice in September – the end of the summer melt period – is the most valuable indicator of the state of the ice cover. On average, sea ice in September covers an area of about seven million km², a little smaller than the continent of Australia.

The scale indicates the per cent by which the local sea ice extent differs above or below the average for the period 1979–2000. The median ice edge for 1979–2000 is indicated by the black outer line. In 2002, total September ice extent was 15 per cent below this average. This represents a reduction equivalent to an area roughly twice the size of Texas or Iraq. From comparisons with records prior to the satellite era, this was probably the least amount of sea ice that had covered the Arctic over the past 50 years.

Quite often, a 'low' ice year is followed by recovery the next year. However, September of 2003 was also extreme, with 12 per cent less ice extent than average. Calculations performed for 30 September 2004 show a sea ice extent loss of 13.4 per cent, especially pronounced north of Alaska and eastern Siberia.

Sea Ice Concentration Anomaly (per cent)

≥+50   +25   0   −25   ≤−50

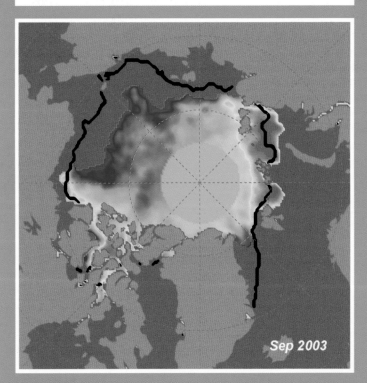

Sep 2003

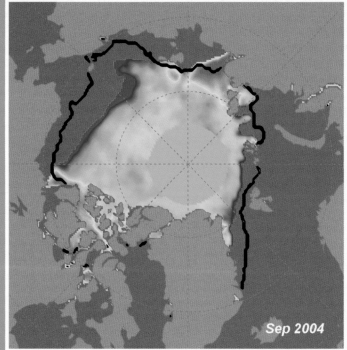

Sep 2004

Source: National Snow and Ice Data Centre News http://nsidc.org/news/press/20041004_decline.html

The Global International Waters Assessment

As common resources, international waters are among the most polluted and overexploited ecosystems on earth. And because they are not easily visible, environmental problems can build up unseen.

The Global International Waters Assessment (GIWA) is designed to fill information gaps. Set up in 1999 as a project of the Global Environment Facility (GEF) and led by UNEP, it is a global assessment of environmental state of all the world's transboundary waters based on existing and continuing studies from all sources.

The state of the waters is assessed by experts on each of the project's environmental and socioeconomic issues. The issues fall into five main focal areas: freshwater shortage, pollution, habitat and community modification, unsustainable exploitation of fish, and impacts of global environmental changes. The information was gathered by regional task teams and typically involved 10 to 15 environmental and socioeconomic experts from each country.

The matrix in the following pages presents a summary of the GIWA results for most of the 66 major water areas of the world (number-keyed on the map below). These geographic units are defined not by political borders but by hydrographic systems: the entire area of one or more catchment areas that drains into a single designated marine system. These marine systems often correspond to Large Marine Ecosystems. In some cases the regions have been further divided into subsystems.

The assessment integrates environmental and socioeconomic data from each country in a region to determine the severity of the impacts of each of the five concerns and their constituent issues on the entire region. The magnitude of the impacts was assessed using the best available information from a wide range of sources and the knowledge and experience of each of the team experts. So as to allow comparisons between different regions, the results were reported as standardized scores according to a four point scale: no known impact, slight impact, moderate impact and severe impact.

It can be seen that very few of the international waters are relatively free of impact so far – among the least affected are the Coral Sea east of New Guinea, and several ocean areas around Greenland, though even these are vulnerable to global change impacts. Among the worst affected across the most categories are the Gulf of Mexico (especially the Rio Grande and Mississippi sub-units) and the Caribbean sea; the Black, Aral and Caspian Seas; the Somali Current waters off the coast of East Africa; and the Sunda, Sulu-Celebes and South China Seas.

The GIWA methodology, progress and resources, with complete regional reports, and a table of the pre-defined criteria can be retrieved from the web site: http://www.giwa.net.

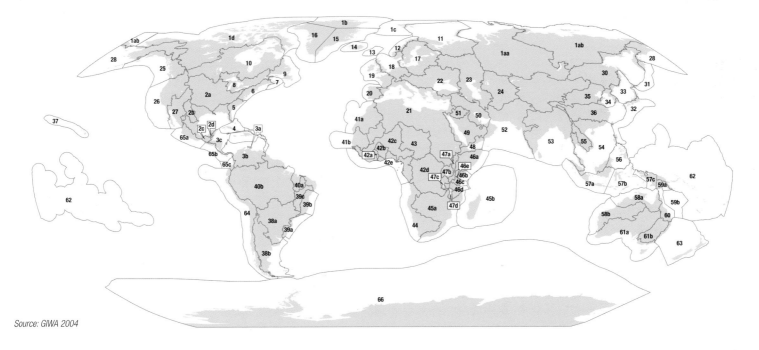

Source: GIWA 2004

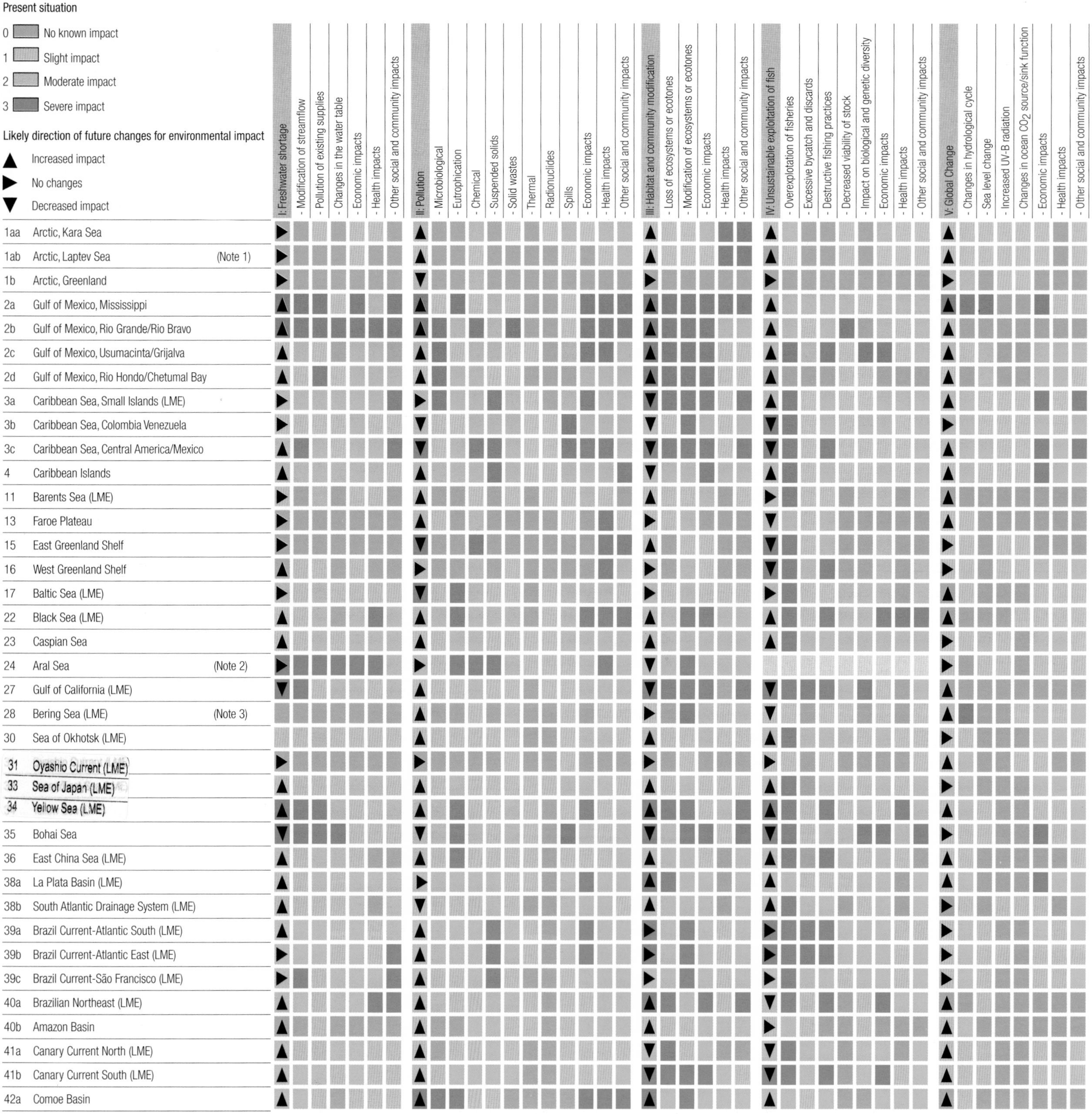

Present situation

- 0 — No known impact
- 1 — Slight impact
- 2 — Moderate impact
- 3 — Severe impact

Likely direction of future changes for environmental impact

- ▲ Increased impact
- ▶ No changes
- ▼ Decreased impact

Column headings

I: Freshwater shortage
- Modification of streamflow
- Pollution of existing supplies
- Changes in the water table
- Economic impacts
- Health impacts
- Other social and community impacts

II: Pollution
- Microbiological
- Eutrophication
- Chemical
- Suspended solids
- Solid wastes
- Thermal
- Radionuclides
- Spills
- Economic impacts
- Health impacts
- Other social and community impacts

III: Habitat and community modification
- Loss of ecosystems or ecotones
- Modification of ecosystems or ecotones
- Economic impacts
- Health impacts
- Other social and community impacts

IV: Unsustainable exploitation of fish
- Overexploitation of fisheries
- Excessive bycatch and discards
- Destructive fishing practices
- Decreased viability of stock
- Impact on biological and genetic diversity
- Economic impacts
- Health impacts
- Other social and community impacts

V: Global Change
- Changes in hydrological cycle
- Sea level change
- Increased UV-B radiation
- Changes in ocean CO_2 source/sink function
- Economic impacts
- Health impacts
- Other social and community impacts

Rows

1aa	Arctic, Kara Sea	
1ab	Arctic, Laptev Sea	(Note 1)
1b	Arctic, Greenland	
2a	Gulf of Mexico, Mississippi	
2b	Gulf of Mexico, Rio Grande/Rio Bravo	
2c	Gulf of Mexico, Usumacinta/Grijalva	
2d	Gulf of Mexico, Rio Hondo/Chetumal Bay	
3a	Caribbean Sea, Small Islands (LME)	
3b	Caribbean Sea, Colombia Venezuela	
3c	Caribbean Sea, Central America/Mexico	
4	Caribbean Islands	
11	Barents Sea (LME)	
13	Faroe Plateau	
15	East Greenland Shelf	
16	West Greenland Shelf	
17	Baltic Sea (LME)	
22	Black Sea (LME)	
23	Caspian Sea	
24	Aral Sea	(Note 2)
27	Gulf of California (LME)	
28	Bering Sea (LME)	(Note 3)
30	Sea of Okhotsk (LME)	
31	Oyashio Current (LME)	
33	Sea of Japan (LME)	
34	Yellow Sea (LME)	
35	Bohai Sea	
36	East China Sea (LME)	
38a	La Plata Basin (LME)	
38b	South Atlantic Drainage System (LME)	
39a	Brazil Current-Atlantic South (LME)	
39b	Brazil Current-Atlantic East (LME)	
39c	Brazil Current-São Francisco (LME)	
40a	Brazilian Northeast (LME)	
40b	Amazon Basin	
41a	Canary Current North (LME)	
41b	Canary Current South (LME)	
42a	Comoe Basin	

I: Freshwater shortage
- Modification of streamflow
- Pollution of existing supplies
- Changes in the water table
- Economic impacts
- Health impacts
- Other social and community impacts

II: Pollution
- Microbiological
- Eutrophication
- Chemical
- Suspended solids
- Solid wastes
- Thermal
- Radionuclides
- Spills
- Economic impacts
- Health impacts
- Other social and community impacts

III: Habitat and community modification
- Loss of ecosystems or ecotones
- Modification of ecosystems or ecotones
- Economic impacts
- Health impacts
- Other social and community impacts

IV: Unsustainable exploitation of fish
- Overexploitation of fisheries
- Excessive bycatch and discards
- Destructive fishing practices
- Decreased viability of stock
- Impact on biological and genetic diversity
- Economic impacts
- Health impacts
- Other social and community impacts

V: Global Change
- Changes in hydrological cycle
- Sea level change
- Increased UV-B radiation
- Changes in ocean CO$_2$ source/sink function
- Economic impacts
- Health impacts
- Other social and community impacts

42b	Volta Basin				
42c	Niger Basin				
42d	Congo Basin				
42e	Guinea Current LME				
43	Lake Chad				
44	Benguela Current (LME)				
45b	Indian Ocean Islands				
46a	Juba-Shebelle Basin				
46b	Tana-Athi-Sabaki Basin				
46c	Wami-Ruvu-Pangani Basin				
46d	Rufiji-Ruvuma Basin				
46e	Lake Jipe-Chala				
47a	Lake Turkana				
47b	Lake Victoria				
47c	Lake Tanganyika				
47d	Lake Malawi				
51	Jordan River Basin				
54	South China Sea (LME)				
56	Sulu-Celebes Sea (LME)				
57a	Ind. Sea, Sunda (LME)				
57b	Ind. Sea, Wallaca (LME)				
57c	Ind. Sea, Sahul (LME)				
58a	North Australian Shelf, Wet tropics				
58b	North Australian Shelf, Dry tropics				
59a	South PNG and Papua				
59b	Coral sea				
60	Great Barrier Rief (LME)				
61a	Great Australian Bight				
61b	Muray Darling Basin				
62	Pacific Islands				
63	Tasman Sea				
64	Humboldt Current (LME)				
65a	Southwest Mexico				
65b	Central Equatorial Pacific				
65c	Pacific Colombian				

Notes: 1: Laptev Sea, East Siberian Sea and Russian Sector of Chukchi Sea. 2: Pollution mainly: salinisation of soils, surface and ground waters. 3: Sub-region 28 East Bering Sea and sub-region 29 West Bering Sea joined into one sub-region 'Bering Sea'.

Source: UNEP/GEF Global International Water Assessment. www.giwa.net

Indian Ocean Tsunami

On 26 December 2004, an undersea earthquake measuring 9.0 on the Richter scale took place in the Indian Ocean, off the west coast of northern Sumatra, Indonesia. It caused one of the deadliest disasters in recent times, as resulting tsunami waves crashed into the coastlines of twelve countries bordering the Indian Ocean, causing massive losses in human life and infrastructure, and damage to marine and terrestrial ecosystems.

This was the fourth largest earthquake in magnitude in the last hundred years (**Table 1**), resulting in one of the deadliest tsunamis in recent times (**Table 2**). Over 220 000 people in Asia were killed by the tsunami, mostly in Indonesia, Sri Lanka, India, and Thailand, with smaller numbers in East Africa (BBC 2005). As the waves moved through the Indian Ocean at over 500 km/h (UNOCHA 2005a) (**Figure 1**), countries as far away as those in East Africa were affected, including Small Island Developing States (SIDS) like Seychelles and Mauritius, and mainland countries like Somalia, Kenya and Tanzania. Casualties were particularly high among children and women – for instance, in India, 40 per cent of the dead were estimated to be children (UNOCHA 2004a).

More than 5 million people were displaced as houses and villages were flattened by giant waves. The province of Aceh in northern Sumatra experienced the greatest impact from waves exceeding 15 metres in height (NASA 2005). The city of Banda Aceh was severely damaged. Bridges were destroyed and ships were overturned as the waves advanced towards the surrounding foothills. In the Maldives, where 53 islands suffered severe damage and 10 per cent of the 1 200 islands and atolls were totally destroyed, approximately 12 200 people were registered as homeless, of whom 8 500 had to be evacuated to other islands (UNOCHA 2005b).

In the short term, millions of people, particularly children, face the risk of disease due to polluted water, damaged sanitation systems and crowded living conditions in camps and the remaining housing (WHO 2005). However, the impact of this disaster will be felt for decades to come. Drinking water sources such as wells and groundwater have been contaminated by saline water, and will take years to recover. Infrastructure has been severely damaged and livelihoods are critically impacted, particularly those related to fisheries, agriculture and tourism.

LOST LIVELIHOODS

Restoring livelihoods will be a key priority in the affected areas in coming years, to help rehabilitate people and prevent large-scale migration to already overcrowded cities (FAO 2004). Fishing communities have been badly affected by the loss of boats, fishing

Table 1: Largest earthquakes in the world since 1900

Date	Location	Magnitude
1960	Chile	9.5
1964	Prince William Sound, Alaska	9.2
1957	Andreanof Islands, Alaska	9.1
1952	Kamchatka, Russia	9.0
2004	Indian Ocean, off the west coast of northern Sumatra	9.0
1906	Pacific Ocean off the coast of Ecuador	8.8
1965	Rat Islands, Alaska	8.7
1950	Assam, India, and Tibet, China	8.6
1923	Kamchatka, Russia	8.5
1938	Banda Sea, Indonesia	8.5
1963	Kuril Islands	8.5

Source: USGS 2005

Figure 1: Simulations of the Indian Ocean tsunami, using the Method of Splitting Tsunami (MOST) model

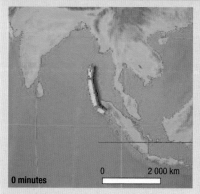   

0 minutes   0   2 000 km

10 minutes

80 minutes

100 minutes

Source: NOAA 2004a

gear, support industries, and aquaculture installations (FAO 2005). Preliminary reports indicate, for instance, that about 80 per cent of the boats in northeast Sri Lanka have been destroyed by the tsunami and more than 5 000 fishing families have been displaced. Ten out of the 12 main fishing harbours in the country have been completely devastated, including infrastructure such as ice plants, cold rooms, workshops and slipways (FAO 2005). The impact on fisheries will need to be assessed.

Arable land has been degraded by saline water and could take decades to recover. Farm animals have been killed and crops have been washed away, along with irrigation and drainage facilities (FAO 2005).

Tourism, a key economic activity in many of the affected areas, has been badly affected by the loss of infrastructure and environmental damage. Tourist resorts, including in Thailand and the Maldives, were hard hit at the peak of seasonal tourism revenue. In the Maldives, where tourism constitutes 95 per cent of the economy and is the country's only source of hard currency (Creel 2003), many diving resorts renowned for their rich marine life were destroyed, along with jetties, harbours and coastal structures (UNOCHA 2005b).

Table 2: Major tsunamis worldwide

Date	Origin*	Effects	Death Toll
1692	Puerto Rico, Caribbean	Port Royal, Jamaica permanently submerged	200
1755	Atlantic Ocean	Lisbon destroyed	60 000
1835	Peru-Chile Trench	Concepción, Chile destroyed	not available
1868	Peru-Chile Trench	Town of Arrica destroyed	10 000–15 000
1883	Krakatoa (volcanic eruption)	Devastation in East Indies	36 000
1896	Japan Trench	Swept the east coast of Japan with waves of 30.5m at Yoshihimama	27 122
1908	Sicily	East of Sicily, including Messina and toe of Italy badly damaged	58 000 (including earthquake victims)
1933	Japan Trench	9 000 houses and 8 000 ships destroyed, Sanriku district, Honshu	3 000
1946	Aleutian Trench	Damage to Alaska and Hawaii	159
1960	South-Central Chile	Coinciding with a week of earthquakes. Damage to Chile and Hawaii	1 500
1964	Anchorage, Alaska	Severe damage to south coast of Alaska	115
1976	Celebes Sea	Devastation in Alicia, Pagadian, Cotabato and Davao, Philippines	8 000
1998	Papua New Guinea, Bismarck Sea	Devastation in Arop, Warapu, Sissano and Malol, Papua New Guinea	2 200
2004	Indian Ocean	11 countries affected across 2 continents	220 000

* Earthquake, unless otherwise specified

Source: NOAA 2004b

ENVIRONMENTAL DAMAGE

The environmental damage caused by the tsunami and the earthquake had not been fully assessed by early 2005 when this publication went to press. It is known to include groundwater contamination from salt intrusion, soil salinization and erosion, damage to biodiversity rich ecosystems such as coral reefs, mangroves, seagrass meadows and estuaries (**Figure 2**), and damage to forests, woodlands, and protected areas.

Figure 2: Damage in the Nicobar Islands, India

The island of Trinkat appears to have been cut in half by the tsunami with a new channel of water approximately five km long stretching from the settlement of Tapiyang to a point on the opposite coast just west of Ol Ol Chuaka. Another channel has possibly been opened up to the south-east of Takasem separating the large mangrove swamp area from the inhabited northern end of the island. The mangrove appears to be relatively intact though several inlets have been created in the east.

The extensive coral reefs visible along the west and east coasts of Trinkat before the tsunami are largely obscured by large plumes of sediments presumably washed from the land. In the later image the coastline has retreated along the east coast enlarging the lagoon. This scouring of terrestrial matter into the lagoon and onto the reefs could have serious consequences for shallow water habitats if sediments settle for longer periods.

Source: UNOSAT

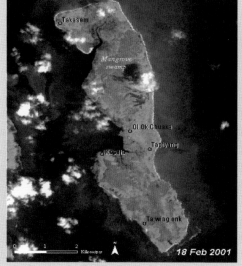

Cement factory along the tsunami-battered coast of Banda Aceh.
Source: Choo Youn-Kong/Reuters/South

Coral reefs and mangroves, which act as buffers against large waves and prevent coastal erosion, are likely to have suffered considerable damage. There are preliminary reports of these ecosystems absorbing the impact of the tsunami in some areas. For instance, according to the MS Swaminathan Research Institute in India, the mangrove forests in Pitchavaram and Muthupet regions of south India acted like a shield and bore the brunt of the tsunami (Venkataramani 2004). The coral reefs around the Surin Island chain on the west coast of Thailand have also been attributed with saving lives by reducing the impact of the waves (Browne 2004).

Besides direct damage from the tsunami, marine ecosystems will also be affected by the resulting sedimentation and debris. Scientists point out that while the coastal beaches and land areas devastated by the tsunami could be restored within a few years, the most severely impacted marine ecosystems could take centuries to fully recover. Debris that ended up in the shallow marine environment, when caught up in strong waves and current, can easily 'bulldoze' corals and marine life, or entangle and drown protected marine mammals. It could also contain hazardous and toxic chemicals, which cause stress to marine ecosystems and disease in corals, algae, fish and other invertebrates. These impacts could be long-lived and may not become apparent to researchers for months or even years (NOAA 2005).

Hazardous or toxic debris and waste, particularly from damaged industrial sites and waste facilities, could also pose a threat. In the Maldives, for example, part of the island that contained the island's waste facilities was washed away. The amount of waste deposited in the ocean as a result has not been established, but a remaining stretch with a two-metre deep layer of waste now extends approximately 30 metres into the water (UNOCHA 2004b).

The tsunami is also likely to have caused damage to coastal forests and protected areas. The infrastructure and management systems of protected areas such as Yala National Park in Sri Lanka and Gunung Leuser National Park in Aceh could also be affected (BirdLife International 2005).

ASSESSING IMPACT AND VULNERABILITY

Following the emergency response to the disaster, detailed assessments of the environmental impact and vulnerability will have to be carried out. Such assessments are necessary not only for rehabilitation activities, but also for future planning to reduce vulnerability and enhance disaster preparedness. A UNEP Asian Tsunami Disaster Task Force, established immediately after the disaster to coordinate UNEP's contribution to the UN wide response and to identify and alleviate the environmental impacts of the disaster, initiated this work soon after it was set up (**Box 1**). In the weeks following the disaster, UNEP mobilized 12 environmental experts to provide environmental assistance to the affected countries and the UN country teams.

The vulnerability of coastal areas to disasters and the need to take this into account in planning and coastal zone management is well known. High population densities, infrastructure and property development in coastal areas all contribute to higher social, economic and environmental consequences in case of disasters. Approximately three billion people, half the world's population, live within 200 km of a coastline. The average population density in coastal areas is about 80 persons/km^2, twice the global average (UNEP 2005b). Of the

---

Box 1: UNEP's role in the response to the disaster

Immediately after the tsunami struck, UNEP's Executive Director established the UNEP Asian Tsunami Disaster Task Force to coordinate and integrate UNEP's contribution to the UN response to the tsunami disaster. UNEP was in direct contact with relevant environmental authorities in the hardest hit countries and received a number of requests for assessing and addressing urgent environmental issues. In order to respond to these, UNEP made US$1 million available for immediate environmental activities and made flash appeals for emergency waste management and environmental assessments, among other purposes.

UNEP also offered remote sensing expertise to the UN system in cooperation with UNDP. Images were obtained and analyzed in order to determine secondary environmental risks from damage to industrial sites. Similar work was undertaken in the areas of biodiversity impacts, particularly with regard to coral reefs, shorelines and protected areas. UNEP also linked to early warning experts and looked into ways of supporting the establishment of an early warning system in cooperation with others.

UNEP developed a five-pillar approach that can be summarized as follows:

- Respond to the requests by affected countries;

- Mobilize immediate environmental assistance by integrating environmental needs into the humanitarian flash appeal;

- Mobilize environmental recovery by integrating environment into the recovery and reconstruction needs assessments;

- Establish and advocate an environmental agenda to reconstruct affected areas; and

- Develop early warning systems.

Source: UNEP 2005a

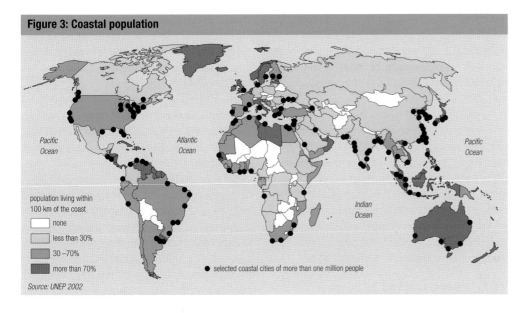

Figure 3: Coastal population

Pacific Ocean

Atlantic Ocean

Pacific Ocean

Indian Ocean

population living within 100 km of the coast
- none
- less than 30%
- 30–70%
- more than 70%

● selected coastal cities of more than one million people

Source: UNEP 2002

Tsunami buoy being deployed in the Pacific Ocean.
Source: NOAA

world's 17 largest cities, 14 are located along coasts – and 11 of these are in Asia. In addition, two-fifths of cities with populations of one million to 10 million people are located near coastlines (**Figure 3**) (Creel 2003).

The vulnerability of SIDS to coastal disasters is of increasing concern, and regional efforts are underway to reduce the impact of such disasters (UNEP 2005c, d and e). However, most of the SIDS have

Rare Indo-Pacific Humpback dolphin rescued from a lake near Phuket, Thailand, where it ended up after the tsunami.
Source: Chaiwat Subprasom/Reuters/South

limited capacity to deal with such disasters and meet their associated costs, and often rely on international assistance to develop capacity for national disaster preparedness and to create appropriate insurance schemes.

The Indian Ocean tsunami once again underlines the increased vulnerability of certain sections of society. UN agencies such as the United Nations Population Fund and the United Nations Development Fund for Women have reported that women and children have been the worst affected both during and after the disaster. For instance, preliminary reports indicate that of the 206 bodies found in one coastal village in Tamil Nadu, India, 26 were men, 96 women, and 84 children (Waldman 2004). In Aceh, which suffered two-thirds of the total death toll of the tsunami, women comprise an estimated 70 per cent of the population due to out-migration of men since the 1980s. As in many other affected parts, women play a central role in society in this province, heading households, sustaining subsistence economies, raising children, and caring for the sick, wounded, and elderly, while bearing the violence of civil war and the burden of poverty (UNOCHA 2005a).

EARLY WARNING

The scale of the disaster highlights the need for reliable and effective early warning systems, both to predict disasters and to keep environmental change under review.

In the case of the Indian Ocean tsunami, many lives could have been saved if an early warning system had existed, especially given the time difference between the earthquake and the impact of the tsunami waves on many land areas. Given the higher occurrence of tsunamis in the Pacific Ocean, an International Tsunami Information Center (ITIC) and Pacific Tsunami Warning Center (PTWC) already exist, but there is no such system for the Indian Ocean. Thailand is a member of the Pacific warning system but all of its ocean buoys, which relay information from wave sensors on the ocean floor, are on its east (Pacific) coast. The need for a tsunami warning programme beyond the Pacific has been raised since 1985 (NOAA 2004a).

Following the recent disaster, there have been proposals to install a warning system similar to the PTWC in the Indian Ocean as a matter of priority, and the UN has announced a 18-month deadline to install such a system (UNESCO 2005). UNEP has offered technical support in its development. In coming months, efforts could be coordinated to achieve regional coverage.

However, there is also the need to establish a global multi-hazard system. It is generally difficult to predict where natural and human-induced disasters will occur, although some areas are at greater risk than others. The Indian Ocean tsunami and the frequent incidence of other disasters globally highlights the need to strengthen early warning and crisis preparedness for disasters worldwide. The development of an Indian Ocean tsunami module of a global early warning system could be a first priority. The system would require the technical capacity to detect earthquakes and tsunamis, and communicate the information to designated national centres; national and regional crisis preparedness capacity, including the capacity to receive and communicate warnings rapidly; and the establishment of coordination and cooperation mechanisms among countries and with the international community. National environmental authorities will have a crucial role to play in such a system – not least to ensure that the role of ecosystems as a buffer against damage from hazardous events is maximized.

A thorough scientific analysis is needed as a basis for the development of such a global, multi-hazard early warning system. An intergovernmental effort will be needed to establish a network of monitoring stations. Once the technical systems are in place, a further challenge will be to strengthen national and regional crisis preparedness capacity, including the capacity to receive, handle and communicate warnings in a timely and effective manner, in ways that reach all sections of society and reduce vulnerability. The potential of indigenous and local knowledge should be taken into account to avoid a focus on top-down priorities and solutions.

Global efforts are also underway to strengthen worldwide monitoring systems, such as plans for a Global Earth Observing System of Systems (GEOSS), a collaborative effort between 54 countries aimed, among other things, at reducing loss of life and property from disasters, protecting and monitoring ocean resources, and understanding the effect of environmental factors on human health and well being.

CHALLENGES FOR THE FUTURE

The most immediate challenges in the aftermath of the tsunami are provision of basic needs such as food, water, sanitation and housing and control of environmental factors that could lead to the spread of disease.

Longer-term efforts to restore livelihoods by addressing environmental impacts will require in-depth assessments of the damage, for instance to fisheries, water sources, the soil and tourism infrastructure. The lessons learnt from this event also need to be carefully recorded, and taken into account in future planning and policies regulating coastal zones. A coordinated global effort to provide reliable and effective early warning systems against such calamities is urgently needed, particularly given that extreme events along coastal areas are expected to increase as a result of climate change.

Even before the Indian Ocean disaster, Munich Re, one of the world's biggest re-insurance companies, announced at the tenth conference of parties to the UN Framework Convention on Climate Change in early December that 2004 was set to go down in history as the costliest natural catastrophe year for the insurance industry worldwide. Insured losses due to weather-related disasters cost the insurance industry an estimated US$35 billion, up from US$16 billion in 2003. When uninsured losses are taken into account, the total cost to the international community from weather-related disasters was much higher – estimated at about US$90 billion, up from about US$65 billion in 2003 (UNEP 2004). Small developing countries with fragile economies were the worst hit.

The Indian Ocean tsunami will add considerably to this estimate, which does not even begin to count the high social and environmental costs. While the focus of the global effort should be to prevent disasters where possible, efforts to reduce the overall costs to society through better disaster preparedness are also urgently required.

REFERENCES

BBC (2005). Asia's tsunami death toll soars. 20 January. http://news.bbc.co.uk/2/hi/asia-pacific/4189883.stn

BirdLife International (2005). Biodiversity impacts of the Asian tsunami tragedy. http://www.birdlife.net/action/ground/asia_tsunami/

Browne, A. (2004). On Asia's Coasts, Progress Destroys Natural Defenses. *The Wall Street Journal*. 31 December.

Creel, L. (2003). Ripple Effects: Population and Coastal Regions. Population Reference Bureau. Washington. http://www.prb.org/Template.cfm?Section=PRB&template=/ContentManagement/ContentDisplay.cfm&ContentID=9513

FAO (2004). FAO assessing damage in countries devastated by tsunamis in South Asia. http://www.fao.org/newsroom/en/news/2004/56521/index.html

FAO (2005). Tsunamis destroyed tens of thousands of fishing boats. http://www.fao.org/newsroom/en/news/2005/88321/index.html

NASA (2005). Earth Observatory, National Aeronautics and Space Administration. http://earthobservatory.nasa.gov/Newsroom/NewImages/images.php3?img_id=16777

NOAA (2004a). NOAA and the Indian Ocean Tsunami. National Oceanic and Atmospheric Administration. www.noaanews.noaa.gov/stories2004/s2358.htm

NOAA (2004b). http://www.prh.noaa.gov/itic/tsunami_events/media/factsheets/major_world_wide_tsunamis.pdf

NOAA (2005). Potential ecological impacts of Indian Ocean Tsunami on nearshore marine ecosystems. http://www.noaanews.noaa.gov/stories2005/s2362.htm

UNEP (2002). *Vital Water Graphics: An Overview of the State of the World's Fresh and Marine Waters*. United Nations Environment Programme. Nairobi.

UNEP (2004). Extreme Weather Losses Soar to Record High for Insurance Industry. UNEP News Centre. http://www.unep.org/Documents.Multilingual/Default.asp?DocumentID=414&ArticleID=4682&l=en

UNEP (2005a). *South Asia Disaster UNEP Situation Report 1*. UNEP South Asian Disaster Task Force. 3 January.

UNEP (2005b). Oceans and Coastal Areas. http://earthwatch.unep.net/oceans/coastalthreats.php

UNEP (2005c). *Atlantic and Indian Oceans Environment Outlook*. United Nations Environment Programme.

UNEP (2005d). *Caribbean Environment Outlook*. United Nations Environment Programme.

UNEP (2005e). *Pacific Environment Outlook*. United Nations Environment Programme.

UNESCO (2005). UNESCO to announce global strategy for establishment of a tsunami early warning system. http://portal.unesco.org/en/ev.php-URL_ID=24450&URL_DO=DO_TOPIC&URL_SECTION=201.html

UNOCHA (2004a). Earthquakes and Tsunami in Asia: Save the Children Emergency Update. United Nations Office for the Coordination of Humanitarian Affairs. New York. http://www.reliefweb.int/w/rwb.nsf/s/82857D66A6481AD585256F7C00602CC7

UNOCHA (2004b). Maldives Situation Report #06/2004. United Nations Office for the Coordination of Humanitarian Affairs. New York. http://www.reliefweb.int/w/rwb.nsf/480fa8736b88bbc3c12564f6004c8ad5/4915ce29d1d3555449256f7d001ede9e?OpenDocument

UNOCHA (2005a). Consolidated Appeals Process (CAP): Flash Appeal 2005 for Indian Ocean Earthquake – Tsunami. United Nations Office for the Coordination of Humanitarian Affairs. New York. http://www.reliefweb.int/w/rwb.nsf/480fa8736b88bbc3c12564f6004c8ad5/40b19a67d90fb4b585256f800073eda1?OpenDocument

UNOCHA (2005b). The tsunami affected the entire population of the Maldives. United Nations Office for the Coordination of Humanitarian Affairs. New York. http://www.reliefweb.int/w/rwb.nsf/480fa8736b88bbc3c12564f6004c8ad5/1472103c6a057a7b49256f8000252c61?OpenDocument

USGS (2005). Earthquake Hazards Program, United States Geological Survey. http://neic.usgs.gov/neis/eqlists/10maps_world.html

Venkataramani, G. (2004). Mangroves can act as shield against tsunami. *The Hindu*. 27 December. Chennai.

Waldman, A. (2004). Motherless and Childless, An Indian Village's Toll. *The New York Times*. 31 December. New York.

WHO (2005). Situation report 6. 3 January. http://www.who.int/hac/crises/international/asia_tsunami/sitrep/06/en/

feature focus

Gender, Poverty and Environment

● GENDER MATTERS ● GENDER, POVERTY
AND ENVIRONMENT: A THREE-WAY INTERACTION
● CHALLENGES FOR THE FUTURE

Gender, Poverty and Environment

Gender is rarely considered as a mainstream issue in environmental policies and programmes. However, a better understanding of the different priorities and perceptions of men and women can be used to maximize policy effectiveness.

GENDER MATTERS

Understanding the relationship between people and the environment is increasingly seen as a key to achieving sustainable development. However, that relationship is extremely complex, both to understand and to manage. There is immense geographic diversity within the environmental resources that provide humans with essential goods and services. Resources are unevenly

Training women in decision making in the Himalayas.
Source: UNEP/ICIMOD Project

distributed, and conditions change over time. On the human side, people interact differently with, and are affected differently by, the environment.

Many of these differences can be traced to the human and social attributes that distinguish different individuals and communities. Gender is one of the

most significant (**Box 1**). It shapes how people impact the environment, and how they, in turn,

Box 1: Some definitions

Gender: A person's sex is biological, but gender is social. Gender is what society makes of sex: it is the accumulation of social norms about what men and women 'should' be and do. For example, the fact that women give birth and men do not is a consequence of their sex. The fact that taking care of children is considered women's work almost everywhere in the world is a gender role. Ideas about gender shape personal relationships and institutions at all scales from the household to governmental agencies. While sex is more or less fixed, gender roles and perception are highly variable and changeable.

Gender analysis: The purpose of gender analysis is to understand the social, cultural and economic relations between women and men in different arenas. Gender analysis is not just about women: men are also part of the picture. It requires an examination of fundamental issues such as:

● The distribution of power between men and women;

● The ways in which notions of masculinity and femininity are defined and enacted in everyday life;

● The social roles and needs of women and men; and

● The gender dimensions of institutions.

Gender mainstreaming: This is the process of assessing the implications for women and men of all planned actions. It is a strategy for making women's as well as men's concerns and experiences an integral dimension when designing, implementing and evaluating policies and programmes in all spheres, so that women and men benefit equally and inequality is not perpetuated (WEDO 2003a).

Gender and Environment Milestones	**1972**	**1979**		**1985**	**1991**	**1992**
	The Stockholm Declaration on Environment articulates the right of people to live in an environment of quality that permits a life of well-being and dignity.	The UN General Assembly adopts the Convention on the Elimination of All Forms of Discrimination against Women (CEDAW), described as the first international bill of rights for women. Although environment is not specified in CEDAW, the Convention defines discrimination against women as "any distinction, exclusion or	restriction made on the basis of sex which has the effect or purpose of impairing or nullifying the recognition, enjoyment or exercise by women, irrespective of their marital status, on a basis of equality of men and women, of human rights and fundamental freedoms in the political, economic, social, cultural, civil or any other field."	The UN Third World Conference on Women, and associated NGO Forum in Nairobi, produces the *Nairobi Forward Looking Strategies*, which recognize women's role in environmental conservation and management.	The Global Assembly on Women and the Environment convenes in Miami.	The United Nations Conference on Environment and Development (UNCED) in Rio recognizes women as a 'major group' in sustainable development and makes specific provisions to advance their position. These include Chapter 24 in *Agenda 21*, entitled 'Global Action for Women towards

are impacted by the environment and environmental change. Sustainable development polices and actions have been found to be more effective when gender factors are taken into account, and when both men and women are involved equally at all stages of identifying and implementing solutions to problems.

The central role of gender in achieving sustainable development has been acknowledged increasingly in development and environment policies, including in Agenda 21, the Millennium Development Goals (MDGs) and the Johannesburg Plan of Implementation (JPOI) of the World Summit on Sustainable Development. However, the focus remains on promoting equity as a goal in itself, rather than on a deeper understanding of how and why gender concerns (which involve both men and women) are important to achieve sustainable development (**Box 2**).

Despite the growing recognition of gender as an important cross-cutting issue, it is rarely addressed in a balanced way. Gender is usually perceived as a synonym for 'women', and women are often treated as a single homogenous social group without much differentiation by age, income or subculture. The majority of gender analyses in the environment field focus on women from poor communities in developing countries. Whilst this focus is understandable because 70 per cent of the world's poor are women (UNDP 1995), and the poor are the most vulnerable to ecological degradation, it does not provide the level of understanding of gender-environment interlinkages needed to include this dimension fully in environmental decision making. To provide comprehensive perspectives, gender

Box 2: The gender perspective in Millennium Development Goals

The Millennium Development Goals were adopted in 2000 as part of the Millennium Declaration, signed by 191 countries, and focus on peace, security, development, environmental sustainability, human rights and democracy.

There are eight goals, which are seen as interconnected and mutually reinforcing agents of sustainable development. A list of 18 quantitative targets and 48 indicators have been identified for the goals, most of which are to be achieved by 2015.

Goal 3 calls for the promotion of gender equality and empowerment of women. It is recognized that this is central to the achievement of the other seven MDGs. Attempting to achieve the MDGs without promoting gender equality will raise the costs and decrease the likelihood of achieving the other goals.

Most signatories to the Millennium Declaration are preparing country level MDG reports as a mechanism for tracking progress. A review of 13 of these reports by the United Nations Development Programme (UNDP) reveals that:

● Gender is not reflected as a cross-cutting issue in any of the reports;

● Goal 3, which deals specifically with gender, is the only goal where gender issues have been consistently addressed by countries;

● Apart from Goal 3, gender issues are most frequently addressed under Goal 5 (maternal mortality);

● Gender issues are mentioned under Goal 1 (poverty) in six reports;

● Women are mentioned under Goal 7 (environment) and Goal 8 (development cooperation) in only one report each (Mozambique and Mauritius respectively).

The UNDP report concludes that including gender as a mainstream issue is still patchy, and is restricted primarily to the obvious sectors of women's empowerment and maternal mortality. The confinement of gender issues within women-specific sectors occurs almost universally – there is no significant difference between reports authored by the UN system, national governments, or independent consultants.

The inclusion of gender perspectives and women's concerns under Goals 5 and 6 (to combat HIV/AIDS, malaria and other diseases), plus the invisibility of women in discussions on Goals 7 (environment) and 8 (development cooperation) in all but two reports, suggests that women are still seen mainly in terms of their vulnerabilities and roles as mothers or victims rather than as actors in development.

Despite the rights-based perspective reflected by most reports in the discussion on Goal 3, recognition of the importance of gender in relation to the other goals continues to be limited. For instance, women's lack of knowledge of care and feeding practices is often cited as a barrier to achieving the goal on reducing child mortality. Such a formulation ignores other gender-related variables that affect child survival, including the role of fathers in parenting and care.

Source: UNDP 2003a

	1993	1994	1995		2000

Sustainable Development'. Rio Principle 20 reads: "Women have a vital role in environmental management and development. Their full participation is therefore essential in achieving sustainable development."

The World Conference on Human Rights in Vienna acknowledges that women's rights are an inalienable part of universal human rights.

The International Conference on Population and Development in Cairo takes major steps forward on women's and girls' rights to control their lives and status in reproductive rights including family planning.

The UN Fourth World Conference on Women in Beijing results in the Beijing Platform for Action, which offers a roadmap for 12 key areas: poverty, education and training, health, violence, armed conflict, the economy, decision making, institutional mechanisms, human rights, the media, the environment and the

girl child. Section K, on women and the environment, asserts that "women have an essential role to play in the development of sustainable and ecologically sound consumption and production patterns and approaches to natural resource management".

Beijing+5: Beijing and Beyond convenes in New York and recognizes several emerging critical issues for women and girls, including work-related rights, gender-based violence, reproductive and sexual rights, education and social security, and access to productive resources. At the Millennium Summit in New York, UN Member

Box 3: Women as participants in programme design and execution

For many years, studies on environmental management portrayed women from poor communities as victims of environmental degradation, particularly water and fuel scarcity. Their role as managers or problem-solvers was overlooked, and policy solutions considered them as passive beneficiaries. Often women were not involved in the analysis of the problem, nor in its solution.

For example, when concerns were raised in the 1970s and 80s about the shortage of biomass fuel for domestic energy in developing countries, and the impact of fuelwood gathering on forests and woodlands, two solutions were proposed: tree planting, and efficient stoves to conserve biomass energy.

The forestry sector largely failed to involve women in afforestation, and many improved stoves were designed in laboratories with little input from the women who would use them. As a result, many early stoves programmes failed to achieve their targets for dissemination and use. Women often rejected them because they were barely more efficient, and did not provide some of the subsidiary benefits of traditional stoves, such as space heating and ability to accommodate different sizes of pots. These failures drew attention to the need for women's participation and consultation, and brought the realization that women could contribute to project success. The emphasis has now shifted to women's participation in planning, design and decision making. However, even women's participation does not always guarantee success, partly because of lack of attention to other gender aspects, such as social relations, women's status in the household or access to income.

Source: Cecelski 2004

have been few systematic attempts to collect gender-related data for the environmental impacts of people on resources, or of environmental impacts on people, except for a limited number of variables.

Gender mainstreaming is also essential but is not occurring on the scale needed (UNDP 2003a). One reason for this could be that sector experts fail to see the importance of women's empowerment for project success. For example, it has been difficult to convince project planners that gender (for energy projects) and energy (for gender/social development projects) are key variables in project success (Cecelski 2004) (**Box 3**).

Governance

A key step in ensuring that women are considered, and take part in, policy-making is that they should be equitably represented in decision-making bodies, at every level from local to national and global.

After almost two decades of attempts to address gender concerns, women still account, on average, for less than 10 per cent of the seats in national parliaments (World Bank 2003). Nowhere in the world do women have equal representation with men in government, and in only 22 countries do they represent 25 per cent or more of legislators (**Figure 1**). The nations with the highest shares of women in elected office are those that enforce explicit policies promoting equality – most notably, the Scandinavian countries (Seager 2003). To date, only Sweden, Denmark, Finland and Norway have achieved a 30 per cent or higher share of seats for women in parliaments or legislatures (World Bank 2003).

analyses must encompass men and women, young and old, from rich and poor backgrounds, in urban and rural situations, as producers and consumers of the planet's resources and as drivers and recipients of environmental change.

Understanding of the different priorities and perceptions of men and women can be used to maximize policy effectiveness. In natural resource management, for instance, men may prioritize income-generation through short-term natural resource use, while women may be more concerned with long-term security for the family in food, water and energy. A World Bank water and sanitation project in Morocco found that men were primarily interested in constructing rural roads and ensuring a supply of electricity.

Women were mainly concerned with the lack of potable water near their homes – many had to walk as far as five kilometres to the nearest source (World Bank 2003).

Policy development also needs to take account of the different environmental hazards and health risks that men and women are exposed to because of their different livelihoods. For example, men may be at greater risk of exposure to toxic chemicals used in mining, while women may be at greater risk from pesticides used in the floriculture industry.

Data inadequacies

Environmental assessment rarely takes gender issues into full consideration. One reason for this may be inadequacies in the data: there

---

2000 continued

States commit themselves to establishing a better, healthier and more just world by 2015. The Millennium Declaration promises "to promote gender equality and the empowerment of women as effective ways to combat poverty, hunger and disease and to stimulate development that is truly sustainable."

Among the eight Millennium Development Goals are:

- Goal One: eradicate extreme poverty and hunger;
- Goal Three: promote gender equality and empower women; and
- Goal Seven: ensure environmental sustainability.

Security Council Resolution 1325 on Women Peace and Security recognizes the impact of war on women, and recommends improving women's protection during conflict as well as women's leadership in peace-building and reconstruction.

2002

The World Summit on Sustainable Development in Johannesburg issues a Political Declaration, and the Johannesburg Plan of Implementation. They confirm the need for gender analysis, gender-specific data and gender mainstreaming in all sustainable development efforts, and the recognition of women's land

rights. Principle 18 of the declaration states: "We are committed to ensure that women's empowerment and emancipation and gender equality are integrated in all the activities encompassed within Agenda 21, the Millennium Development Goals and the Plan of Implementation of the Summit".

2003

The 11th session of the UN Commission on Sustainable Development decides that gender equality will be a cross-cutting issue in all forthcoming work up until 2015.

The 2004–05 UNEP programme of work identifies gender as a cross-cutting priority in all UNEP's activities.

Figure 1: Women in government, 2002

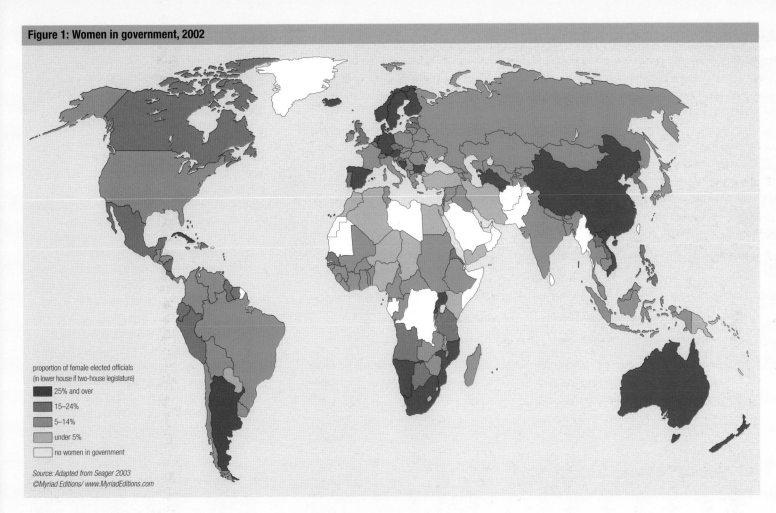

proportion of female elected officials
(in lower house if two-house legislature)

- 25% and over
- 15–24%
- 5–14%
- under 5%
- no women in government

Source: Adapted from Seager 2003
©Myriad Editions/ www.MyriadEditions.com

The Beijing Platform for Action, developed at the Fourth World Conference on Women in 1995, calls for at least 30 per cent representation by women in national governments. Quota or reservation systems that ensure a minimum level of female representation are now in place in more than 25 countries. An increasing number of women are active in local governance, in city councils and mayoralties. In India, for instance, there were close to a million elected women leaders at the village level in 2001 (Seager 2003). At the level of international governance, in both developed and developing countries, women are in the minority in positions of authority where decisions that affect the environment are taken. While global environmental processes have reiterated the need to empower and involve women, the Stockholm Convention on Persistent Organic Pollutants, which came into force in 2004, is the first treaty to clearly call for a balanced inclusion of women in the convention process itself. One positive development, however, is the formation of a Network of Women Ministers of the Environment, aimed at strengthening

2004

The First Meeting of the Global Women's Assembly on Environment is held in Nairobi at UNEP. The resulting Manifesto engages to "continue the struggle for a peaceful, just and healthy planet for all… and to continue to work, develop, and support activities that contribute to gender justice, a cleaner safer environment, and a better life for our communities."

2005

Implementation of the MDGs within the context of gender and environment is a special topic for consultation at the 23rd session of UNEP's Governing Council / Global Ministerial Environment Forum.

Box 4: Network of Women Ministers of the Environment

In March 2002, 22 women ministers for the environment and 28 women leaders of intergovernmental and non-governmental environmental organizations in Africa, Asia, Europe, North and South America met in Helsinki, Finland. The meeting resulted in the creation of a Network of Women Ministers of the Environment (NWME) with a secretariat in Washington DC.

NWME is part of a new architecture of organizations founded to advance global democracy, excellence in governance and gender equality. It operates under the auspices of the Council of Women World Leaders, founded in 1996, and the International Assembly of Women Ministers, created in 2002.

NWME recognizes that women constitute a majority of the world's poor, but are severely under-represented in policy-making roles. Given that women can bring to the table new ideas, approaches and strategies for protecting people and natural resources, the Network focuses on increasing the involvement of women in sustainable development issues. Some of its activities include:

● Developing recommendations for practical solutions to environmental problems confronting nations and the world;

● Building partnerships with appropriate civil society, non-governmental and intergovernmental agencies;

● Exchanging best-practice experiences in order to implement more effective policies; and

● Creating a critical mass of leadership to influence international and national policy.

For 2004–05, NWME has identified demography and sanitation, fresh water, energy and sustainable security as priority issues. In 2005, for the tenth anniversary of the Beijing Conference on women, the Network will explore gender and environmental perspectives of the Beijing goals.

Source: NWME 2004

women's positions in environmental decision making (**Box 4**).

Progress is being made within the United Nations system in advancing gender mainstreaming. Key UN agencies devoted specifically to gender issues include the United Nations Development Fund for Women (UNIFEM), United Nations International Research and Training Center for the Advancement of Women, United Nations Division for the Advancement of Women, and the Commission on the Status of Women. These institutions provide leadership on substantive gender issues and processes of gender mainstreaming.

Women's environmental action has been most effective at the local level, where they have greatest voice and autonomy. At the grassroots, women have often become major forces for environmental change. The 'Chipko' or 'hug the trees' movement was started by women protecting their natural resource base in the Himalayas from logging in the 1970s (**Box 5**). It provided inspiration to environmentalists across the world, and contributed to a better understanding of the

Box 5: Women defend the trees

The Uttarakhand region in the Himalayan foothills in India is rich in forest resources such as timber, limestone, magnesium, and potassium, which have been commercially exploited over the centuries. Forest conservation policies traditionally restricted the access of local communities to these forests. Combined with large-scale deforestation due to logging, these policies resulted in large-scale migration from the region. In the 1960s, entire villages were depopulated.

Women often stayed behind in the villages. They faced increasing difficulties as environmental degradation deepened and spread, resulting in acute water, fuelwood and fodder shortages. Communities gave up raising livestock, adding to the problems of malnutrition in the region. Natural disasters increased in intensity as watersheds were deforested and flooding and erosion increased.

The increasing adversity of hill life prompted local people to resist the destruction of their land and livelihoods. The first confrontation occurred when a forest concession was granted to an outside company rather than to local interests. Activists fanned out across the Himalayas to organize communities against commercial logging operations that threatened their livelihoods.

In 1974, state government and contractors diverted the men of Reni village to a fictional compensation payment site, while labourers disembarked from trucks to start logging operations. Under the leadership of Gaura Devi, a 50-year old illiterate woman, women left their homes to hug the trees and prevent them from being cut. A four-day standoff ended in victory for the villagers.

The actions of the women of Reni were repeated in several other places in the region, as hill women demonstrated their new-found power as non-violent activists. Their spontaneous movement eventually culminated in the banning of tree felling above 1 000 metres in 1980, by India's then Prime Minister, Indira Gandhi.

Source: Rawat 1996

Bali Devi, one of the leaders of the Chipko movement, at the 2004 meeting of Women as the Voice for the Environment.

Source: IISD

Gender imbalance is often apparent at international meetings.
Source: IISD

links between poverty and the environment. It was commonly believed then that environmental concerns were the luxury of the rich. The drastic steps taken by the local community showed that environmental concerns were in fact a matter of life and death for the poor.

In Kenya, the Green Belt Movement, started by Nobel laureate Wangari Maathai, demonstrated that tree planting can improve the lives of women, provide sustainable livelihoods, and conserve the environment. Professor Maathai founded the movement on Earth Day 1977. Since then, 50 000 people have planted 30 million indigenous trees on farms and school and churchyards all over Kenya. They were paid for every seedling that survived. A Pan African Green Belt Network has been set up, and similar initiatives established in other countries including Ethiopia, Lesotho, Malawi, Tanzania, Uganda and Zimbabwe.

The Green Belt initiative has multiple benefits. It empowers women, provides them with a sustainable livelihood, and promotes self-sufficiency. It provides them with fuel wood, prevents soil erosion, protects catchments, provides shade, and creates windbreaks for crops. In recent years, the movement has broadened to include issues of food security and production of indigenous food crops, many of which had been abandoned in favour of export crops such as coffee, tea and flowers. As Professor Maathai remarked, "Implicit in the act of planting trees is a civic education, a strategy to empower people and to give them a sense of taking their destiny into their own hands" (Maathai 2004).

Time to participate

In many rural communities in the developing world, one of the obstacles to more equitable gender participation in governance and decision making relates to women's work burden and its effect on the time available for other matters.

Experts in the late 1970s began to argue that the 'real energy crisis' was not a shortage of biomass energy, but of women's time. Work burdens also affect other factors needed for informed participation: they limit girls' and women's opportunities to receive training and education which could enhance their understanding of problems and possible solutions (Cecelski 2004). The schooling gap between boys and girls in many countries and regions still exists. In times of hardship, girls are the first to be pulled from school. An estimated 860 million people in the world are illiterate, and two-thirds of these are women (UNESCO 2003b).

Detailed studies of time allocation since the late 1970s showed that women and girls worked longer hours than men and boys, and more of their work was unpaid. There was also considerable diversity in the division of labour between men and women. Certain tasks, such as weeding, child care, cooking, fuel collection, food processing and water carrying were typically done by women, while other tasks such as ploughing and home repair were done by men (Cecelski 2004).

In response to such studies, the International Labour Organisation (ILO) recommended in the 1980s that the definition of 'labour activities' in labour market censuses should cover subsistence and domestic activities, as well as wage-earning and the production and sale of goods and services (Cecelski 2004). In 1995, UNDP estimated that if unpaid activities were treated as market transactions at prevailing wages, global output would increase by US$16 trillion of currently non-monetized contributions. Of this, US$11 trillion would correspond to women's 'invisible contribution' and the rest to men's (UNDP 1995).

Such studies also drew attention to the need for time-saving technologies for women, to free up time for other income generating activities and for education. More equal education of women would bring a range of benefits. Education has been found to have a profound effect on health and population growth. A study of 25 developing countries showed that, all else being equal, one to three extra years of maternal schooling would

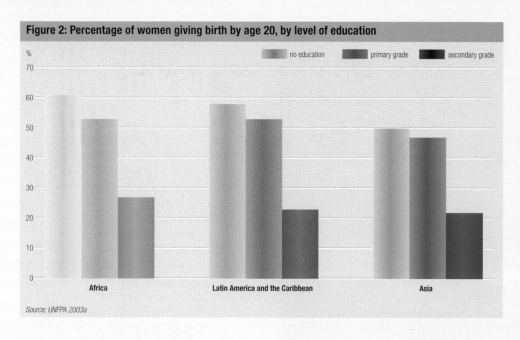

Figure 2: Percentage of women giving birth by age 20, by level of education

%

Legend: no education | primary grade | secondary grade

Categories: Africa | Latin America and the Caribbean | Asia

Source: UNFPA 2003a

Shanty town in Bangladesh.

Source: Mark Edwards/Still Pictures

reduce child mortality by 15 per cent, whereas similar increases in paternal schooling would achieve a 6 per cent reduction (Kirk and Pillet 1998). Education, especially if pursued beyond the first few years, also reduces fertility rates (UNFPA 2003a) (**Figure 2**).

GENDER, POVERTY AND ENVIRONMENT: A THREE-WAY INTERACTION

In many parts of the world, women tend to be the poorest of the poor in a very literal sense. In addition to being the majority among the poor, they are often denied the most basic rights and access to critical resources such as land,

inheritance or credit. Their labour and knowledge are undervalued. Their needs are often overlooked. They are more vulnerable to disease and disasters and the situation is made worse by their poverty. Cultural and social norms sometimes complicate matters further by placing additional expectations, restrictions and limitations on women. Gender gaps are widespread, and in no region of the world are women equal to men in legal, social and economic rights (World Bank 2003) (**Figure 3**).

In recent years the definition of poverty has broadened from its traditional focus on per capita income, to encompass other dimensions such as lack of empowerment, opportunity, capacity and security (World Bank 2003). Analysts argue that improving women's access to economic opportunities is critical to the MDG of halving world poverty. Some of the causes of poverty are embedded in how resources are distributed, and this is linked to the power relations between men and women (Kabeer 2003). The MDGs of gender empowerment and poverty eradication are therefore seen as mutually reinforcing.

Integrating poverty and gender analyses in policy-making is a challenging task. The World Bank's Gender and Development Group took stock of the Bank's Poverty Reduction Strategy Papers (PRSPs) in 2001 and found that incorporation of gender had been minimal – less than half the PRSPs discussed gender issues in any detail. Even fewer integrated gender analysis into their strategy, resource

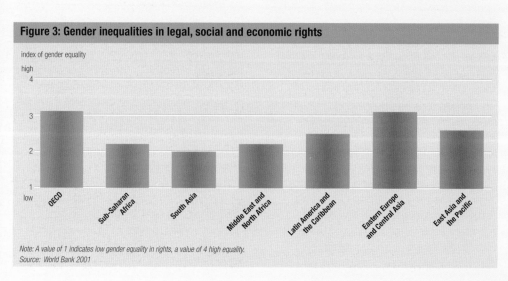

Figure 3: Gender inequalities in legal, social and economic rights

index of gender equality

Categories: OECD | Sub-Saharan Africa | South Asia | Middle East and North Africa | Latin America and the Caribbean | Eastern Europe and Central Asia | East Asia and the Pacific

Note: A value of 1 indicates low gender equality in rights, a value of 4 high equality.
Source: World Bank 2001

allocation and monitoring and evaluation sections (Kabeer 2003).

Even more challenging than integrating poverty and gender is integrating environment as well into a three-way interaction. Gender is often the one that disappears in the analysis (Seager and Hartmann 2004).

The synergies between the goals of gender equity, poverty alleviation and environmental sustainability are explored below in terms of addressing poverty among women – including energy and water poverty, health, climate change, natural disasters and creating sustainable livelihoods by empowering women in the realms of agriculture, forest and biodiversity management.

Energy, environment and gender

The synergies between gender, environment and the energy sector were first recognized in relation to biomass energy. Women were recognized as users and collectors of fuel wood, and as victims of environmental deterioration that caused energy scarcity.

Time use surveys have shown that women spend long hours in fuel collection. The burden increases as deforestation worsens, and this affects the time available to women for other activities including income-generating activities, education and participation in decision making. In Sudan, for instance, deforestation in the last decade led to a quadrupling of the time women spent gathering fuelwood (PRB 2001). This stimulated efforts to promote afforestation and design more fuel-efficient stoves. Funding petered out, however, when the improved stoves and forestry projects were not as successful as anticipated (see also **Box 3**).

Attention to biomass energy and its impact on women's lives has recently revived. A 2002 report by the World Health Organisation ranked indoor air pollution, mainly from woodfuel smoke, as the fourth largest health problem in developing countries (WHO 2002). It is estimated to kill 2 million women and children in developing countries every year (World Bank 2003), and also causes respiratory and eye diseases. There are differences in exposure according to age and economic status, and in some cultures

women tend to undervalue their own health, leading to under-reporting of problems (Cecelski 2004).

In many developing countries communal lands remain a crucial source of biomass energy, yet privatization of these lands

Deforestation increases the time women spend in meeting energy needs.
Source: Shehzad Noorani/Still Pictures

Air pollution from biomass smoke mostly affects women and children.
Source: Jorgen Schytte/Still Pictures

continues apace – reducing free access to fuelwood, and removing yet another area where cooperative decisions could be made on sustainable management of fuelwood sources (Agarwal 1986).

In developed countries, the links between gender, environment and energy have been explored mainly in the areas of equal opportunity in the energy professions, decision making in energy policy, pollution and health, preferences for energy production systems, access to scientific and technological education and the division of labour in the home (Clancy and Roehr 2003). There is also some indication in industrialized countries that women's preferred research agendas may differ from men's: they tend to be more skewed towards research on renewable energy and social aspects of energy (Clancy and Roehr 2003).

A key lesson for energy policy makers is that the involvement of both sexes in planning and decision making is central to the success or failure of energy interventions.

Transportation choices affect energy use and harmful emissions.
Source: Permdhai Vesmaporn/UNEP/Still Pictures

Climate change and gender

Climate change is predicted to cause displacement of populations due to sea level rise. In many parts of the developing world it is expected to increase water scarcity, to increase the disease burden, to negatively impact agriculture, and to cause more frequent extreme weather events (IPCC 2001).

Analysts have assumed that the effects of climate change are very likely to differ by gender, because of the strong relationship between poverty and vulnerability, and the fact that women as a group are poorer and less powerful than men (Skutsch 2002). But the discussion has remained largely speculative, with little research to support it. Neither the impact of climate on a gender basis, nor the respective roles of men and women in addressing climate change have been considered in global negotiations under the UN Framework Convention on Climate Change (UNFCCC).

The potential value of gender as a factor in deciding on policies and programmes to reduce greenhouse gas emissions has received even less attention. For example, as

users of household energy, women can play a key role in energy conservation, as well as in promoting renewable energy technologies.

Both sexes make decisions about the forms of transport they use and how frequently they travel, and there are gender differences in the choices they make. In developed countries, for example, women tend to use public transport more than men.

To encourage a policy focus on these areas, more gender-disaggregated research is needed on energy and climate change topics, including vulnerability to climate change and adaptive capacity among different social groups (Denton and Parikh 2003). Other areas for gender-disaggregated research include:

- Environmental aspects of energy production including biomass;
- Environmental awareness and attitudes about energy issues including renewable/ alternative energy;
- Energy consumption, use and saving;
- Impacts of privatizing energy markets; and
- Policy instruments in the energy sector, including policies on climate change.

Land tenure and agriculture

Time use studies challenged the commonly held belief that women play a marginal role in agriculture. It was found, for instance, that women produced most of the food in Africa (Cecelski 2004) (**Figure 4**). Official statistics recognize that women now make up about 40 per cent of the agricultural labour force worldwide, and about 67 per cent in developing countries (Seager 2003).

Despite this key role in agriculture, most of the world's women do not equally own, inherit or control land and other property. Discriminatory inheritance and property ownership laws restrict women's ability to ensure long-term food security for the family, and to get loans using land as collateral. They also have important consequences for soil and land management – it is widely acknowledged that owners of land take more care to ensure soil conservation. Improved access to agricultural support systems, including credit, technology, education, transport, extension and marketing services, is essential to improving agricultural

Small scale farming in Mozambique.
Source: Jorgen Schytte/Still Pictures

productivity and promoting environmentally sustainable practices – yet often women have no access to these services.

The division of labour between men and women in agricultural production varies considerably between cultures. However, as a broad generalization, it is usually men who are responsible for large-scale cash cropping, especially when it is highly mechanized, while women take care of household food production and some small-scale, low technology cultivation of cash crops. This has important implications for biodiversity. Gender-differentiated local knowledge systems play a decisive role in conserving, managing and improving genetic resources for food and agriculture. In Kenya, researchers have found that men's knowledge of traditional crops and practices is actually declining as a result of formal schooling and migration to urban areas. By contrast, women retain a widely shared level of general knowledge about wild foods, craft and medicinal plants, and acquire new knowledge about natural resources as their roles and duties change (Rocheleau and others 1995).

The 1992 United Nations Convention on Biological Diversity (CBD) recognizes the vital role that women play in the conservation and sustainable use of biological diversity, and affirms the need for their participation at all levels of policy-making and implementation. Women from farming communities in developing countries have also played a key role in opposing the patenting of plant and animal species by corporations, and continue to campaign to protect their access to seeds and medicinal plants essential to their survival (Diverse Women for Diversity 2004).

Water

Lack of access to clean potable water has been recognized as a factor increasing women's work burdens in those parts of the world where they are responsible for collecting water for basic needs like cooking, cleaning and hygiene. In some cases water collection can take up to 60 per cent of their working time (UNESCO 2004a).

In rural Africa, women and girls spend as much as three hours a day fetching water, using up more than one-third of their daily caloric energy intake (WEHAB Working Group 2002). This limits the time available for them to engage in wage-earning economic and social activities and development projects. Lack of clean water is also responsible for water-borne diseases among children – one of the major causes of child disease and mortality. This further adds to women's childcare responsibilities.

The lack of easily accessible water has health implications for women as well. Carrying heavy water jars over long distances during pregnancy can result in premature births, prolapsed uterus or back injuries

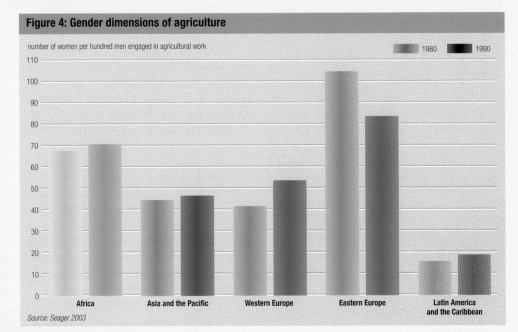

Figure 4: Gender dimensions of agriculture

number of women per hundred men engaged in agricultural work   ■ 1980 ■ 1990

Source: Seager 2003

Gender-aware water policies are needed at every level.

Source: Finbarr O'Reilly/Reuters/South

Box 6: Women ensuring their own water supplies

In several parts of the world, women have taken matters into their own hands to solve their water problems. In India, the Self-Employed Women's Association (SEWA), a trade union of 215 000 poor, self-employed women, launched a ten-year campaign to revive water sources in drought-prone districts of Gujarat. Women made up seven out of eleven members of the watershed committees set up at village meetings, and the chairperson was also required to be a woman. The committees performed soil and water conservation work, and created green belts and grass cover for better retention of water. The projects reduced soil salinity, resulting in more fertile land and a more sustainable source of income, while generating direct employment opportunities for about 240 women.

In Honduras, women in low-income urban neighbourhoods have taken on and managed their own licensed water-vending points, to fight back against high water prices from private vendors and license holders. The result has been lower and more reliable water prices, part-time employment for poor single women with children, and use of the group's surplus for neighbourhood projects. Women have used the local water supply for income generation through beer brewing, teashops and a launderette.

Source: WEDO 2003a

(UNFPA 2003b). Constant exposure to water while collecting, washing clothes, cleaning and cooking puts women at greater risk of contracting water-related diseases. For instance, in eastern Tanzania, urinary schistosomiasis, a water-related disease, was most common among boys, and also among girls and women between the ages of 10 and 40. The incidence among boys was associated with swimming. Among women and girls, it was associated with the local practice of washing clothes while standing in schistosomiasis-infested water (WEDO 2003a).

The importance of involving women in water management in local communities has been well documented over the years. A review of 271 World Bank projects by the International Food Policy Research Institute shows that when women are consulted, sustainability of projects is increased by 16 per cent (IFPRI 2000). Yet, in most parts of the world, women are involved only at the lower echelons of water monitoring and management. Men still take most decisions on water, particularly at the national and global level. The global trend towards privatization of public services may make matters worse, if increased water and energy prices result in decreased access to clean water for poor women. Women have been central in struggles against the privatization of public water services (WEDO 2003b) (**Box 6**).

Non-governmental, governmental, and academic interests have recently begun gender analyses of water resources, management, and supply issues. Support for integrating gender into water resource management has come from the recent World Water Forums – in Marrakech 1997, The Hague 2000, and Kyoto 2003. Despite these commitments, a fully gender-aware water agenda has yet to be taken on board by governments and multilateral agencies.

Such an agenda would include the development of gender-aware water policies at all levels; comprehensive data collection to better understand the gender aspects of water supply, use and informal water management in household economies; gender-sensitive impact studies of water

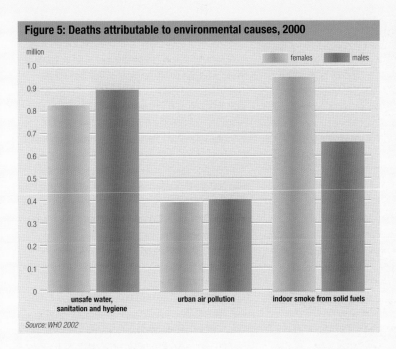

Figure 5: Deaths attributable to environmental causes, 2000

million

females　males

Source: WHO 2002

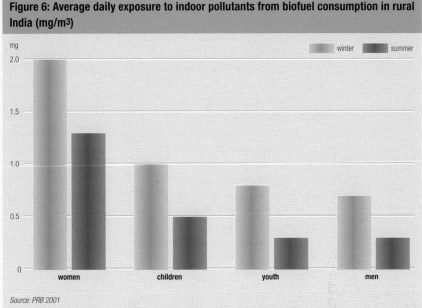

Figure 6: Average daily exposure to indoor pollutants from biofuel consumption in rural India (mg/m³)

mg

winter　summer

Source: PRB 2001

privatization; and the involvement of women in decision making on water use and management. The benefits of such an agenda for women would include increased awareness of health and hygiene in water management, and increased income-generating capacity through time saved in fetching water (Joshi and Fawcett 2001).

Health

The link between health and the environment has been widely recognized, if not fully acted upon, in recent years (**Figure 5**). Unclean water and untreated sewage are responsible for the spread of water-borne diseases such

as cholera and intestinal parasites (**Box 7**). Limited access to water may be responsible for the spread of germs. Pollutants in the environment (including air pollutants from transport and industry, chemical toxins and heavy metals from industrial processes, and dioxins from waste incineration) pose a constant threat to the human body. Climate change is expected to increase the burden of disease considerably by allowing vectors to breed in latitudes or altitudes where current temperatures prevent them.

Men and women are exposed differently to environmental risks, and their bodies may respond differently even to the same threats. For instance, the incidence of respiratory illnesses is considerably higher among women and young children, who are constantly exposed to indoor air pollution, than among men (**Figure 6**).

Poor nutritional levels can make people particularly vulnerable to infectious diseases, and age and gender may exacerbate this risk. Malaria, for example, is more likely to cause serious problems or death in young children or pregnant women. During pregnancy, it can cause severe anaemia, and it can also harm the foetus, increasing the chances of abortion, premature birth, stillbirth, intrauterine growth retardation and low infant birth weight.

Malnutrition, persistent bouts of diarrhoea from unclean water and intestinal worms in the mother can also retard the growth of the foetus by causing anaemia. Estimates attribute 20 per cent of maternal deaths in

Box 7: Sanitation

Women have a vested interest in promoting sanitation systems, to ensure better hygiene for their families and hence a reduced disease burden. This interest was reflected in a study in Indonesia and Cambodia, which showed that the process for acquiring family latrines was mostly initiated by women. Women's interest was higher despite evidence that the extra work involved in keeping toilets clean and ready for use fell to women alone (Mukherjee 2001).

Table 1: HIV/AIDS prevalence by gender, 2003

Percentage of the population aged 15–49 living with HIV/AIDS

	Total	Men	Women
Northern Africa	<0.1	na	na
Sub-Saharan Africa	7.2	6.2	8.3
Latin America and Caribbean	0.7	0.9	0.5
Eastern Asia	0.1	0.2	<0.1
Southern Asia	0.7	0.8	0.5
South-Eastern Asia	0.5	0.7	0.3
Western Asia	<0.1	na	na
Oceania	0.5	0.7	0.3
Commonwealth of Independent States (Asia)	0.1	0.1	<0.1
Commonwealth of Independent States (Europe)	1.1	1.5	0.8
Developed Regions	0.5	0.6	0.3

Note: na – not available

Source: UN Statistics 2004

Africa and 23 per cent in Asia to anaemia during pregnancy (Murray and Lopez 1996).

Scientists now regard certain chemicals such as PCBs, dioxins, DDT and at least 80 other pesticides as 'endocrine disrupters,' which may interfere with normal hormone function, undermining disease resistance and reproduction. Some of them may cause declining sperm counts among men, infertility among women, miscarriages, and early puberty in girls (UNFPA 2003b). People of both sexes need to be better informed of these threats, so that they may exert pressure on governments to find safer alternatives, support pre-market testing of chemicals and integrate the precautionary approach into chemicals management policies (Patton 2004).

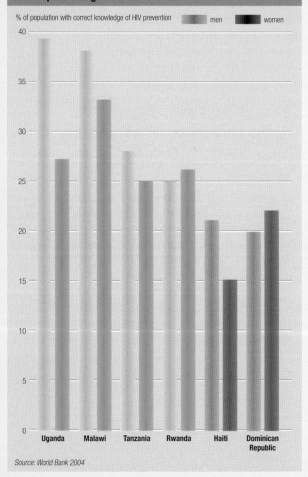

Figure 7: Knowledge difference between men and women about preventing HIV

% of population with correct knowledge of HIV prevention — men / women

Source: World Bank 2004

One of the newest threats to health and social welfare is the spread of HIV/AIDS. Both sexes are affected, but to different extents in different parts of the world (**Table 1**). Globally, men account for 52 per cent of infected adults. Lack of information among women on how the disease is transmitted confounds the problem in many regions (**Figure 7**). In sub-Saharan Africa, 55 per cent of those infected are women (World Bank 2003). In this region, women grow most of the food, and women's agricultural labour often shows the first signs of wider community disruption by HIV/AIDS. For example, in Malawi, Mozambique, Zambia and Zimbabwe where women are responsible for most food production, there has been a progressive shift from maize production to less labour-intensive, and less nutritious, cassava production to compensate for the labour lost through HIV/AIDS (De Waal and Whiteside 2003).

A study in South Africa showed that in almost half the households surveyed the primary caregiver for an HIV/AIDS patient has taken time off from formal or informal employment, or from schooling. The primary caregiver is most frequently female. Women and girls may lose as much as 60 per cent of their time from other housework or cultivation tasks, affecting the ability of poor households to grow food for consumption or sale (Heyzer 2004).

Urbanization

Until recently, the link between gender, the environment and urbanization was mostly seen as rural women being left behind in rural areas to take care of agriculture, while men migrated to cities in search of a better income. This focus has slowly expanded to include the impact of urban environments on women.

In many developing countries, people migrating as unskilled labourers to a city face a challenge in accessing even basic necessities such as food, water, and housing, and they are vulnerable to exploitation and economic abuse.

Air and water pollution can be extreme in urban settings, and sanitation and waste treatment poor or non-existent in low-cost residential areas and slums. Housing tenure patterns in towns and cities are sometimes gender distorted: it is often harder for women to have secure tenure of their housing or land. In addition, inequitable inheritance practices leave female-headed households extremely vulnerable, especially where land grabbing occurs. Many urban households have female heads, and typically these are poorer and more vulnerable than households with a couple (Seager 2003).

Flower workers are often exposed to pesticides. Holambra, Brazil.
Source: Ron Giling/Still Pictures

Men and women may be exposed to different hazards.

Source: Peter Frischmuth/Still Pictures

Environmental disasters

Disasters do not strike evenly by social class or gender. However, it is well established that the poor are more exposed to environmental and other disasters, and also more vulnerable to them when they occur. They are more likely to live in disaster-prone areas, in vulnerable, badly built and badly sited housing, and with few resources to pay for rescue or rehabilitation.

Anyone who is located (socially and/or spatially) 'out of the loop' of information supplied by early warning systems is likely to suffer more from disasters. In some countries, these individuals are more likely to be women than men. The 1991 cyclone in Bangladesh resulted in a disproportionate number of female deaths (71 per 1 000 women as against 15 per 1 000 men). This was partly because warnings of the cyclone were displayed in public places, less frequented by women. Researchers also found that women delayed leaving their houses for much longer, in order to avoid the impropriety of being alone in public. Women were also less likely to have been taught how to swim (Khonder 1996).

On the other hand, men sometimes treat disaster warnings less seriously. More men than women died in Florida and the Caribbean during Hurricane Mitch in 1998, in part because they ventured into the storm (Nelson

and others 2001). The earthquake in Kobe, Japan in 1995 demonstrated clear gender-differentiated impacts both during and after the event (**Box 8**). The Food and Agriculture Organization of the United Nations (FAO) has developed gender guidelines for emergency preparedness. These include key questions to be asked in an emergency situation to help ensure that emergency interventions will be sensitive to gender differences (FAO 2001). Several other disaster-relief NGOs, including OXFAM, have done similar work.

CHALLENGES FOR THE FUTURE

Many countries are introducing policies to address gender issues, including positive action measures, often called 'gender mainstreaming' tools. These include measures geared at improving equity such as legislation for gender-balanced quotas and targets, gender-sensitive budgets, equal education of girls and boys at all levels, and support for women's networks. They also include institution-building measures such as gender-mainstreaming advisors, gender impact assessments of old and new practices and policies, gender analysis and gender audits, and visioning about the future of institutions to weed out discriminatory practices.

The full success of forward-looking strategies for bringing gender into

environmental analysis – and vice versa – may hinge on four major areas of activity.

First, improving and supporting women's capacity to participate and shape environmental policy and action at all levels from grassroots to government. Worldwide, women are still very poorly represented in governments and other decision-making bodies. There has been an improvement in women's participation in development programmes, but their role still falls far short of men's. Part of the solution is to prepare women for greater participation by equalizing education and literacy rates for girls and women with those of boys and men.

Second, adjusting government priorities so that awareness and promotion of gender equality are integrated into financial planning. In 20 countries so far, UNIFEM has supported the development of gender-responsive budgets that examine how the allocation of public resources benefits women and men, and addresses gender equality requirements. In Mexico, the government earmarked the equivalent of 0.85 per cent of the total budget in 2003 for programmes promoting gender equity. Fourteen ministries are required to report quarterly on the status of these programmes.

Third, improving institutional capacities to incorporate gender-related environmental analysis. Much of modern environmental analysis is framed by the technical/scientific paradigm and relies mostly on quantitative biophysical data. Much of the work on gender and environment, on the other hand, is framed by a social science approach relying more on qualitative material, case study narratives, and anecdotal evidence. Merging these two paradigms will be a challenge.

It is difficult enough to mainstream social considerations within environmental work; adding gender as a third dimension is even more challenging. Many people in the environmental field see issues such as climate change or loss of biodiversity as urgent, first-

"As agents of change, bound together by our commitment to justice, equality and peace, we can sustain our environment and our common future."

Women as the Voice for the Environment Manifesto

order global problems. Bringing a gender perspective into the discussion is often dismissed as trivial – or at least not essential to priority problem solving. It is not unusual for environmentalists to consider that attention to gender diverts energy and time away from pressing issues; it is "like rearranging the chairs on the Titanic", one environmentalist was recently cited as saying (UNDP 2003b). Part of this challenge is to convince technical experts that gender matters, and that analyses of gender balance and equity do not weaken or delay, but actually strengthen and sharpen environmental analyses, policies and programmes.

Gender-related environmental analysis at all scales, in all regions, and across all topics is hampered by the lack of appropriate data and indicators. Thus there is also need for gender-disaggregated and gender sensitive data. Since most social and environmental data are still not disaggregated, analysts need to be

trained to use a gender-sensitive lens when analyzing them. Time budgets are increasingly used to document livelihood activities by gender, and changes in these budgets can be used as early warnings of environmental stress. A future challenge will be to develop gender sensitive criteria and indicators in all areas of sustainable development, covering social, cultural, economic and institutional aspects. This will require gender-disaggregated data for assessment and monitoring purposes.

Finally, there is a need for explicit commitment to bring issues of gender into the environmental arena. The 2004 Global Assembly of Women on Environment called on UNEP and the world's governments to bring to the table indigenous and women's perspectives on sustainable development, and to implement the World Summit on Sustainable Development commitments from a gender equality perspective (UNEP 2004).

REFERENCES

Agarwal, B. (1986). *Cold hearths and barren slopes: The woodfuel crisis in the Third World.* Zed Books, London

Cecelski, E. (2004). Re-thinking gender and energy: Old and new directions. *Energy, Environment and Development.* ENERGIA/EASE, Netherlands

Clancy, J. and Roehr, U. (2003). Gender and Energy: Is there a Northern Perspective? *Energy for Sustainable Development,* 7, 3, 44-9

De Waal, A. and Whiteside, A. (2003). New Variant Famine: AIDS and Food Crisis in Southern Africa. *The Lancet,* 362, 1234-7

Denton, F. and Parikh, J. (2003). Gender – A Forgotten Element. *Tiempo: A Bulletin on Climate and Development.* Issue 47

Diverse Women for Diversity (2004). http://www.diversewomen.org/Issues.htm

FAO (2001). *SEAGA Guidelines for Emergency Preparedness.* United Nations Food and Agriculture Organization, Rome

Government of Japan (2003). *Towards a research methodology for gender-sensitive program planning and implementation.* Interim report of the Working Team of Impact Assessment, Gender Equality Bureau, Cabinet Office, Tokyo. http://www.gender.go.jp/danjo-kaigi/eikyou/houkoku/index_hei1511.html

Heyzer, N. (2004). Peace of Mind, Peace of Land. *Our Planet,* 15, 2, 11-2

IFPRI (2000). *Women – The key to Food Security: Looking into the Household. Information brochure.* International Food Policy research Institute, Washington, D.C.

IPCC (2001). *Climate Change 2001: Impacts, Adaptation, and Vulnerability. Contribution of Working Group II to the Third Assessment Report of the Intergovernmental Panel on Climate Change.* Cambridge University Press, Cambridge, UK

Joshi, D. and Fawcett, B. (2001). *Water Projects and Women's Empowerment.* Paper for the 27th WEDC Conference: People and Systems for Water, Sanitation and Health, Lusaka, Zambia

Kabeer, N. (2003). *Gender mainstreaming in poverty eradication and the Millennium Development Goals: How readdressing gender inequalities can help achieve the MDGs.* International Development Research Centre, Ottawa, Canada

Khonder, H. H. (1996). Women and Floods in Bangladesh. *International Journal of Mass Emergencies and Disasters,* 14, 3, 281-92

Kirk, D. and Pillet, B. (1998). Fertility levels, trends, and differentials in Sub-Saharan Africa in the 1980s and 1990s. *Studies in Family Planning,* 29, 1, 1-22

Maathai, W. (2004). The Green Belt Movement. http://www.greenbeltmovement.org/biographies.htm

Mukherjee, N. (2001). *Achieving sustained sanitation for the poor.* Water and Sanitation Program for East Asia and the Pacific. Jakarta, Indonesia

Murray, C.J.L. and Lopez, A.D. eds. (1996). *The Global Burden of Disease: A comprehensive Assessment of Mortality and Disability from Diseases, Injuries and Risk Factors in 1990 and Projected to 2020.* Harvard School of Public Health, Cambridge, Massachusetts

Nelson, V., Meadows, K., Cannon, T., Morton, J., and Martin, A. (2001). Uncertain predictions, invisible impacts, and the need to mainstream gender in climate change adaptations. *Gender and Development* 10, 2, 51-9.

NWME (2004). The Network of Women Ministers of the Environment. http://www.womenworldleaders.org

Patton, S. (2004). Toxic Trespass. *Our Planet,* 15, 2, 24-6

PRB (2001). *Women, Men and Environmental Change: The gender dimensions of environmental policies and programs.* Population Reference Bureau, Washington DC

Rawat, R. (1996). *Women of Uttarakhand on the Frontiers of the Environmental Struggle.* http://www.bostonglobalaction.net/UK/chipko.html

Rocheleau, D., Thomas-Slayter, B. and Edmunds, D. (1995). Gendered Resource Mapping: Focusing on Women's Spaces in the Landscape. *Cultural Survival Quarterly,* 18, 4, 62-8

Saksena, S., Prasad, R., Pal, R.C., and Joshi, V. (1992). Patterns of daily exposure to TSP and CO in the Garhwal Himalaya. Atmospheric Environment, 26A, 2125-34

Seager, J. and Hartmann, B. (2004). *A Gender Assessment of DEWA and United Nations Environment Programme.* Unpublished report to DEWA, United Nations Environment Programme, Nairobi

Seager, J. (2003). *The Penguin Atlas of Women in the World.* Penguin Group, London

Skutsch, M. (2002). Protocols, treaties, and action: the 'climate change process' viewed through gender spectacles. *Gender and Development* 10, 2, 30-9

UNDP (1995). *Human Development Report 1995.* United Nations Development Programme, New York

UNDP (2003a). *Millennium Development Goals National Reports. A Look through a Gender Lens.* United Nations Development Programme, New York

UNDP (2003b). *Human Development Report 2003: Millennium Development Goals.* United Nations Development Programme. Oxford University Press, Oxford

UNEP (2004). *Report of the Global Women's Assembly on Environment on the Work of its First Meeting,* United Nations Environment Programme, UNEP/DPDL/WAVE/1. United Nations Environment Programme, Nairobi

UNESCO (2004a). *Women and Water.* United Nations Education, Scientific and Cultural Organization. http://www.unesco.org/water/ihp/women_and_water.html

UNESCO (2004b). *Education: World Literacy in Brief.* http://portal.unesco.org/education/en/ev.php-URL_ID=12874&URL_DO=DO_PRINTPAGE&URL_SECTION= 201.html

UNFPA (2003a). *State of World Population 2003.* United Nations Population Fund, New York

UNFPA (2003b). *Global Population and Water, Access and Sustainability. Population and Development Strategies, Number 6.* United Nations Population Fund, New York

UN Statistics (2004). *Millennium Indicators.* http://unstats.un.org/unsd/mi/mi_worldregn.asp

WEDO (2003a). Untapped Connections: Gender, Water and Poverty. Women's Environment and Development Organization. http://www.wedo.org/sus_dev/untapped1.htm

WEDO (2003b). *Diverting the Flow: A Resource Guide to Gender Rights and Water Privatization.* Women's Environment and Development Organization. http://www.wedo.org/sus_dev/diverting_final.pdf

WEHAB Working Group (2002). *A Framework of Action on Water and Sanitation.* Paper presented at the World Summit on Sustainable Development, Johannesburg, South Africa. http://www.johannesburgsummit.org/html/documents

WHO (2002). *The World Health Report 2002. Reducing Risks, Promoting Healthy Life.* World Health Organization, Geneva

World Bank (2001). *Engendering Development Through Gender Equality in Rights, Resources, and Voice.* World Bank, Washington D.C.

World Bank (2003). *Gender Equality and the Millennium Development Goals.* World Bank, Washington D.C.

World Bank (2004). *2004 World Development Indicators.* World Bank, Washington D.C.

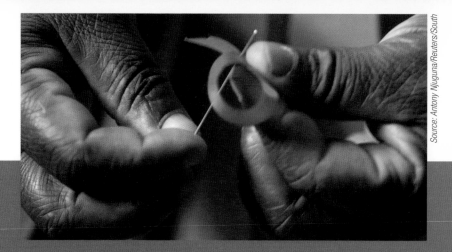

Emerging Challenges – New Findings

● EMERGING AND RE-EMERGING INFECTIOUS DISEASES: LINKS TO ENVIRONMENTAL CHANGE ● ABRUPT CLIMATE CHANGE: OCEAN SALINITY CHANGES AND POTENTIAL IMPACTS ON OCEAN CIRCULATION

Emerging Challenges – New Findings

This section presents some of the latest evidence from scientific research that can shed new light on ongoing and emerging environmental complexities and priority issues. This year's issues – the links between environmental change and emerging and re-emerging infectious diseases, and the possible consequences of reduced ocean salinity – were identified in consultation with the Scientific Committee on Problems of the Environment (SCOPE) of the International Council for Science (ICSU).

Emerging and Re-emerging Infectious Diseases: Links to Environmental Change

Environmental factors are major contributors to many emerging and re-emerging infectious diseases. Although the pathways and extent of the environmental role are not always fully known, the disease burden and the economic impact can be significantly reduced by improved environmental management.

In recent years new diseases such as Severe Acute Respiratory Syndrome (SARS), and newly resurgent familiar diseases such as tuberculosis, have caused suffering, international disruption and alarm. Frequent environmental changes are key factors. Environmental policy sometimes has a crucial role to play in controlling emerging and re-emerging diseases.

Infectious diseases remain the leading cause of death in the world, accounting for about 15 million deaths per year – approximately 25 per cent of total global mortality (Morens and others 2004). The impact is greatest in the developing world (WHO 2003a). In Africa and South Asia, infectious diseases are the underlying cause of two thirds of all deaths, killing mostly children and young adults. Infectious diseases are also a major cause of permanent disability and poor health and well-being for tens of millions of people, hindering economic development and sustainability in many parts of the world.

The economic and social burden of diseases such as malaria is enormous (Sachs and Malaney 2002, WHO 2003a). In addition to the long-term effects, short-term epidemics of emerging or re-emerging infectious diseases, such as SARS in Hong Kong, Taiwan, and Toronto and plague in India, have each cost billions of dollars. These recent epidemics underscore the fact that we live in a worldwide community that is tightly linked, and that all of us are susceptible to the burden of infectious diseases (Morens and others 2004, Weiss and McMichael 2004).

FROM OPTIMISM TO CONCERN

The beginning of the latter half of the 20th century was marked by optimism about the conquest of infectious diseases. The discovery of antibiotics produced treatments for tuberculosis and other major infectious diseases, while insecticide use initially caused a decline in vector-borne diseases. Smallpox was eradicated and vaccines were developed for polio and other major childhood diseases. Fifty years later, due to the emergence of newly recognized infectious diseases and the re-emergence of known ones, optimism has been replaced by grave concern and, in some cases, dread (McMichael 2004, Institute of Medicine 1992 and 2001).

This growing concern in part reflects a recognition of the difficulties associated with preventing, controlling, or eradicating

Box 1: Some definitions

Infectious diseases are caused by the invasion and unwanted growth of living organisms within the body.

Infectious disease vectors are agents that transfer pathogens from one organism to another, for instance, mosquitoes that transmit malaria parasites.

Emerging diseases are those that have recently increased in incidence or in geographic or host range (such as Lyme disease, West Nile virus, Nipah virus); that are caused by pathogens that have recently evolved (such as new strains of influenza virus, SARS, drug resistant strains of malaria); or that are newly discovered (such as Hendra virus, Hantavirus pulmonary syndrome or Ebola virus).

Re-emerging diseases are those that have been controlled in the past, but are now rapidly increasing in incidence or geographic range (such as tuberculosis). Re-emergence typically occurs because of breakdowns in public health measures for previously controlled infections, or as co-infections, such as occur with HIV.

Irrigation of rice fields can create excellent breeding sites for mosquitoes.

Source: Joerg Boethling/Still Pictures

infectious diseases. Medical interventions have been unable to keep up with all infectious diseases because many disease-causing agents and vectors have developed resistance to available drugs and pesticides (Morens and others 2004, Singh and others 2004, WHO 1992). Resistance to antibiotics has been fostered by their overuse or misuse medically and in animal husbandry (Smith and others 2002, Horrigan and others 2002). In addition, the pace of vaccine and new drug development has been slower than anticipated, and the expense of new drugs has often limited their availability in developing countries. For many infectious diseases, such as malaria and dengue, vaccines are still not available.

These difficulties, along with the increasing evidence that environmental change is a major player and that effective environmental management may provide more cost-effective and sustainable control measures than using drugs and pesticides, suggest a need to refocus on potentially preventable environmental factors to reverse the trend of emergent and re-emergent infectious diseases (Chivian 2002, Patz and others 2004).

DRIVING FORCES

Population growth and distribution and consumption patterns have been major driving forces of social and environmental changes in relation to land use, deforestation, agricultural practices, and water management. Research increasingly shows that many of these changes are linked to patterns of infectious disease.

Human migration, whether due to poverty, conflict, or climate-induced habitat changes, can foster the spread of emerging and re-emerging infectious diseases. Migration introduces diseases to new locations and exposes susceptible resident populations to new vector species. The devastating impact of infectious disease patterns was a common change of the initial contact of Native American groups and Pacific Islanders with Europeans. Modern transportation patterns are also having an impact. For example, the mosquito *Aedes albopictus*, which can breed in stagnant water in discarded tyres, has been globally distributed from Asia through transportation of used tyres on cargo freighters (Schaffner and others 2004, Madon and others 2002). The transfer of SARS in 2003, from South Asia to Toronto in Canada, could be traced to a single infected human who made the

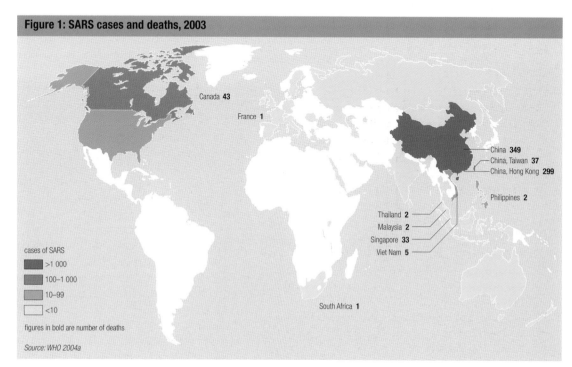

Figure 1: SARS cases and deaths, 2003

Canada **43**

France **1**

China **349**
China, Taiwan **37**
China, Hong Kong **299**

Philippines **2**

Thailand **2**
Malaysia **2**
Singapore **33**
Viet Nam **5**

South Africa **1**

cases of SARS
>1 000
100–1 000
10–99
<10

figures in bold are number of deaths

Source: WHO 2004a

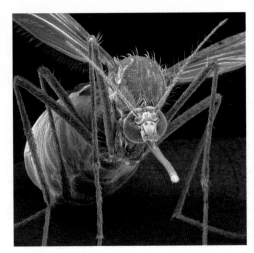

Aedes aegypti – the principal vector of dengue and yellow fever.
Source: David Scharf/Still Pictures

journey by commercial jet while incubating the disease (**Figure 1**). HIV/AIDS was spread widely throughout southern and central Africa by long-distance truckers, and globally by air travellers.

Unplanned rapid urbanization has resulted in inadequate housing and lack of water, sewer and waste management

Deforestation and agricultural practices can alter habitat availability for disease vectors.
Source: Tran Cao Bao Lond/UNEP/Still Pictures

systems for large numbers of people in different parts of the world. When crowded human populations live in close association with large populations of mosquitoes, rodents, and other vermin, there is a dramatic increase in epidemics of diseases borne by water, food, mosquitoes and rodents, as well as in communicable diseases.

Urbanization has been the major driving force in the dramatic global resurgence of epidemic dengue and the re-emergence of its complication, dengue hemorrhagic fever (DHF) (Gubler 2004, Ko and others 1999). The global prevalence of dengue has grown dramatically in recent decades. Before 1970 only nine countries had experienced DHF epidemics: that number increased more than four-fold by 1995. It is now endemic in more than 100 countries, with South-east Asia and the western Pacific most seriously affected.

Some 2 500 million people are now at risk from dengue. In the 1950s an average of 908 DHF cases were reported to the World Health Organization (WHO) each year. This rose to an average of 514 139 cases a year for the period 1990–98. In 2001, there were more than 609 000 reported cases of dengue in the Americas alone, more than twice the number of dengue cases in 1995 (WHO 2004b).

In coastal areas, population pressure leading to coastal degradation have increased epidemics of waterborne diseases such as cholera. This may also have increased the impact of toxins resulting from algal blooms known as red tides.

ENVIRONMENTAL CHANGE AND INFECTIOUS DISEASE EMERGENCE

The various domains of environmental policy provide a framework for analyzing relationships between environmental drivers and pressures, and specific infectious diseases (**Table 1**). These linkages are further explained below.

Land

Decisions about land use can have direct and indirect impacts on infectious disease. Demand for land for agriculture and settlement has led to widespread

Discarded plastic and standing water can increase the risk of vector-borne infectious disease.
Source: Friedrich Stark/Still Pictures

Table 1: Emerging and re-emerging infectious diseases and links to environmental change

Examples of drivers of change and pressures	Examples of impacts caused by drivers and pressures	Examples of infectious disease implications	Examples of infectious diseases potentially affected
Deforestation	Ecosystem fragmentation. Destruction of natural balance leading to decrease in natural predators and changes in species dominance. Easy access by farmers/workers/hunters to new land and natural areas. Habitat disturbance.	More favourable conditions for propagation of disease vectors. Increased number of vectors in human settlements. Vector numbers and habitats increase. Increased contact with animal reservoirs and vectors.	Yellow fever, malaria, Kyasanur forest disease, Ebola and other hemorrhagic fevers, zoonotic diseases that exist normally in animals, but can infect humans.
Reforestation and expansion of housing	Housing expands into woodland/forest fringes.	Humans brought into closer contact with tick vectors and animal reservoirs (deer and rodents).	Lyme disease.
Agriculture	Monoculture destroys the natural balance, allowing propagation of vectors. Concentration of domestic animals/cattle close to humans. Land erosion and gullying – more habitat for vectors. Environmental pollution (including contamination with pesticides).	More favourable conditions for propagation of disease vectors. Vector numbers and habitats increase. Increased contact with vectors. Development of resistance by disease vectors.	Western and Venezuelan equine encephalitides, typhus.
Dam building and irrigation	More open water. More stagnant water. More fertile soil and sand beds. Environmental pollution.	Increased habitat and breeding sites for vectors and carriers.	Schistosomiasis, West Nile fever, Japanese encephalitis.
Rapid and unplanned urbanization	Ecosystem fragmentation. Destruction of natural balance. Lack of water, sewerage and waste management systems.	More sites and more favourable conditions for propagation of disease vectors. Spread of vectors and parasites. Increased contact with infected people.	Tuberculosis, dengue hemorrhagic fever, plague, Hantavirus pulmonary syndrome.
Untreated drinking water and waste water Inadequate sanitation	Settlements without clean water and sanitation. Water pollution (including accidents).	Increased contact with infection and increased mobility of infection in case of poor water management or accidents.	Leptospirosis, malaria, cholera, cryptosporidia, diarrhoeal diseases.
Industry Transport	Deteriorating air quality. Anthropogenic greenhouse gas emissions leading to global warming.	Impaired lung function. Increased mobility of infected people. Spread of diseases and vectors into high latitudes and altitudes.	(Aggravated) respiratory diseases and infections, meningitis, cholera.
Chemical use Antibiotics in livestock and livestock waste	Antibiotics in livestock products and waste.	Developing resistance in bacteria.	Hepatitis, dengue, antibiotic-resistant bacterial diarrhoeal disease.

Notes: This table is selective and illustrative. Some diseases have more than one environmental 'driver'. Many of the underlying drivers are primarily cultural, economic, demographic, and social.

deforestation and land cover change affecting wildlife habitat. These practices have resulted in an increase in zoonotic diseases (in which animals are the reservoirs of the infectious agent) in those areas where the populations of carrier animals have expanded or their contact with humans increased. Land use changes account for a majority of emerging and re-emerging infections, including major parasitic diseases such as Chagas disease, trypanosomiasis, leishmaniasis and onchocerciasis (Molyneux 1998), each of which has one or more animal reservoirs in the wild.

Habitat changes also alter the availability and reproductive capacity of vectors that transmit and sometimes also act as reservoirs of diseases. For example, some of the major vector-borne infectious diseases, including malaria, Japanese encephalitis, and dengue hemorrhagic fever, are transmitted by various species of mosquito (Gubler 2002). Opportunities for mosquito breeding in standing water are often increased by habitat and land-use change, by changes in natural water flows, by environmental degradation caused by human activities, and even by human-made containers such as discarded automobile tyres and non-biodegradable plastic (Gubler 1998). Environmental and public health management practices that decrease unnecessary standing water can often reduce the risk of vector-borne infectious disease.

Road building to open up wilderness for agriculture, mining, forestry, or other purposes can alter vector habitat, promoting the spread of vectors that favour more open areas. New roads can also lead to the migration of susceptible human populations to areas in which infectious disease pathogens and their vectors are present (**Boxes 2** and **3**).

Box 3: Bushmeat, Ebola and HIV/AIDS

Humans are susceptible to many of the same diseases that plague the great apes (chimpanzees, bonobos, gorillas and orangutans). Historically there has been little contact between people and apes, so little opportunity for diseases to transfer. But in Central Africa, the growing migration of human populations and increased access to forest habitats have allowed the trade in wild meat ('bushmeat') to flourish.

Recent analyses have linked the first human cases in Ebola outbreaks to the handling of meat from infected apes (Leroy and others 2004). The Ebola virus, discovered in 1976, is fatal in a high proportion of cases in humans and great apes. Outbreaks in Central Africa have killed hundreds of people and thousands of apes in the last few years. Disease transmission is a strong argument against the consumption of primate meat.

Retroviruses including HIV and simian foamy virus (SFV) have also been contracted this way (Wolfe 2004). HIV/AIDS is suspected to have originated from the fusion of two Simian Immunodeficiency Viruses, possibly acquired by humans through direct exposure to animal blood and secretions through hunting, butchering, or consumption of uncooked contaminated meat (Hahn and others 2000).

Ebola outbreaks, 1976–2004

Year	Country	Cases	Deaths	Fatality (%)
1976	Sudan	284	151	53
1976–77	Zaire	319	281	88
1979	Sudan	34	22	65
1994	Gabon	52	31	60
1994	Côte d'Ivoire	1	0	0
1995	Liberia	1	0	0
1995	Democratic Republic of Congo (formerly Zaire)	315	250	81
1996–97	Gabon	97	66	68
1996	South Africa	1	1	100
2000–01	Uganda	425	224	53
2001–02	Gabon	65	53	82
2001–03	Republic of Congo	237	201	85
2004	Sudan	17	7	41
Total		**1848**	**1287**	

Source: WHO 2004c

Bushmeat on sale for passing motorists, Central Africa.

Source: Martin Harvey/Still Pictures

The way that land is used for agriculture can also have widely divergent effects on the habitat for infectious disease vectors, depending on the prevalence of irrigation, agroforestry, prior felling of forests and so on. For example, irrigation of rice fields will create excellent breeding sites for mosquitoes. The use of insecticides however sometimes has a greater detrimental effect on natural predators of mosquitoes than on mosquitoes themselves.

Natural habitats

Intact ecosystems can help control diseases by providing a balance of species potentially involved in the life cycle of infectious diseases, along with predators and other agents that control or limit the animal reservoirs, vectors and pathogens. Disease agents that live much of their life cycle outside the human host, such as those responsible for water- and vector-borne diseases, are highly susceptible to environmental conditions. It is these diseases for which the greatest linkages to surrounding ecology have been found.

Anopheline mosquito species occupy a variety of ecological niches that can be altered by environmental changes (Keating and others 2003). For example, partial deforestation, with subsequent changes in land use and human settlement patterns, has coincided with an upsurge of malaria and its Anopheline mosquito vectors in Africa, Asia, and Latin America (Walsh and others 1993). In eastern and southern Africa, the proportion of under-five deaths due to malaria doubled between 1982–89 and 1990–98 (**Figure 2**). Climate change,

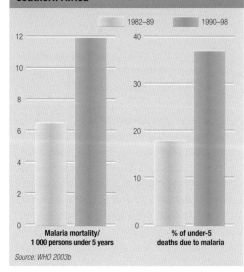

Figure 2: Malaria resurgence in eastern and southern Africa

1982–89   1990–98

Malaria mortality/ 1 000 persons under 5 years

% of under-5 deaths due to malaria

Source: WHO 2003b

resistance to drugs, and the spread of HIV/AIDS causing depressed immune function, are also factors in the increased incidence of malaria (WHO 2003b).

The incidence of onchocerciasis (river blindness) can be affected by land use change.

Source: Mark Edwards/Still Pictures

Forest destruction can lead to a decrease or increase in onchocerciasis (river blindness, caused by the filarial worm *Onchocerca volvulus*), depending upon the impact of such factors as remaining forest cover and new stream flow regimes on the habitat of the black fly which transmits the larvae (Walsh and others 1993). On the other hand, reforestation can also take its toll. In northeastern United States it has enhanced the spread of Lyme disease (**Box 4**).

Water

Traditionally, concern about water and human health has focused on the diseases that result from inadequate or unsafe water supplies or sanitation. For example, the presence of human and animal wastes in surface waters has resulted in devastating outbreaks of cryptosporidiosis in North America and in cholera in many parts of the world (Colwell 1996, Rodo and others 2002).

However, there are many other ways in which environment-related changes in human use and management of, and contacts with, water can affect disease incidence and transmission, at every scale from the puddle in the yard to a major irrigation system. Dam construction is a driving force in infectious disease because it alters the nature of aquatic habitats and affects species survival (Patz and others 2004). The construction of large dams has caused an increased incidence of schistosomiasis (**Box 5**). By providing habitats for infectious disease vectors, irrigation has resulted in dramatic increases in morbidity and mortality due to malaria in Africa and to Japanese encephalitis in Asia.

Climate

Emissions of carbon dioxide, methane, and other greenhouse gases from land use change and industrial activities are contributing to climate change, and thus may be indirectly involved in emerging and re-emerging infectious diseases (IPCC 2000).

Changes in climate inevitably lead to changes in habitat and a resultant change in the location of vectors (Kovats and others 2003). While the net effect globally remains uncertain and somewhat controversial (Reiter 2001, Hay and others 2002, Confalonieri 2003), local changes in the risk of vector borne infectious disease are virtually certain (Patz 2002). Certain microbial organisms, such as *Neisseria meningitidis*, a common cause of meningitis, can be borne many miles on the wind in dusty conditions following exacerbated

Box 4: Reforestation, biodiversity loss, and Lyme disease

Lyme disease is a bacterial disease occurring in North America, Europe, and Asia that is transmitted by the bite of infected deer ticks. It was first named in 1977, but was recognized earlier. The major reservoir hosts for the bacteria are rodents, while deer are the major host for the tick vectors (Steere and others 2004).

Patchy reforestation of the northeastern United States led to a dramatic increase in the deer population, which in turn increased the tick population. Habitat changes also decreased rodent predators, resulting in an expansion of rodent hosts for the Lyme disease pathogen. Wet conditions in late spring and early summer were associated with an increase in Lyme disease incidence in the northeast of the country possibly by increasing tick survival and activity (McCabe and Bunnell 2004).

These environmental changes have been combined with increased human use of this habitat for homes and recreation. Because new homes are often built in wooded areas, transmission of Lyme disease near homes has become an important problem. Dutchess County, a semi-rural peri-urban county north of New York City, has one of the highest incidences of Lyme disease in the United States, with a crude mean annual incidence rate of 400 cases per 100 000 persons per year during the period 1992–2000 (Chow and others 2003). Specific strategies such as clearing leaf litter, and brush- and wood-piles in gardens can reduce deer, mouse and tick habitat thereby reducing the tick population and likelihood of disease (CDC 2004a, CDC 2004b).

The female deer tick, *Ixodes dammini*, is the vector for Lyme disease.

Source: Kent Wood/Still Pictures

Box 5: Irrigation, schistosomiasis and West Nile Virus

Snails serve as an intermediate reservoir host for schistosomiasis, and irrigation canals can provide an ideal habitat. Increasing fecundity and growth of freshwater snails are related to decreased water salinity and increased alkalinity following irrigation development along the Senegal River, and to water flow changes associated with the Aswan Dam in Egypt (Abdel-Wahab and others 1979).

Irrigation ponds, canals, and ditches can also provide larval habitat for vector mosquito species such as *Culex tarsalis*. As it bites both animals and humans, *Culex tarsalis* is a major bridge vector for enzootic diseases (diseases constantly present in animal populations) such as St. Louis encephalitis in the western United States (Mahmood and others 2004). As West Nile virus has moved into the region in the past three years, this species has emerged as the principal mosquito vector, resulting in a major epidemic in humans, and in birds and horses (Reisen and others 2004).

Schistosome snails, *Biomphalaria glabrata*, shedding schistosome larvae which burrow into people and cause schistosomiasis.

Source: Darlyne A. Murawski/Still Pictures

droughts in the Sahel (Cunin and others 2003). Cholera outbreaks are also influence by climate events such as El Niño (**Box 6**).

Chemicals

Chemical pesticides have been successful in controlling vectors responsible for infectious disease – but this has to be balanced carefully against their potential for short- and long-term adverse impacts on health and the environment. The cost-benefit issues will differ for different diseases and in different parts of the world, depending in part on the impact, incidence, and prevalence of the vector-borne disease.

Public health pesticides have played a major role in the successful control of vector-borne diseases. The Global Malaria Eradication Programme, which successfully

controlled malaria and saved tens of millions of lives over much of Asia, Oceania, and the Americas, was based on indoor spraying of DDT. This and related compounds were also instrumental in the successful mosquito eradication programme in the American tropics, to control epidemics of yellow fever and dengue. Misuse of pesticides has been primarily associated with broad scale agricultural use, rather than with disease control (Horrigan and others 2002).

Significant concern also exists that a variety of chemical pollutants have an adverse impact on human resistance to infectious disease. Furthermore, the development of insect resistance to pesticides has meant that many chemical agents are no longer effective, and there is a likelihood that resistance will develop to new chemical agents. Many other chemicals, including certain flame-retardants used in electronic equipment, are suspected of disrupting the human endocrine system.

POLICY IMPLICATIONS AND CONCLUSIONS

In some parts of the world, illness and death from infectious diseases affect such a high proportion of the population that they severely threaten sustainable development. The current

toll of human death and disability, as well as the social and economic disruptions caused by emerging and re-emerging infectious diseases, warrant a high priority for developing effective prevention and control measures (Sachs and Malaney 2002).

Because environmental change, in many cases, plays a major role in the emergence and re-emergence of infectious diseases, environmental policy can have a significant impact on the incidence and cost of these diseases.

Areas of potential action are very wide-ranging, covering many fields and potentially impacting the incidence of many diseases. They include protection of land, air, water, and natural habitats, and regulation of industrial chemicals and pesticides use. Effective disease prevention requires an inter-sectoral effort: environment, public health, industrial, agricultural, and urban policies need to be developed and implemented in concert. These efforts should occur in the context of existing national and international activities including those focused on global climate change and biodiversity.

Environmental ministries and agencies may have a crucial role to play in human health. Emerging and re-emerging infectious disease should be a new area of policy concern, alongside more traditional concerns of pollution, quality of the environment and nature conservation. In some countries, governments may wish to consider adding routine infectious disease considerations, including the impact of habitat changes on hosts and vectors, to environmental impact assessments and to health impact assessments.

The role of other stakeholders in preventing emerging and re-emerging infections must be enhanced by promoting inter-sectoral cooperation at every level. Because the interactions of environmental factors with infectious disease vectors and pathogens are so complex, effective understanding and response will require personnel with diverse disciplinary and cross-disciplinary knowledge. Developing, using and linking effective health and environmental monitoring systems will be crucial (Patz and others 2004). Incorporating

Box 6: Climate and cholera

The bacterial species responsible for cholera proliferate in warm waters. Copepods, tiny zooplankton that feed on algae, can serve as reservoirs for *Vibrio cholerae* and other enteric pathogens. In Bangladesh, cholera follows seasonal warming of sea surface temperature that can increase plankton blooms. El Niño and La Nina events seem to intensify the pattern of cholera incidence – cholera increases after warm events and decreases after cold events (Rodo and others 2002, Kovats and others 2003).

geographic information systems into monitoring systems already shows much promise (Eisele and others 2003).

Collaborative multidisciplinary and multinational research will be needed to explore the linkages among environmental dynamics, disease vectors, pathogens, and human susceptibility. The role of the environment in emerging and re-emerging infectious diseases should be considered in future scenarios of global change – including the possibility of health benefits from greenhouse gas mitigation (Cifuentes and others 2001).

Local measures such as reduction of unnecessary standing water to prevent malaria together with worldwide efforts to ensure safe water and improved sanitation could lead to public health triumphs. But they can only be achieved by giving a high priority to preventable health problems caused by environmental conditions.

As the global SARS epidemic demonstrated, even a small number of cases of an emerging infection can cause major international social and economic disruption. In a globalizing world undergoing rapid environmental change, local actions must be combined with enhanced cooperation at global and regional levels.

REFERENCES

Abdel-Wahab, M.F., Strickland, G.T., El-Sahly, A., El-Kady, N., Zakaria, S. and Ahmed, L. (1979). Changing pattern of schistosomiasis in Egypt 1935–79. *Lancet*, Aug 4, 2, 8136, 242-4

CDC (2004a). *Lyme Disease and Animals*. Centers for Disease Control and Prevention. http://www.cdc.gov/healthypets/diseases/lyme.htm

CDC (2004b). *Lyme Disease Vector Ecology*. Centers for Disease Control and Prevention http://www.cdc.gov/ncidod/dvbid/lyme/history.htm

Chivian, E. (ed.) (2002). Chapter 5: Ecosystem Disturbance, Biodiversity, and Human Infectious Diseases. In Biodiversity: *Its Importance to Human Health*. Center for Health and the Global Environment, Harvard Medical School

Chow, C.C., Evans, A.S.Jr, Noonan-Toly, C.M., White, D., Johnson, G.S., Marks, S.J., Caldwell, M.C. and Hayes, E.B. (2003). Lyme disease trends – Dutchess County, New York, 1992-2000. *Mt Sinai J Med*. May, 70, 3, 207-13

Cifuentes, L., Borja-Aburto, V.H., Gouveia, N., Thurston, G. and Davis, D.L. (2001). Hidden Health Benefits of Greenhouse Gas Mitigation. *Science*, 293, 1257-9

Colwell, R.R. (1996). Global Climate and Infectious Disease: The Cholera Paradigm. *Science*, 274, 5295, 2025-31

Confalonieri, U.E.C. (2003). Variabilidade Climática, vulnerabilidade social e saúde no Brasil. *Terra Livre, S. Paulo*, 19-I, 20, 193-204

Crompton, P., Ventura, A.M., deSouza, J.M., Santos, E., Strickland, G.T. and Silbergeld, E. (2002). Assessment of Mercury Exposure and Malaria in a Brazilian Amazon Riverine Community. *Environmental Research*, 90, 69-75

Cunin, P., Fonkoua, M-C., Kollo, B., Bedifeh, B.A., Bayanak, P. and Martin, P.M.V. (2003). Serogroup A Neisseria meningitidis outside meningitis belt in southwest Cameroon. *Emerg Infect Dis* [serial online] http://www.cdc.gov/ncidod/EID/vol9no10/03-03-0170.htm

Eisele T.P., Keating J., Swalm C., Mbogo C.M., Githeko A.K., Regens J.L., Githure J.I., Andrews L. and Beier J.C. (2003). Linking Field-based Ecological Data with Remotely Sensed Data Using a Geographic Information System in Two Malaria Endemic Urban Areas of Kenya. *Malaria Journal*, 2, 1, 44

Gubler, D.J. (1998). Resurgent Vector-borne Disease As a Global Health Problem. *Emerging Infectious Diseases*, 4, 3, 442-50

Gubler, D.J. (2002). The Global Emergence/Resurgence of Arboviral Diseases as Public Health Problems. *Science Direct*, 33, 4, 330-42

Gubler, D.J. (2004). Cities Spawn Epidemic Dengue Viruses. *Nature Medicine*, 10, 2, 129-30

Hahn, B.H., Shaw, G.M., De Cock, K.M. and Sharp, P.M. (2000). AIDS as a Zoonosis: Scientific and Public Health Implications. *Science*, 287, 607-14

Hay, S.I., Cox J., Rogers, D.J., Randolph, S.E., Stern, D.I., Shanks, G.D., Myers, M.F. and Snow, R.W. (2002). Climate change and the resurgence of malaria in the East African highlands. *Nature*, 415, 6874, 905-9

Horrigan, L., Lawrence, R.S., and Walker, P. (2002). How Sustainable Agriculture Can Address the Environmental and Human Health Harms of Industrial Agriculture. *Environmental Health Perspectives*, 110, 5, 445-56

Institute of Medicine (1992). *Emerging Infections: Microbial Threats to Health in the United States*. Report of a study by a committee of the Institute of Medicine, Division of Health Sciences Policy and Division of International Health. Lederberg, J., Shope, R.E., and Oaks, S.C. Jr., eds. National Academy Press, Washington D.C.

Institute of Medicine (2001). *Emerging Infectious Diseases from the Global to the Local Perspective: Workshop Summary Board on Global Health*. Davis, J.R. and Lederberg, J., eds. National Academy Press, Washington D.C.

IPCC (2000). *Summary for Policymakers. Special Report Emissions Scenarios*. Intergovernmental Panel on Climate Change, Geneva

Keating, J., MacIntyre, K., Mbogo, C., Githeko, A., Regens, J.L., Swalm, C., Ndenga, B., Steinberg, L.J., Kibe, L., Githure, J.I., and Beier, J.C. (2003). A Geographic Sampling Strategy for Studying Relationships Between Human Activity and Malaria Vectors in Urban Africa. *American Journal of Tropical Medical Hygiene*, 68, 3, 357-65

Ko, A.I., Galvao Reis, M., Ribeiro Dourado, C.M., Johnson, W.D. Jr., and Riley, L.W. (1999). Urban epidemic severe leptospirosis in Brazil. *Lancet*, 354, 820-5

Kovats, R.S., Bouma, M. J., Hajat, S., Worrall, E. and Haines, A. (2003). El Nino and health. *The Lancet*, 362, 1481-9

Leroy E.M., Rouquet P., Formenty, P., Souquiere, S., Kilbourne, A., Froment, J.-M., Bermejo, M., Smit, S., Karesh, W., Swanepoel, R., Zaki, S.R. and Rollin, P.E. (2004). Multiple Ebola virus transmission events and rapid decline of Central African wildlife. *Science*, 303, 387-90

Madon, M.B., Mulla, M.S., Shaw, M.W., Kluh, S., and Hazelrig, J.E. (2002). Introduction of Aedes albopictus (Skuse) in southern California and potential for its establishment. *Journal of Vector Ecology*, 27, 1, 149-54

Mahmood, F., Chiles, R.E., Fang, Y., Barker, C.M. and Reisen, W.K. (2004). Role of nestling mourning doves and house finches as amplifying hosts of St. Louis encephalitis virus. *Journal of Medical Entomology*. 41, 965-72

McCabe, G.J. and Bunnell, J.E. (2004). Precipitation and the Occurrence of Lyme Disease in the Northeastern United States. *Vector-Borne and Zoonotic Diseases* 4, 143-8

McMichael A.J. (2004). Environmental and Social Influences on Emerging Infectious Diseases: Past, Present and Future. *Transactions of the Royal Society of London*, 359, 1447, 1049-58

Molyneux, D.H. (1998). Vector-Borne Parasitic Diseases- an Overview of Recent Changes. *International Journal for Parasitology*, 28, 927-34

Morens, D.M., Folkers, G. K. and Fauci, A.S., (2004). The Challenge of emerging and re-emerging infectious diseases. *Nature*, 430, 242-9

Patz, J.A. (2002). A Human Disease Indicator for the Effects of Recent Global Climate Change. *Proceedings of the National Academy of Sciences of the United States of America*, 99, 20, 12506-8

Patz, J.A., Daszak, P., Tabor, G. M., Aguirre, A.A., Pearl, M., Epstein, J., Wolfe, N.D., Kilpatrick, A.M., Foufopoulos, J., Molyneaux, D., Bradley, D.J., and Members of the Working Group on Land Use Change and Disease Emergence (2004). Unhealthy Landscapes: Policy Recommendations on Land Use Change and Infectious Disease Emergence. *Environmental Health Perspectives*, 112, 10, 1092-8

Reisen, W., Lothrop, H., Chiles, R., Madon, M., Cossen, C., Woods, L., Husted, S., Kramer, V. and Edman, J. (2004). West Nile virus in California. *Emerging Infections Diseases*. 10, 8, 1369-78

Reiter, P. (2001). Climate Change and Mosquito-Borne Disease. *Environmental Health Perspectives*, 109, 141-61

Rodo, X., Pascual, M., Fuchs, G., and Faruque, A.S. (2002). ENSO and cholera: a nonstationary link related to climate change? *Proceedings of the National Academy of Sciences of the United States of America*, 99, 20, 12901-6

Sachs, J. and Malaney, P. (2002). The Economic and Social Burden of Malaria. *Nature*, 415, 6872, 680-5

Schaffner, F., Van Bortel, W. and Coosemans, M. (2004) First Record of Aedes (Stegomyia) albopictus in Belgium. *Journal of the American Mosquito Control Association*, 20, 2, 201-3

Singh, N., Nagpal, A.C., Saxena, A. and Singh, M.P. (2004). Changing scenario of malaria in central India, the replacement of *Plasmodium vivax* by *Plasmodium falciparum (1986-2000)*. *Tropical Medicine & International Health*, 9, 3, 364-71

Smith, D.L., Harris, A.D., Johnson, J.A., Silbergeld, E.K. and Morris, J.G. Jr. (2002). Animal Antibiotic Use Has an Early but Important Impact on the Emergence of Antibiotic Resistance in Human Commensal Bacteria. *Proceedings of the National Academy of Sciences of the United States of America*, 99, 9, 6434-9

Steere, A.C., Coburn, J. and Glickstein, L. (2004). The Emergence of Lyme Disease. *Journal of Clinical Investigation*, 113, 1093-101

Walsh, J.F., Molyneux, D.H. and Birley, M.H. (1993). Deforestation: Effects on Vector-Borne Disease. *Parasitology*, 106, 55-75

Weiss, R.A., and McMichael, A.J. (2004). Social and environmental risk factors in the emergence of infectious diseases. *Nat Med*. Dec,10 (12 Suppl), S70-6

WHO (1992). *Vector resistance to pesticides. Fifteenth report of the WHO Expert Committee on Vector Biology and Control*. World Health Organization Technical Report Series 818, Geneva

WHO (2003a). *Global Defense Against the Infectious Disease Threat*. Kindhauser, M.K., WHO/CDS/2003.15. World Health Organization, Geneva. http://www.who.int/infectious-disease-news/cds2002/intro.pdf

WHO (2003b). *Africa Malaria Report 2003*. World Health Organization.http://www.rbm.who.int/amd2003/amr2003/amr_toc.htm

WHO (2004a). *Summary of probable SARS cases*. http://www.who.int/csr/sars/country/table2004_04_21/en/

WHO (2004b). *Dengue and dengue haemorrhagic fever*. World Health Organization.http://www.who.int/mediacentre/factsheets/fs117/en/

WHO (2004c). *Ebola outbreak chronology*. World Health Organization. http://www.who.int/mediacentre/factsheets/fs103/en/index1.html

Wolfe, N.D., Switzer, W.M., Carr, J.K., Bhullar, V.B., Shanmugam, V., Tamoufe, U., Prosser, A.T., Torimo, J.N., Wright, A., Mpoudi-Ngole, E., McCutchan, F.E., Birx, D.L., Folks, T.M., Burke, D.S. and Heneine, W. (2004) Naturally acquired simian retrovirus infections in central African hunters. *Lancet*, 363, 932-7

Yapabandara, A.M., Curtis, C.F., Wickramasinghe, M.B. and Fernando, W.P. (2001). Control of malaria vectors with the insect growth regulator pyriproxyfen in a gem-mining area in Sri Lanka. *Acta Trop*. Dec 21, 80, 3, 265-76

Abrupt Climate Change: Ocean Salinity Changes and Potential Impacts on Ocean Circulation

Global warming is increasing high latitude precipitation and river runoff while also melting Arctic ice-caps and glaciers, causing more freshwater to enter the oceans in northern high latitudes. The freshwater lowers ocean salinity – and since salinity is one of the key drivers of the long-distance ocean circulation that distributes the planet's heat, this could have serious consequences.

Ocean-Atmosphere-Climate dynamics

Records from Greenland ice cores (Cuffey and Clow 1997) illustrate that abrupt temperature oscillations were the norm over much of the past 100 000 years. Shifts between warm and cold climates occurred rapidly, sometimes within a decade (Alley and others 1993, Alley and others 2003). This suggests that such abrupt changes could occur again.

Over the past 8 000 years these oscillations have been absent, and the Earth has experienced several millennia of relatively stable climate. Modern human civilization developed during this period. It was and is based on permanent agriculture, which depends upon a stable climate with predictable patterns of temperature and rainfall. If abrupt change were to recur, there would be unique challenges to human societies, and to natural ecosystems which have great difficulty adapting to rapid change.

A major factor involved in the abrupt climate changes of the past appears to have been changes in the ocean circulation, which distributes heat from the equator toward the poles. This circulation is controlled in part by differences in seawater density, which is determined by the temperature and salt content of the water. The colder and saltier the water, the more dense it is, and the more readily it sinks. Flows within the oceans related to variations in temperature and salt are called the 'thermohaline circulation' ('thermo' for heat and 'haline' for salt) or the 'Conveyor' (Broecker 1995) (**Figure 1**).

As the waters of the warm Gulf Stream-North Atlantic current system flow northward, the surface waters cool and thus become denser. In some locations, the salty surface waters become dense enough to sink into the deep ocean (**Figure 2**). This sinking is called ventilation or deep convection and generally occurs in the Greenland, Iceland, Norwegian and Labrador Seas as well as in the subpolar gyre of the North Atlantic (**Figure 1**).

When the surface waters sink, they pull in additional waters and ultimately form the North Atlantic Deep Water that flows southward. In turn, this draws more warm water at the surface northward (**Figure 2**).

The northward-flowing compensating flow of warm water has a crucial climatic function for northern and western Europe and some parts of northeastern America. It carries heat from lower latitudes, losing much of this to the atmosphere as it moves northward. In doing so it makes northern and western Europe

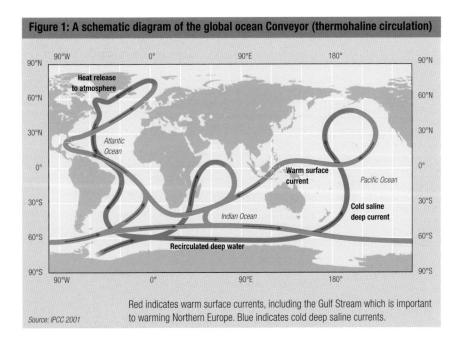

Figure 1: A schematic diagram of the global ocean Conveyor (thermohaline circulation)

Red indicates warm surface currents, including the Gulf Stream which is important to warming Northern Europe. Blue indicates cold deep saline currents.

Source: IPCC 2001

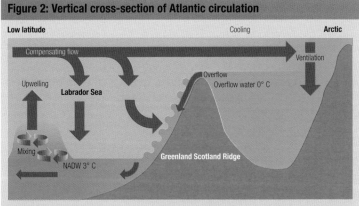

Figure 2: Vertical cross-section of Atlantic circulation

A diagram depicting the northern flow of surface waters (compensating flow), the deep sinking of dense surface waters in the Greenland, Norwegian and Labrador Seas (ventilation) and the combining of Nordic overflow waters, carried down and mixed with the deep waters of the western North Atlantic waters and Labrador Sea ventilation waters to form the southward flow of North Atlantic Deep Water (NADW). Background colours distinguish the blue Nordic Sea waters from red North Atlantic waters and purple NADW. Green arrows indicate flows.

Source: Modified from Hansen and others 2004

warmer in winter than the west coast of North America at similar latitudes.

The sinking that drives the global thermohaline circulation depends critically on the water being sufficiently cold and salty. Anything that makes the water less cold and less salty can jeopardize the circulation, with potentially serious impacts.

Observations over recent decades suggest that changes in the factors that govern this circulation are occurring, possibly as a result of human activities. This raises concerns about possible abrupt climate changes in the future.

Six steps to abrupt climate change

Theory had already predicted that such changes were possible. In the 1980s, it was suggested that climate warming could add enough freshwater to key places in the oceans to slow or even shut down the thermohaline circulation, leading to reorganization of ocean and atmospheric circulation patterns (Broecker 1987, Broecker and others 1985). Climate model results (Manabe and Stouffer 1988, Rahmstorf 1994) soon lent further support to this theory, and projected substantial cooling in the northern hemisphere, especially in the North Atlantic region, if a shutdown occurred (**Figure 3**) (Rahmstorf 2002).

Recent records suggest that the changes predicted by theory and modelling may be actually under way. Measurements of evaporation, precipitation, runoff, ocean salinity, and ocean circulation show these factors changing in ways that may reduce the density of North Atlantic subpolar waters. We may now be observing the early stages of processes that could lead to changes in ocean circulation (Curry and others 1997, Dickson and others 2002, Hansen and others 2001).

The following six steps (**Figure 4**) lay out one possible sequence of events by which human activities could lead to abrupt climate change.

Step 1: Higher carbon dioxide (CO_2) emissions increase atmospheric CO_2 concentrations.

The burning of fossil fuels (coal, oil and natural gas) and land-use changes have already

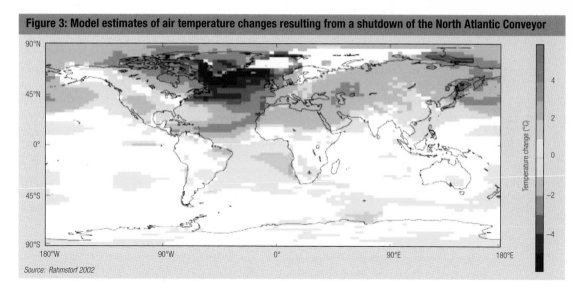

Figure 3: Model estimates of air temperature changes resulting from a shutdown of the North Atlantic Conveyor

Source: Rahmstorf 2002

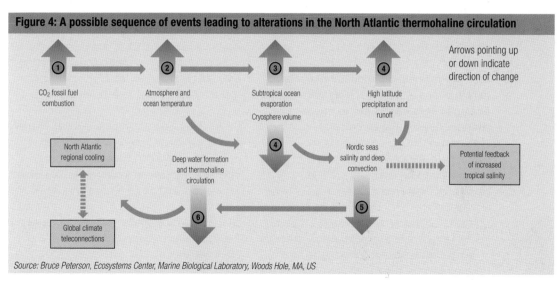

Figure 4: A possible sequence of events leading to alterations in the North Atlantic thermohaline circulation

Arrows pointing up or down indicate direction of change

① CO_2 fossil fuel combustion

② Atmosphere and ocean temperature

③ Subtropical ocean evaporation
Cryosphere volume

④ High latitude precipitation and runoff

North Atlantic regional cooling

Deep water formation and thermohaline circulation

④ Nordic seas salinity and deep convection

Potential feedback of increased tropical salinity

⑤

Global climate teleconnections

⑥

Source: Bruce Peterson, Ecosystems Center, Marine Biological Laboratory, Woods Hole, MA, US

created a large increase in the concentration of CO_2 in the atmosphere. CO_2 concentrations have increased by about 35 per cent since the start of the industrial revolution to the current level of 379 parts per million by volume (ppmv) (CDIAC 2004). Concentrations are projected to rise much more if emissions are not sharply reduced (IPCC 2001).

Step 2: This increases global temperatures.

CO_2 and other greenhouse gases in the Earth's atmosphere cause an increase in the air temperature near the surface of the Earth. Global average surface air temperature has already risen by 0.6° C over the past

100 years (IPCC 2001). It is projected to rise by another 1.4 to 5.8° C over the next 100 years, according to the range of climate models evaluated by the Intergovernmental Panel on Climate Change (IPCC 2001).

Step 3: Ocean evaporation and surface salinity increase in subtropical latitudes.

The atmospheric warming increases the evaporation of water from the surface of the subtropical oceans, increasing their salinity. A 5–10 per cent increase in evaporation has already been observed in the subtropical Atlantic Ocean over the past 40 years, equivalent to 5–10 cm of surface ocean water

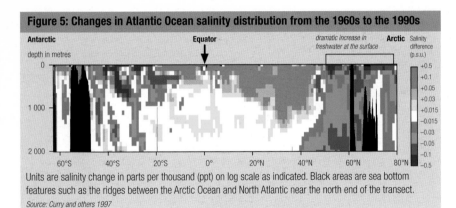

Figure 5: Changes in Atlantic Ocean salinity distribution from the 1960s to the 1990s

Units are salinity change in parts per thousand (ppt) on log scale as indicated. Black areas are sea bottom features such as the ridges between the Arctic Ocean and North Atlantic near the north end of the transect.

Source: Curry and others 1997

each year (Curry and others 1997). **Figure 5** shows the resulting increase in surface water salinity in the subtropical Atlantic as calculated and interpolated from direct measurements of salinity. Similar trends in salinity have been observed in the Pacific and Indian Oceans (Wong and others 1999).

Step 4: Precipitation, runoff and glacial melt increase in northern high latitudes, adding excess freshwater to the ocean surface layers in these regions.

The increased moisture evaporated from the subtropical oceans condenses in the atmosphere at higher latitudes, leading to increased precipitation. There has in fact been an increase in precipitation of 6–12 per cent in the northern high latitudes over the last century (IPCC 2001), resulting in increased freshwater runoff from rivers in Russia. The most dramatic increases have occurred in recent decades (Peterson and others 2002) (**Figure 6**). Increased melting from the

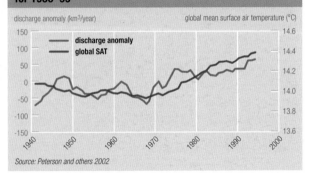

Figure 6: Eurasian river discharge anomaly, and global surface air temperature (SAT) expressed as 10 year running means for 1936–99

Source: Peterson and others 2002

Greenland Ice Sheet and other arctic glaciers has also added more freshwater to the Arctic Ocean over the past 40 years (Dyurgerov and Carter 2004). By comparison, the construction of dams and the melting of permafrost have had minor impacts on the long-term pattern of change in river discharge (McClelland and others 2004).

Melting sea ice adds a further source of additional freshwater, because sea ice contains little salt as it rejects most of its salt as it forms. Sea ice extent has declined by 2–3 per cent per decade since 1978 (Comiso and Parkinson 2004). The arctic sea ice is not just shrinking in area but also thinning, leading to predictions that the Arctic Ocean may be free of ice in summer by the end of this century (Yu and others 2004, Laxon and others 2003). These warming-induced increases in precipitation, runoff, glacial melt and sea ice melt could potentially reduce the salinity of surface waters in the Arctic and North Atlantic Oceans.

Step 5: Surface ocean salinity decreases at key locations of deep convection in the North Atlantic.

The Conveyor described above depends on delicately balanced processes. If surface waters in the Greenland, Iceland, Norwegian and Labrador Seas and the subpolar gyre of the North Atlantic are made less salty by an increase in freshwater input due to rising precipitation and runoff, or if temperatures are not sufficiently cold, these waters will not sink as usual. Instead, they will remain on top of the denser saltier waters below, capping them in much the same way as a layer of oil rests above a layer of water. This would stop the initiation of the deep convection that links the surface and bottom portions of the Conveyor.

There is evidence that freshening has been occurring for several decades in the North Atlantic and adjacent seas (**Figures 5** and **7**).

For example, the volume of dense deep water (water of temperature <0.5° C, and of density greater than 1 028 kg/m^3) in the Norwegian Sea has been decreasing for the last 50 years. This has led to a decline in the overflow of this deep water (a precursor to North Atlantic Deep Water) via the Faroe Bank Channel into the North Atlantic (Hansen and others 2001) (see **Figures 2** and **7**).

Similarly, the stock of dense deep waters in the Greenland Sea has declined during the period from the 1970s to the 1990s, and a cap of less saline water has accumulated (Curry and others 1997, Curry and Mauritzen *in print*). The density gradient that drives the overflow across the Denmark Strait Sill has decreased by about 10 per cent, suggesting that the overflow of this second precursor to North Atlantic Deep Water (NADW) may also have declined.

These trends of declining salinity and density in the Nordic Seas are supported by evidence for four decades of salinity decline in deep waters in the North Atlantic and Labrador Sea at additional locations downstream of these overflows (Dickson and others 2002) (**Figure 7**).

Step 6: There is a slowing or stopping in the ocean circulation that distributes the planet's heat, potentially causing abrupt climate change.

The final step of the process would occur if the sinking of surface water and southward flow of the deep water part of the Conveyor slowed or stopped. If this happened, the warm subtropical waters would not flow northward as they do now.

Direct measurements of a decline in the northward transport of tropical Atlantic Ocean waters have not yet been made, although the multi-decadal slowdown in the overflows of dense deep waters from the Norwegian and Greenland Seas (Hansen and others 2004) suggest that some slowing of the northern-most segment might already be occurring. There is also evidence that some of the freshwater is being carried down and mixed with the deep waters of the western North Atlantic and Labrador Sea (Dickson and others 2002), so while the Conveyor is still operating, it is now carrying more freshwater to depth than in previous decades (**Figures 5** and **7**).

Perspectives

Has the modest 0.6° C global warming of the past century left such a widespread imprint on the global hydrological cycle that the first five steps leading to a potential shutdown of the thermohaline circulation are already measurable?

The trends in the data suggest that the changes in subtropical evaporation, high latitude precipitation and runoff, and ocean salinity predicted by General Circulation Models (GCMs) for greenhouse warming scenarios may be under way (Curry and others 1979, Hansen and others 2004, Manabe and Stouffer 1994). We must learn how to better distinguish natural changes from those caused by human activities such as fossil fuel burning, before we can definitely attribute the changes in the hydrological cycle and ocean salinity to global warming. Natural climate variability, such as natural shifts in atmospheric circulation patterns, may be responsible for some of the changes (Dickson and others 2002).

The changes observed thus far have not been large enough to greatly impact the ocean Conveyor circulation. However, a further projected warming of 1.4 to 5.8° C during the remainder of this century (IPCC 2001) would have a larger impact. The chain of events – from the increase in low latitude evaporation; to increasing high latitude precipitation, runoff and glacier melt; to the reduction in high latitude surface ocean salinity; to declining deep convection and slowing of Nordic Seas overflows – are converging to suggest that the North Atlantic thermohaline circulation may be moving in the direction of a significant weakening, or a possible collapse.

Most GCMs project that the thermohaline circulation would be slowed as a result of several degrees of global warming during this century (IPCC 2001). However, most paleo evidence for abrupt changes comes from *glacial* climate regimes. In contrast we now have a *warm* climate becoming even warmer. We do not know if there is a threshold beyond which the Conveyor would inevitably shut down under contemporary warm climate conditions.

Several model studies of greenhouse warming suggest that the North Atlantic

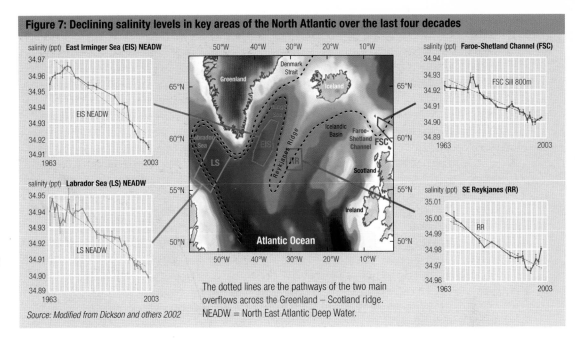

Figure 7: Declining salinity levels in key areas of the North Atlantic over the last four decades

salinity (ppt) East Irminger Sea (EIS) NEADW
salinity (ppt) Labrador Sea (LS) NEADW
salinity (ppt) Faroe-Shetland Channel (FSC)
salinity (ppt) SE Reykjanes (RR)

The dotted lines are the pathways of the two main overflows across the Greenland – Scotland ridge.
NEADW = North East Atlantic Deep Water.

Source: Modified from Dickson and others 2002

thermohaline circulation might collapse at CO_2 levels of roughly 800 to 1 000 ppm and temperature increases of 4 to 6° C (Manabe and Stouffer 1994, Schmittner and Stocker 1999, Rahmstorf and Ganopolski 1999). These are within the upper bounds of the IPCC 2001 projections for the end of this century, but may not be reached. Most of the greenhouse warming model runs performed for the IPCC Third Assessment exhibited a substantial decline in the overturning circulation by 2100 but not a complete shutdown of the Conveyor.

However, the models do not include the melting of the Greenland ice cap and arctic glaciers and therefore underestimate the freshwater forcing. Since the CO_2 and temperature projections attain maximum values *after* 2100, the model simulations are most likely to show that the largest impacts on the thermohaline circulation will occur after that date. Experiments with models also indicate that the likelihood of thermohaline circulation collapse is greater at higher rates of CO_2 release to the atmosphere (Stocker and Schmittner 1997). A slower release of the same amount of CO_2 would be less likely to cause a collapse.

While observations suggest that five of the six steps described above may be already

underway, it is possible that processes that are not currently understood or accounted for in all models could alter the course of the sixth stage in unpredictable ways. Such processes might decrease the severity of the changes that might occur – or they might increase it. For example, as salty water from the subtropics moves northward, increased salinity (created by increased subtropical evaporation under global warming) may offset the freshening from high latitude precipitation and melting, thereby stabilizing the Conveyor (Latif and others 2000).

If a collapse were to occur, disruption of the Conveyor circulation might begin erratically, leading to unpredictable climatic conditions as the circulation weakened (Knutti and Stocker 2001). Alternatively, a shutdown might occur abruptly with little warning. A shutdown could lead to a regional cooling of from 2 to 5° C concentrated in the North Atlantic, including Greenland, Iceland, the British Isles, and Northern Europe (**Figure 3**), with major effects on ecological conditions both in oceans and on land. If a shutdown were to occur relatively soon, then there would be a big temperature drop. However, if the region were already warmer due to global climate change, the immediate temperature change relative to current climate conditions would be less. But even in the latter case, over time the CO_2 peak would go down as fossil fuel supplies were depleted or there was a major switch to alternative energy sources. As the CO_2 concentration dropped, the Earth's temperature would cool and, as long as the thermohaline circulation remained shut down, this region would become colder (Rahmstorf and Ganopolski 1999).

If a collapse of the Conveyor circulation were to occur, it is not clear how long it might take to restart. Evidence from ice cores and modelling suggests that it might require hundreds or thousands of years (Rahmstorf and Ganopolski 1999). In the interim, the atmospheric and ocean currents that redistribute heat from the equator toward the poles would reorganize. Prediction of the new pattern of currents is a topic of current research.

Global Ramifications

While the most apparent impact of a slowdown or shutdown in the Conveyor circulation is projected to be a climatic cooling in the North Atlantic region, more widespread impacts of a thermohaline shutdown can be illustrated from modeling studies such as the warming in the southern hemisphere (**Figure 3**).

Correlations between climate changes in the North Atlantic and in distant regions have been found in the paleo records. These distant linkages between climate conditions in one location with conditions in remote regions are termed teleconnections. For example, the strength of the Arabian Sea monsoon correlates with changes in North Atlantic climate (Schulz and others 1998). Likewise, shifts in climate and vegetation of the South American tropics correlate closely with climatic events recorded in the Greenland ice core (Hughen and others 2004). It appears that either the Conveyor circulation may have impacts far beyond the North Atlantic region or that the distant events may have a common cause. However, the teleconnections that operated during the colder glacial periods may have depended on sea ice cover in the North Atlantic whereas sea ice will not be present under contemporary warm climate conditions. Thus these teleconnections may be weaker or absent.

Slowing the thermohaline circulation would have other global effects. Deep water formation is one mechanism for carrying anthropogenic carbon dioxide down into the deep ocean. Slowing of the circulation might allow carbon dioxide in the atmosphere to build up more rapidly, possibly leading to more intense global warming (Sabine and others 2004).

CONCLUSIONS

Given the current range of uncertainties it is wise to consider model projections as indications of what *might* happen rather than predictions of what *will* happen. Obtaining a clearer outlook will require improved understanding of ocean physics, improved climate simulations, and a more precise estimate of future warming. The global freshwater cycle and ocean circulation will require close monitoring.

The scientific evidence reviewed here suggests that minimizing the buildup of CO_2 in the atmosphere would lower the projected temperature increase and therefore minimize the acceleration of the hydrological cycle. The result would be a lower probability of forcing a reorganization of the North Atlantic thermohaline circulation – and a better chance of maintaining a stable climate in the North Atlantic region and elsewhere.

The actions required to minimize the probability of abrupt climate change are the same as those needed to allow successful adaptation of natural and managed systems to global warming: that is, to reduce the rate of increase and the overall intensity of greenhouse forcing by reducing our output of greenhouse gases.

REFERENCES

Alley, R.B., Meese, D.A., Shuman, C.A., Gow, A.J., Taylor, K.C., Grootes, P.M., White, J.W. C., Ram, M., Waddington, E.D. Mayewski, P.A. and Zielinski, G.A. (1993). Abrupt increase in Greenland snow accumulation at the end of the Younger Dryas event. *Nature*, 362, 527-9

Alley, R.B., Marotzke, J., Nordhaus, W.D., Overpeck, J.T., Peteet, D.M., Pielke, Jr., R.A., Pierrehumbert, R.T., Rhines, P.B., Stocker, T.F., Talley, L.D. and Wallace, J.M. (2003). Abrupt climate change. *Science*, 299, 2005-10

Broecker, W.S. (1987). Unpleasant surprises in the greenhouse? *Science*, 328, 123-7

Broecker, W.S. (1995). *The Glacial World According to Wally*, 2nd edition. Eldigio Press, Lamont- Docherty Geological Observatory of Columbia University, Palisades, N.Y.

Broecker, W.S., Peteet, D.M. and Rind, D. (1985). Does the ocean-atmosphere system have more than one stable mode of operation? *Nature*, 315, 21-6

CDIAC (2004). Carbon Dioxide Information Analysis Center. http://cdiac.esd.ornl.gov

Comiso, J.C. and Parkinson, C.L. (2004). Satellite-observed changes in the Arctic. *Physics Today*, August 2004, 38-44

Cuffey, K.M. and Clow, G.D. (1997). Temperature, accumulation, and ice sheet elevation in central Greenland through the last glacial transition. *J. Geophys. Res.*, 102, 383-96

Curry, R., Dickson, B. and Yashayaev, I. (2003). A change in the freshwater balance of the Atlantic Ocean over the past four decades. *Nature*, 426, 826-9

Curry, R. and Mauritzen, C. (In print). *On the freshwater balance of the Greenland Sea from 1950 to 1990*

Dickson, R.R., Yashayaev, I., Meincke, J., Turrel, W., Dye S. and Holfort, J. (2002). Rapid freshening of the deep North Atlantic over the past four decades. *Nature*, 416, 832-7

Dyurgerov, M.B. and Carter, C.L. (2004). Observational evidence of increases in freshwater inflow to the Arctic Ocean. *Arctic, Antarctic and Alpine Research* 36, 117-22

Hansen, B., Turrell, W.R. and Østerhus, S. (2001). Decreasing overflow from the Nordic Seas into the Atlantic Ocean through the Faroe Bank channel since 1950. *Nature*, 411, 927-30

Hansen, B., Osterhus, S., Quadfasel, D. and Turrell, W. (2004). Already the day after tomorrow? *Science*, 305, 953-4

Hughen, K.A., Eglinton, T.I., Xu, L. and Makou, M. (2004). Abrupt tropical vegetation response to rapid climate changes. *Science*, 304, 1955-9

IPCC (2001). *Climate Change 2001: The Scientific Basis: Summary for Policy Makers and Technical Summary of the Working Group 1 Report*. Intergovernmental Panel on Climate Change. Cambridge University Press, Cambridge

Knutti, R. and Stocker, T.F. (2001). Limited predictability of the thermohaline circulation close to a threshold. *Journal of Climate*, 15, 179-86

Latif, M., Roeckner, E., Mikolajewicz, U.R. and Voss, R. (2000). Tropical stabilization of the thermohaline circulation in a greenhouse warming simulation. *Journal of Climate*, 13, 1809-13

Laxon, S., Peacock, N. and Smith, D. (2003). High interannual variability of sea ice thickness in the Arctic region. *Nature*, 425 (6961), 947-50

Manabe, S. and Stouffer, R.J. (1988). Two stable equilibria of a coupled ocean-atmosphere model. *Journal of Climate*, 1, 841-66

Manabe, S. and Stouffer, R.J. (1994). Multiple-century response of a coupled ocean-atmosphere model to an increase of atmospheric carbon dioxide. *Journal of Climate*, 7, 5-23

McClelland, J.W., Holmes, R.M., Peterson, B.J. and Stieglitz, M. (2004). Increasing river discharge in the Eurasian Arctic: Consideration of dams, permafrost thaw, and fires as potential agents of change. *J. Geophysical Research* 109, D18102, doi:10.1029/2004JD004583

Peterson, B.J., Holmes, R.M., McClelland, J.W., Vorosmarty, C.J., Lammers, R.B., Shiklomanov, A.I., Shiklomanov, I.A. and Rahmstorf, S. (2002). Increasing river discharge to the Arctic Ocean. *Science*, 298, 2171-3

Rahmstorf, S. (1994). Rapid transitions in a coupled ocean-atmosphere model. *Nature*, 372, 82-5

Rahmstorf, S. (2002). Ocean circulation and climate during the past 120,000 years. *Nature*, 419, 207-14

Rahmstorf, S. and Ganopolski, A. (1999). Long-term warming scenarios computed with an efficient coupled climate model. *Climatic Change*, 43, 353-67

Sabine, C.L., Feeley, R.A., Gruber, N., Key, R.M., Lee, K., Bullister, J.L.R. Wanninkhof, R., Wong, C.S., Wallace, D.W.R., Tilbrook, B., Millero, F.J., Peng, T-H., Kozyr, A., Ono T. and Rios, A. (2004). The oceanic sink for anthropogenic CO_2. *Science*, 305, 367-71

Schmittner, A. and Stocker, T.F. (1999). The stability of the thermohaline circulation in global warming experiments. *Journal of Climate*, 12, 1117-33

Schulz, H., von Rad, U., Erlenkeuser, H. (1998). Correlation between Arabian Sea and Greenland climate oscillations of the past 110 000 years. *Nature*, 393 (6680), 54-7

Stocker, T.F. and Schmittner, A. (1997). Influence of CO2 emission rates on the stability of the thermohaline circulation. *Nature*, 388, 862-5

Wong, A.P.S., Bindoff, N.L. and Church, J.A. (1999). Large-scale freshening of intermediate waters in the Pacific and Indian Oceans. *Nature*, 400, 440-3

Yu, Y., Maykut, G.A. and Rothrock, D.A. (2004). Changes in the thickness distribution of Arctic sea ice between 1958-1970 and 1993-1997. *Journal of Geophysical Research-Oceans* 109(C8): article number C08004 Aug 6

Source: Wim Van Cappellen/Still Pictures

Source: J.P.Delobelle/Still Pictures

GEO
Indicators

Source: Robert J. Ross/Still Pictures

● ATMOSPHERE ● DISASTERS CAUSED BY
NATURAL HAZARDS ● BIODIVERSITY ● COASTAL AND
MARINE AREAS ● FRESHWATER ● URBAN AREAS
● GLOBAL ENVIRONMENTAL ISSUES

GEO Indicators

The set of GEO indicators gives a compact, illustrated overview of global trends in major issues related to the environment, depicting changes over the last years. The selected data are a mix of environmental pressures, states, impacts and responses.

The overall data situation continues to improve steadily – if slowly – although many data gaps and shortcomings still persist. The availability of data on threatened species and ozone depleting substances has significantly improved recently. Many data sets have been updated during the year – including the use of energy resources, carbon dioxide (CO_2) emissions, protected areas and catch of living marine resources. Others are updated on a more occasional basis. Currently the most problematic data are those for consumption and quality of freshwater, household and other wastes, urban air pollution, forest cover change, land degradation, and data related to coastal and marine areas.

The graphics incorporate the most recent year for which data are available. Compared to the *GEO Year Book 2003*, indicators have been added for renewable energy supply, consumption of hydrochlorofluorocarbons (HCFCs) and methyl bromide, marine protected areas, freshwater quality and urban air pollution. The indicators for use of freshwater and forest cover were not included this year, because there are no new comprehensive data available.

In the course of 2004, the set of GEO indicators was reviewed as part of an assessment of sustainability indicators by a consortium of the Scientific Committee on Problems of the Environment (SCOPE), UNEP, the International Human Dimensions Programme on Global Environmental Change (IHDP) and the European Environment Agency. Where possible, the recommendations of the review have been reflected in the current key set.

The indicators are grouped by thematic areas and environmental issues. Where appropriate the corresponding indicator for the environmental targets of the Goals in the Millennium Declaration is given. Definitions of terms used, information sources and technical notes are provided in an **Annex**. The data are presented at the global, regional and, in a few cases, sub-regional level, based on the regional classification used in the GEO assessment (UNEP 2002). All data and documentation have been extracted from the GEO Data Portal, which holds the reference database for use in the GEO assessment and reporting process (http://geodata.grid.unep.ch/).

Theme: **ATMOSPHERE**
Issues: **Climate change**
Stratospheric ozone depletion
Indicators: **Energy use per unit of GDP***

Renewable energy supply index
CO_2 emissions, total
CO_2 emissions, per capita**
Consumption of CFCs*, HCFCs and methyl bromide**

* *MDG indicator no. 27 under Target 9, Goal 7*

** *MDG indicator no. 28(a) under Target 9, Goal 7*

*** *MDG indicator no. 28(b) under Target 9, Goal 7*

Energy use

Energy use per unit of Gross Domestic Product (GDP) is gradually decreasing, indicating that energy is being used more efficiently (**Figure 1**). There are not enough data to show the line for West Asia.

The total renewable energy supply has risen considerably over the last decade, with the index up to 119 in 2002 compared to 1990 (100) (**Figure 2**). Wind and solar energy in particular have seen sharp increases in absolute terms. However, overall energy use has increased in parallel, so the overall share of renewable energy has remained stable since 1990 at about 13.5 per cent of total energy use.

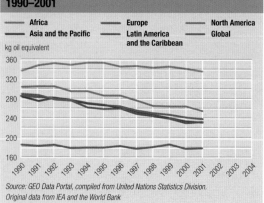

Figure 1: Energy use (kg oil equivalent) per US$1 000 Gross Domestic Product by region and global, 1990–2001

Africa — Europe — North America
Asia and the Pacific — Latin America and the Caribbean — Global

kg oil equivalent

Source: GEO Data Portal, compiled from United Nations Statistics Division. Original data from IEA and the World Bank

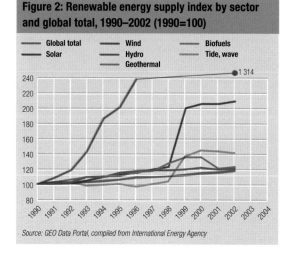

Figure 2: Renewable energy supply index by sector and global total, 1990–2002 (1990=100)

Global total — Wind — Biofuels
Solar — Hydro — Tide, wave
Geothermal

1 314

Source: GEO Data Portal, compiled from International Energy Agency

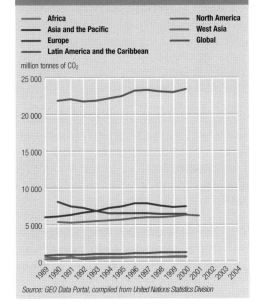

Figure 3: Total carbon dioxide emissions (million tonnes of CO₂) by region and global, 1989–2001

Africa
Asia and the Pacific
Europe
Latin America and the Caribbean
North America
West Asia
Global

million tonnes of CO₂

Source: GEO Data Portal, compiled from United Nations Statistics Division

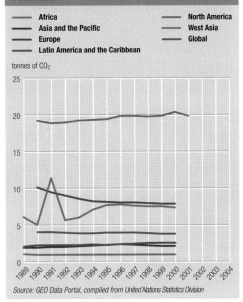

Figure 4: Total carbon dioxide emissions (tonnes of CO₂) per capita by region and global, 1989–2001

Africa
Asia and the Pacific
Europe
Latin America and the Caribbean
North America
West Asia
Global

tonnes of CO₂

Source: GEO Data Portal, compiled from United Nations Statistics Division

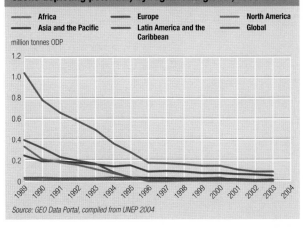

Figure 5: Consumption of chlorofluorocarbons (tonnes of ozone depleting potential) by region and global, 1989–2003

Africa
Asia and the Pacific
Europe
Latin America and the Caribbean
North America
Global

million tonnes ODP

Source: GEO Data Portal, compiled from UNEP 2004

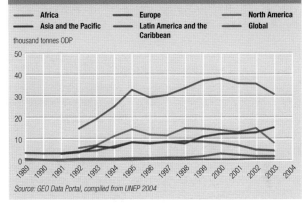

Figure 6: Consumption of hydrochlorofluorocarbons (tonnes of ozone depleting potential) by region and global, 1989–2003

Africa
Asia and the Pacific
Europe
Latin America and the Caribbean
North America
Global

thousand tonnes ODP

Source: GEO Data Portal, compiled from UNEP 2004

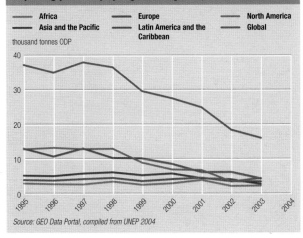

Figure 7: Consumption of methyl bromide (tonnes of ozone depleting potential) by region and global, 1995–2003

Africa
Asia and the Pacific
Europe
Latin America and the Caribbean
North America
Global

thousand tonnes ODP

Source: GEO Data Portal, compiled from UNEP 2004

Carbon dioxide emissions

The concentration of CO_2 in the Earth's atmosphere has increased from about 280 ppm before the industrial age, and accelerated during recent years to an all time high of 379 ppm in 2004 (NOAA 2004).

Global anthropogenic emissions of CO_2 were slightly higher in the latest reported year (2000) (**Figure 3**), while per capita figures seem to be levelling off (**Figure 4**). Figures for other greenhouse gases such as nitrous oxide (N_2O) and methane (CH_4) are not available yet for all major regions of the world. Total aggregated anthropogenic greenhouse gas emissions decreased by about three per cent from 1990 to 2000 in countries which are Annex I Parties to the United Nations Framework Convention on Climate Change (UNFCCC).

Stratospheric ozone depletion

While the consumption of chlorofluorocarbons (CFCs) has decreased steadily in most regions of the world (**Figure 5**), the use of substitutes belonging to the group of HCFCs rose until around 2000 (**Figure 6**). Although data are not complete, the years 2000–03 showed a noticeable decline due to reversing trends in Europe, Latin America and the Caribbean and North America. HCFCs are much less ozone depleting than CFCs, but do have a large global warming potential. The use of methyl bromide increased during the 1990s, but is now decreasing in all regions of the world, largely due to reductions in usage for soil fumigation (**Figure 7**) (UNEP 2004). There are not enough data to show the lines for West Asia.

Theme: DISASTERS CAUSED BY NATURAL HAZARDS
Issue: **Human vulnerability to extreme natural events**
Indicator: **Number of people killed by disasters**

For 2003, the reported number of deaths from natural disasters reached almost 80 000, considerably more than the estimated yearly average of 65 000 measured over the last 30 years. The fatalities in 2003 are mainly attributed to earthquakes such as the one in Bam, Iran, and the heat waves that occurred in Europe. For the year 2004, the reported fatalities amounted to 12 000 by October. The figure for the whole of 2004 will need to be completed and revised dramatically in the light of more recent events, most notably the unprecedented tsunami disaster in the Indian Ocean on 26 December. As of mid-January 2005, the death toll reportedly exceeded 220 000. The data on the number of people killed due to natural hazards in 2004 will be included in the next issue of the GEO Year Book series.

The figures here relate to earthquakes, volcanic eruptions, droughts, extreme temperatures, insect infestations, floods, landslides, wave/surges, wild fires

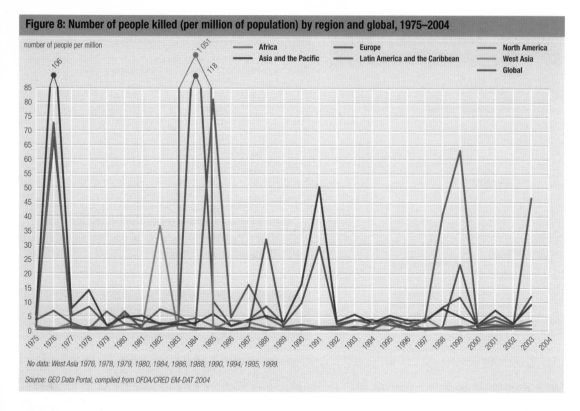

Figure 8: Number of people killed (per million of population) by region and global, 1975–2004

number of people per million

Africa
Asia and the Pacific
Europe
Latin America and the Caribbean
North America
West Asia
Global

No data: West Asia 1976, 1978, 1979, 1980, 1984, 1986, 1988, 1990, 1994, 1995, 1999.

Source: GEO Data Portal, compiled from OFDA/CRED EM-DAT 2004

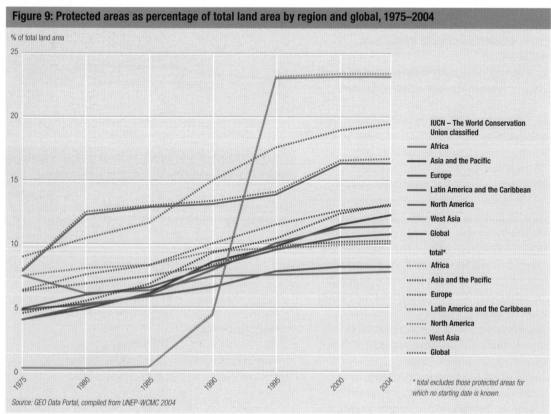

Figure 9: Protected areas as percentage of total land area by region and global, 1975–2004

% of total land area

IUCN – The World Conservation
Union classified

Africa
Asia and the Pacific
Europe
Latin America and the Caribbean
North America
West Asia
Global
total*
Africa
Asia and the Pacific
Europe
Latin America and the Caribbean
North America
West Asia
Global

* total excludes those protected areas for which no starting date is known

Source: GEO Data Portal, compiled from UNEP-WCMC 2004

and wind storms (**Figure 8**). On average, since 1975 for the world as a whole, 31 per cent of reported fatalities are related to droughts, 30 per cent to earthquakes, 16 per cent to wind storms and 10 per cent to floods. Different hazards affect different parts of the world. In Africa, droughts are by far the predominant disaster type (95 per cent of reported fatalities), in Europe, West Asia, and Asia and the Pacific earthquakes predominate (56, 49 and 43 per cent respectively), in Latin America floods (32 per cent) and in North America wind storms cause most fatalities (64 per cent) (OFDA/CRED EM-DAT 2004).

Theme: **BIODIVERSITY**
Issues: **Species loss**
Habitat loss
Indicators: **Number of threatened species**
Ratio of area protected to maintain biological diversity to surface area*

*MDG indicator no. 26 under Target 9, Goal 7

Threatened species

The number of threatened animal and plant species indicates the extent to which biodiversity is at risk from human activities and pressures on the environment, such as the destruction of habitat. The number of threatened species continues to increase and has now reached about 6 700 animals and 8 300 plant species (**Table 1**). The considerably higher figure for threatened amphibians in 2004 (31 per cent compared to 2.9 per cent in 1983) is mainly due to preliminary results for Brazil, based on a different categorization method.

These figures need to be treated with caution. The total number of existing species is unknown, and the data on threatened species are incomplete (IUCN 2004). This is especially true for insects, molluscs, crustaceans and plants, since only small portions of these groups have been evaluated to date.

Protected areas

Although the reported data are incomplete, the trend indicates a steady increase in protected areas over the last decades at regional and global levels (**Figure 9**). The jump for West Asia between 1990 and 1995 is due to the establishment of a single large protected area in Saudi Arabia in 1994.

Excluding areas for which no starting data are known, the total protected area (terrestrial and marine) in the world is estimated to be 19.5 million km² (as in November 2004), or about 13 per cent of the total land area (3.8 per cent of the Earth's surface).

Table 1: Threatened species

	Number of described species	Number of threatened species					Threatened species in 2004 as percentage of described species
		1996/98*	2000	2002	2003	2004	
Mammals	5 416	1 096	1 130	1 137	1 130	1 101	20
Birds	9 917	1 107	1 183	1 192	1 194	1 213	12
Reptiles	8 163	253	296	293	293	304	4
Amphibians	5 743	124	146	157	157	1 770	31
Fishes	28 500	734	752	742	750	800	3
Insects	950 000	537	555	557	553	559	0.06
Molluscs	70 000	920	938	939	967	974	1
Crustaceans	40 000	407	408	409	409	429	1
Plants	287 655	5 328	5 611	5 714	6 774	8 321	2.9

* 1996 – animals, 1998 – plants

Source: IUCN 2004

Theme: **COASTAL AND MARINE AREAS**
Issue: **Unsustainable use of living marine resources**
Indicators: **Marine capture**
Marine Protected Areas as percentage of Large Marine Ecosystem areas

Marine capture

The catch of living marine resources (fish, crustaceans and molluscs) is an indication of human pressure on marine ecosystems and their environmental sustainability. In 2002, reported global marine capture totalled about 84.5 million tonnes of fish, crustaceans and molluscs (**Figure 10**). This is a little higher than the average for the period since 1990 when the catch began to oscillate around the figure of 83 million tonnes (FAO 2004).

Marine Protected Areas as percentage of Large Marine Ecosystem areas

Large Marine Ecosystems (LMEs) are regions of ocean space encompassing coastal areas from river basins and estuaries to the seaward boundaries of continental shelves and the outer margins of the major current systems. They are relatively large regions of between 221 324 km^2 (Gulf of California) up to 6 429 232 km^2 (Arctic Ocean) in extent, and are characterised by distinct bathymetry, hydrography, productivity, and trophically dependent populations. On a global scale, the 64 LMEs account for 95 per cent of the world's annual

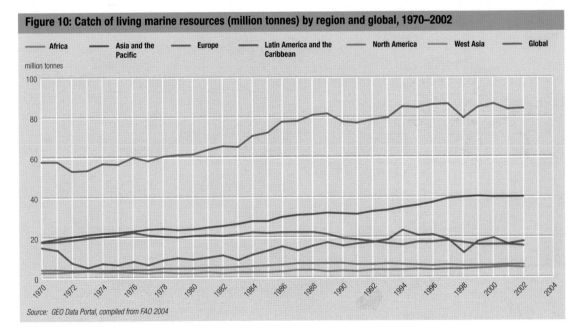

Figure 10: Catch of living marine resources (million tonnes) by region and global, 1970–2002

Legend: Africa — Asia and the Pacific — Europe — Latin America and the Caribbean — North America — West Asia — Global

Source: GEO Data Portal, compiled from FAO 2004

marine fishery biomass yields and most of the ocean pollution. Resource harvesting and pollution have led to severe coastal habitat degradation.

Although significantly increased in number and surface area over the last decades (**Figures 11** and **12**), marine areas remain under-represented in the global protected area system (Chape and others 2003). However, the share of protected areas in marine ecosystems and ocean zones has doubled since 1990

and now amounts to 1.6 per cent of the total LME area, or almost 73 million km^2. The level of protection within LMEs varies significantly. For example, in the Northeast Australian Shelf 26.7 per cent of the 1 285 097 km^2 is protected, mainly due to the substantial area that has been devoted to protecting the Great Barrier Reef. In the Indonesian Sea, an equally important marine ecosystem area, only 1.1 per cent out of 2 269 581 km^2 is protected (Spalding and others *in press*).

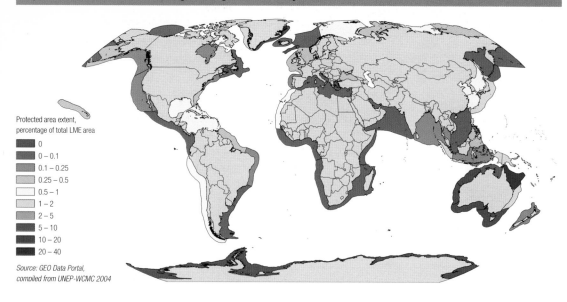

Protected area extent,
percentage of total LME area

- 0
- 0 – 0.1
- 0.1 – 0.25
- 0.25 – 0.5
- 0.5 – 1
- 1 – 2
- 2 – 5
- 5 – 10
- 10 – 20
- 20 – 40

*Source: GEO Data Portal,
compiled from UNEP-WCMC 2004*

Figure 12: Protected areas coverage of Large Marine Ecosystems in 2004

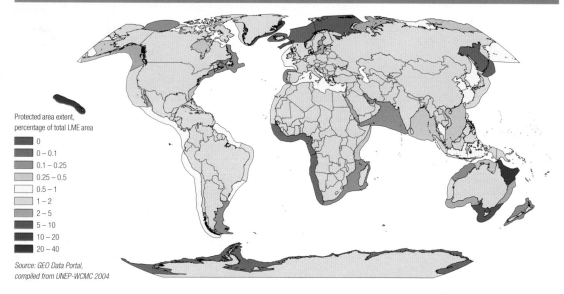

Protected area extent,
percentage of total LME area

- 0
- 0 – 0.1
- 0.1 – 0.25
- 0.25 – 0.5
- 0.5 – 1
- 1 – 2
- 2 – 5
- 5 – 10
- 10 – 20
- 20 – 40

*Source: GEO Data Portal,
compiled from UNEP-WCMC 2004*

Theme: **FRESHWATER**

Issues: **Water quality**

Access to improved water supply and sanitation

Indicators: **Concentration of dissolved nitrogen in surface waters**

Biological oxygen demand (BOD) in surface waters

Proportion of population with access to improved water supply*

Proportion of population with access to improved sanitation**

*MDG indicator no. 30 under Target 10, Goal 7

**MDG indicator no. 31 under Target 10, Goal 7

Water quality

Freshwater quality changes at the global, continental and drainage basin levels. In general, water pollution is growing, but there are also areas of improvement. Indicators for water quality include parameters for dissolved nitrogen and biological oxygen demand (BOD).

In water, nitrogen occurs as nitrates and nitrites. Sources of nitrogen in water bodies include fertilizer washed from agricultural land, acid rain and untreated or partially treated human and animal wastes. While surface water nitrogen levels in some parts of the world have gone down, in most regions they have remained stable or increased (**Figure 13**). Excessive nitrogen can harm human health and result in undesirable water quality conditions, including excessive algal and plant growth, and deoxygenation when plants and algae die and the oxygen is consumed as part of the decay process.

Concentrations of nitrates occur naturally in surface waters up to 5 mg/l NO_3-N. Higher concentrations usually indicate pollution by human or animal waste, or fertilizer run-off. For drinking water, a maximum limit of 11.3 mg/l NO_3-N is recommended. Higher concentrations can represent a significant human health risk (UNESCO/WHO/UNEP 1996).

Organic matter is decomposed by microorganisms in water and this process 'demands' oxygen. BOD is an indicator of the amount of organic matter present in freshwater. High BOD levels may indicate that water is contaminated with coliform bacteria and other pathogens and unfit for human consumption. Rivers in Europe and North America have shown a reduction in BOD levels over the past two decades (**Figure 14**). Unpolluted waters typically have a BOD of 2 mg/l O_2 or less, while those receiving wastewaters or other organic residues can have up to 10 mg/l O_2 or more (UNESCO/WHO/UNEP 1996).

Water supply and sanitation

New data show that between 1990 and 2002, access to improved drinking water supply rose from 77 to 83 per cent of the world's population (**Figure 15**). Significant progress was made in Asia and the Pacific (+9 per cent). Progress in sub-Saharan Africa was also very impressive: from 49 to 58 per cent. In Latin America and the Caribbean, almost 90 per cent now have access to an improved supply (WHO/UNICEF 2004). However more than one billion people continue to use water from unimproved sources, nearly two thirds of whom live in Asia.

Global sanitation coverage rose from 49 per cent in 1990 to 58 per cent in 2002 (**Figure 16**). About 2.6 billion people – half of the developing world – still live without improved sanitation. Though major progress was made in the Asia and the Pacific region, less than half of its population currently have access to improved sanitation. In Africa, coverage has increased by 4 per cent to 43 per cent over the same period of time.

Figure 13: Mean concentration of dissolved nitrogen (nitrate + nitrite, mg/l N) in surface waters by selected region, 1979–90 and 1991–99

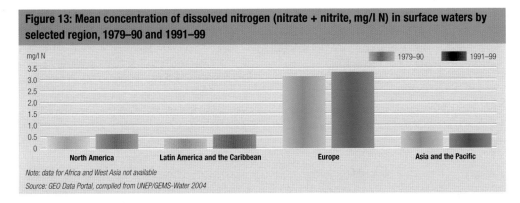

Note: data for Africa and West Asia not available

Source: GEO Data Portal, compiled from UNEP/GEMS-Water 2004

Figure 14: Mean BOD (mg/l O₂) in surface waters by selected region, 1979–90 and 1991–99

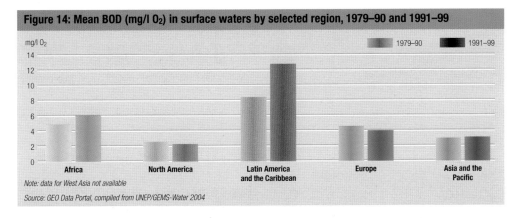

Note: data for West Asia not available

Source: GEO Data Portal, compiled from UNEP/GEMS-Water 2004

Figure 15: Population with access to improved water supply (% of total) by region and global, 1990 and 2002

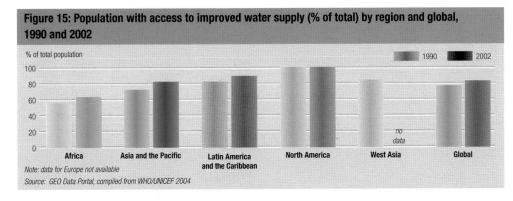

Note: data for Europe not available

Source: GEO Data Portal, compiled from WHO/UNICEF 2004

Figure 16: Population with access to improved sanitation (% of total) by region and global, 1990 and 2002

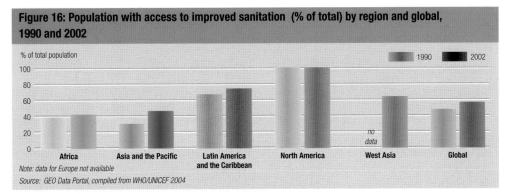

Note: data for Europe not available

Source: GEO Data Portal, compiled from WHO/UNICEF 2004

Theme: **URBAN AREAS**

Issue: **Urban air quality**

Indicators: **Concentrations of lead, particulate matter (PM) sulphur dioxide (SO₂) and nitrogen dioxide (NO₂) in air**

Urban air quality

The air in cities may be severely polluted not only by transport but also by the burning of fossil fuels in power plants, factories, office buildings, and homes and by the incineration of garbage. There are no up-to-date and comprehensive data on city air quality for most regions of the world. However, selected data collected by OECD indicates that lead is becoming less of a problem in developed regions and its levels are now well below the WHO guideline value (WHO 2000) (**Figure 17**). In many of the cities the concentrations of particulate matter and sulphur dioxide are also decreasing (**Figures 18** and **19**), while nitrogen dioxide

Figure 17: Concentrations of lead (μg/m3) in air in selected cities, 1985–99

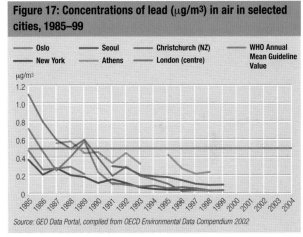

Source: GEO Data Portal, compiled from OECD Environmental Data Compendium 2002

Figure 18: Concentrations of PM (μg/m3) in air in selected cities, 1985–2000

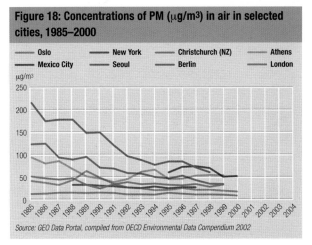

Source: GEO Data Portal, compiled from OECD Environmental Data Compendium 2002

Figure 19: Concentrations of SO₂ (μg/m³) in air in selected cities, 1985–2000

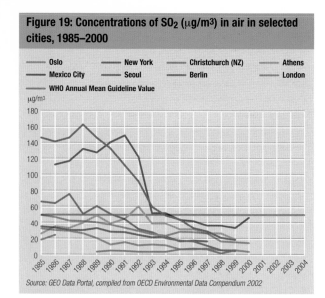

Source: GEO Data Portal, compiled from OECD Environmental Data Compendium 2002

Figure 20: Concentrations of NO₂ (μg/m³) in air in selected cities, 1985–2000

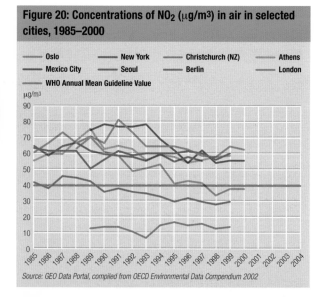

Source: GEO Data Portal, compiled from OECD Environmental Data Compendium 2002

levels are still high (**Figure 20**) (OECD 2002). The decrease in pollutant levels has usually been brought about through controls on emissions and changing fuel use patterns.

Theme: **GLOBAL ENVIRONMENTAL ISSUES**
Issue: **International environmental governance**
Indicator: **Number of parties to multilateral environmental agreements**

Ratification of major multilateral environmental agreements (MEAs) has progressed, indicating increasing commitment of countries to addressing environmental issues (**Figure 21**). Recently the Kyoto Protocol to the UN Framework Convention on Climate Change gained sufficient ratifications to come into force in early 2005. On chemicals, the Rotterdam Convention on Prior Informed Consent, and the Stockholm Convention on Persistent Organic Pollutants, both entered into force in 2004. All the selected MEAs have seen the number of ratifications grow steadily, and many are approaching the maximum number of parties by now. Taking all 13 MEAs together 75 per cent of possible ratifications have been made for the world as a whole. In every region at least 60 per cent of the potential ratifications have been made (**Table 2**).

Figure 21: Number of parties to multilateral environmental agreements, 1971–2004

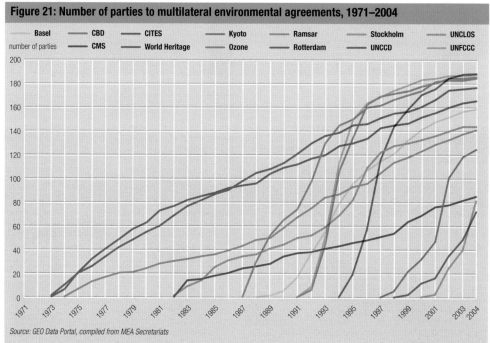

Source: GEO Data Portal, compiled from MEA Secretariats

Table 2: Number of parties to multilateral environmental agreements, by GEO region

	CBD	CMS	CITES	Heritage	Kyoto	Ozone	Ramsar	PIC	POPs	UNCCD	UNCLOS	UNFCCC	Basel	Total	Potential	%
Africa (53)	52	29	51	45	26	51	40	22	23	53	38	52	39	521	689	76
Asia + Pacfic (45)	45	9	30	40	33	43	24	13	18	45	33	44	33	410	585	70
Europe (49)	46	36	44	48	36	46	46	22	23	46	36	47	46	522	637	82
LAC (34)	32	8	32	31	27	33	25	9	13	33	27	33	30	333	442	75
North America (2)	1	0	2	2	1	2	2	1	1	2	1	2	1	18	26	69
West Asia (12)	10	3	7	11	2	10	4	5	3	10	9	10	10	94	156	60
Global (195)	186	85	166	177	125	185	141	72	81	189	144	188	159	1898	2535	75

See Annex for full convention names.
Source: GEO Data Portal, compiled from MEA Secretariats

REFERENCES

Chape, S., Blyth, S., Fish, L., Fox, P. and Spalding, M. (compilers). (2003). *2003 United Nations List of Protected Areas*. World Conservation Union, Gland, and United Nations Environment Programme World Conservation Monitoring Centre, Cambridge

FAO (2004). *FISHSTAT Plus system*. Food and Agriculture Organization. http://www.fao.org/fi/statist/FISOFT/FISHPLUS.asp

IUCN (2004). *2004 IUCN Red List of Threatened Species*.IUCN – The World Conservation Union. http://www.redlist.org/

NOAA (2004). Climate Monitoring and Diagnostics Laboratory of the National Oceanic and Atmospheric Administration. http://www.cmdl.noaa.gov/

OECD (2002). *Environmental Data Compendium 2002*. Organization for Economic Cooperation and Development, Paris

OFDA/CRED EM-DAT (2004). *The OFDA/CRED International Disaster Database*. Brussels, Université Catholique de Louvain. http://www.em-dat.net/

Spalding, M., Jenkins M. and Chape, S. (in press). *The World's Protected Areas: Status, Values and Prospects in the 21st Century*. University of California Press, Berkeley

UNEP (2002). *Global Environment Outlook 3. Past, Present and Future Perspective*. London, Earthscan

UNEP (2004). *Information Provided by the Parties in Accordance With Article 7 of the Montreal Protocol on Substances That Deplete the Ozone Layer*. UNEP/OzL.Pro/16/4. 18 October 2004. Sixteenth Meeting of the Parties to the Montreal Protocol on Substances That Deplete the Ozone Layer. Prague, 22-26 November 2004. http://www.unep.org/ozone/Meeting_Documents/mop/16mop/16mop-4.e.pdf

UNEP/GEMS-Water (2004). UNEP Global Environment Monitoring System (GEMS) Water Programme. http://www.gemswater.org/

UNEP-WCMC (2004). *World Database on Protected Areas*. UNEP World Conservation Monitoring Centre. http://sea.unep-wcmc.org/wdbpa/

UNESCO/WHO/UNEP (1996). *Water Quality Assessments – A Guide to Use of Biota, Sediments and Water in Environmental Monitoring – Second Edition*. E&FN Spon, London. http://www.who.int/water_sanitation_health/resourcesquality/wqa/en/

WHO (2000). *Guidelines for Air Quality*. World Health Organization, Geneva

WHO/UNICEF (2004). *Meeting the MDG drinking water and sanitation target: a mid-term assessment of progress*. WHO/UNICEF Joint Monitoring Programme for Water Supply and Sanitation. http://www.who.int/water_sanitation_health/monitoring/en/jmp04.pdf

ANNEX

Indicator, unit of measurement and source(s)	Notes
Energy use per unit of GDP Unit of measurement: kilogram of oil equivalent per US$1 000 of GDP, converted from national currencies using purchasing power parity (PPP) conversion factors for the year 1995. *Source: UN Statistics Division (UNSD), compiled from the International Energy Agency (IEA) and the World Bank.*	Energy use is calculated by the IEA as production of fuels + inputs from other sources + imports − exports − international marine bunkers + stock changes. It includes coal, crude oil, natural gas liquids, refinery feedstocks, additives, petroleum products, gases, combustible renewables and waste, electricity and heat. Real GDP comes from the national income accounts deflated by reference to PPP tables prepared by the International Comparisons Program.
Renewable energy supply index. Unit of measurement: none (index). *Source: IEA*	Renewable energy data refer to Total Primary Energy Supply, originally expressed in Mtoe, for all the countries of the world from 1990 to 2002. The included renewable energy categories are: hydro, geothermal, wind, solar, biomass (solid, liquid and gas) and tide/wave/ocean. The data are based on submissions from national administrations to the IEA Secretariat. The database contains time series of annual renewables and wastes data for OECD countries from 1990 to 2002, together with estimates for 2003 that are the latest renewable energy data available at the moment.
Emission of CO_2 is the total amount of CO_2 emitted by a country as a consequence of human production and consumption activities. **Emission of CO_2 per capita** is the above divided by the population of the country. Unit of measurement: tonne. *Source: UNSD, compiled from the United Nations Framework Convention on Climate Change (UNFCCC) and Carbon Dioxide Information Analysis Center (CDIAC).*	In the CO_2 emission estimates of the CDIAC, the calculated country emissions of CO_2 include emissions from consumption of solid, liquid and gas fuels; cement production; and gas flaring. National reporting to UNFCCC that follows the Intergovernmental Panel on Climate Change guidelines is based on national emission inventories and covers all sources of anthropogenic CO_2 emissions as well as carbon sinks.
Consumption of CFCs, HCFCs and MeBr is defined as production plus imports minus exports of controlled substances, as reported to the Secretariat of the Montreal Protocol by parties. Unit of measurement: tonne of ozone-depleting potential. *Source: UNEP (Ozone Secretariat).*	Ozone-depleting potential (ODP) is the ratio of the impact on ozone of a chemical compared to the impact of a similar mass of CFC-11. Thus, the ODP of CFC-11 is defined as 1.0. The five CFCs compiled for MDG indicator no.28 are CFC-11, CFC-12, CFC-113, CFC-114 and CFC-115. Not all parties meet reporting deadlines in time. Illegal production and trade occur and are not covered by the reporting process. The HCFCs to be phased out are HCFC-22, HCFC-123, HCFC-124, HCFC-133a, HCFC-141b, HCFC-142b, HCFC-225ca and HCFC-225cb. Methyl bromide, MeBr or CH_3Br, is to be phased out by 2005 in developed countries and by 2015 in developing countries (except for critical use). In 2004, 11 developed countries which faced a year-end deadline for phasing out methyl bromide were granted limited 'critical use exemptions'.
Number of people killed by natural disasters is the number of persons confirmed as dead and persons missing and presumed dead. Unit of measurement: number. *Source: OFDA/CRED EM-DAT.*	A disaster is a situation or event, which overwhelms local capacity, necessitating a request to national or international level for external assistance; an unforeseen and often sudden event that causes great damage, destruction and human suffering. The data were revised in 2004 by OFDA/CRED, resulting in changed figures for past years, including the casualties in Africa in 1984.
Number of threatened species. Unit of measurement: number. *Source: IUCN Red List of Threatened Species.*	The term 'threatened species' includes species listed as Critically Endangered, Endangered and Vulnerable i.e. those facing an extremely high risk, very high risk or high risk of extinction in the wild, respectively, according to the relevant criteria for population size, range, and maturity as established under the IUCN Red List system. Regional time-series data cannot be presented because reporting and definitions have changed over the years. Only a small proportion of described species has been evaluated for threatened status. For animals, only birds and mammals are (almost) all evaluated (100 and 99 per cent respectively). Less than 0.1 per cent of insect species have been evaluated. For plants, gymnosperms (mainly the conifers and cycads) are the only major group to be almost completely evaluated (93 per cent). Due to changes in the classification system, the plant figures do not include some species from the 1997 IUCN Red List of Threatened Plants. The data on species threatened in each group do not mean that the remainder are not threatened. A number of species are listed as Near Threatened or Data Deficient. Species assessed as 'of Least Concern' are often not reported, and are not included. The numbers evaluated as threatened are therefore probably an underestimate.
Ratio of area protected to maintain biological diversity to surface area. Unit of measurement: per cent. *Source: UNEP-WCMC (World Database on Protected Areas).*	Protected area is the area of land and/or sea especially dedicated to the protection and maintenance of biological diversity, and of natural and associated cultural resources, and managed through legal or other effective means. The six IUCN management categories provide an internationally agreed framework within which countries can structure their protected area systems. IUCN management categories are Strict Nature Reserve (Ia); Wilderness Area (Ib); National Park (II); Natural Monument (III); Habitat/Species Management Area (IV); Protected Landscape/Seascape (V); Managed Resource Protected Area (VI).
Marine capture is the nominal catch of fish, crustaceans and molluscs in marine areas. Unit of measurement: tonne. *Source: FAO (FISHSTAT Plus).*	Fish categories include demersal, pelagic and other marine fish and freshwater and diadromous fish caught in marine areas, as taken for commercial, industrial, recreational and subsistence purposes. The harvest from mariculture, aquaculture and other kinds of fish farming is excluded. Catches are expressed in live weight – the weight of the organisms at the time of capture. Data include all quantities caught and landed for food and feed purposes but exclude discards. Data on illegal fish catch are not available. The general availability of fisheries data has not improved significantly over the last two decades, and although the available statistics probably reflect general trends reliably, the annual figures and the assessments involve some uncertainty.

Indicator, unit of measurement and source(s)	Notes
Protected areas in Large Marine Ecosystems gives the share of protected area in major marine ecosystems (LMEs). Unit of measurement: per cent. *Source: UNEP-WCMC (World Database on Protected Areas).*	In the World Database on Protected Areas, sites indicated as marine are currently undergoing verification. The site information supplied often has only the 'total protected area' without a breakdown between marine and terrestrial components. Difficulty arises when trying to account for the marine proportion of a site especially where no polygon information is held. Efforts have been made to mitigate this problem in the data presented here. Data and calculations as of November 2004.
Dissolved nitrogen and BOD in surface waters. Units of measurement: mg/l . *Source: UNEP GEMS/Water Programme.*	Surface waters include rivers and lakes. Nitrate is the principal form of combined nitrogen found in natural waters. Total nitrogen is usually calculated as the sum of particulate nitrogen (i.e. does not pass a 0.45 μm filter) and the resultant dissolved nitrate. Nitrogen (N) is measured in a number of forms in water samples; specifically as ammonium ions (NH_4), ammonia gas (NH_3), nitrate ions (NO_3^-) and Nitrite ions (NO_2^-). Biological oxygen demand (BOD) measures the level of organic material in a water body, based on the fact that microorganisms use the oxygen dissolved in water to decompose organic matter in polluted water through a biochemical process which produces the carbon they need to survive. The data are derived from the GEMS/Water Programme database. The figures should be used with caution since the existing database is fairly sparse in regions such as Africa and parts of Latin America and the Caribbean.
Proportion of population with access to improved water supply. Unit of measurement: per cent. *Source: WHO/UNICEF (Joint Monitoring Programme for Water Supply and Sanitation).*	'Improved' water supply technologies are: household connection, public standpipe, borehole, protected dug well, protected spring, rainwater collection. 'Not improved' are: unprotected well, unprotected spring, vendor-provided water, bottled water (based on concerns about the quantity of supplied water, not concerns over the water quality), tanker truck-provided water. It is assumed that if the user has access to an 'improved source' then such source would be likely to provide 20 litres per capita per day at a distance no further than 1 km. In 1990, data for 89 per cent of world population were available. In 2002, data for 94 per cent of world population were available. Time series cannot be shown due to lack of data.
Proportion of population with access to improved sanitation. Unit of measurement: per cent. *Source: WHO/UNICEF (Joint Monitoring Programme for Water Supply and Sanitation).*	'Improved' sanitation technologies are: connection to a public sewer; connection to septic system; pour-flush latrine; simple pit latrine; ventilated improved pit latrine. The excreta disposal system is considered adequate if it is private or shared (but not public) and if it hygienically separates human excreta from human contact. In 1990, data for 87 per cent of regional population were available. In 2002, data for 91 per cent of regional population were available. Time series cannot be shown due to lack of data. In 2004, revisions to earlier reported data were made based on additional information, more detailed definitions of sanitation facilities and a more stringent method used to estimate coverage. Data for the year 1990 were adjusted accordingly.
Concentrations of lead, PM, SO_2, NO_2 in air. Unit of measurement: μg/m³. *Source: OECD Environmental Data Compendium 2002.*	The data provide an indication of trends in ambient air quality in cities. The use of the data is limited because often only one measurement site is available for trend purposes, and in some cities the number of trend sites will change significantly from one year to the next. One measurement site is not sufficient when trying to assess citywide trends. While no firm rule exists, five or more sites are recommended as a minimum number from which to derive such trend information, assuming a distribution of sites that represents multiple areas of a city. Caution is needed when interpreting these data, especially because of the large differences in the number of monitoring sites used in the calculation of citywide averages. The variation in the number of sites may sometimes introduce a bias to the trend within an individual city. Sometimes monitoring is carried out only at sites where there is a severe problem, leading to a bias towards higher concentrations. Because of different PM measurement techniques applied in different cities extreme caution is needed in comparing the figures. (Mexico City: data refer to the Metropolitan area. New York: particulates smaller than 10 μm. Seoul: data refer to total suspended particulate. Christchurch: particulates smaller than 50 μm. Berlin: particulates smaller than 15 μm. Oslo: particulates smaller than 10 μm. London: data refer to black smoke.)
Number of parties to multilateral environmental agreements is the number of countries and political and/or economic integration organizations, which have deposited their instrument of ratification, accession, acceptance or approval of each of the 13 multilateral environmental agreements (MEAs) listed on the right. The list also includes secretariats' Web pages showing status of ratification. Unit of measurement: number. *Source: MEA Secretariats.*	Convention on Biological Diversity (CBD): http://www.biodiv.org/world/parties.asp Convention on the Conservation of Migratory Species of Wild Animals (CMS): http://www.cms.int/about/intro.htm Convention on International Trade in Endangered Species of Wild Fauna and Flora (CITES): http://www.cites.org/eng/disc/parties/index.shtml Convention Concerning the Protection of the World Cultural and Natural Heritage (World Heritage): http://whc.unesco.org/nwhc/pages/doc/main.htm Kyoto Protocol to the UN Framework Convention on Climate Change (Kyoto): http://unfccc.int/essential_background/kyoto_protocol/status_of_ratification/items/2613.php Vienna Convention for the Protection of the Ozone Layer and its Montreal Protocol on Substances that Deplete the Ozone Layer (Vienna/Montreal): http://www.unep.ch/ozone/ratif.shtml Convention on Wetlands of International Importance Especially as Waterfowl Habitat (Ramsar): http://www.ramsar.org/key_cp_e.htm Rotterdam Convention on the Prior Informed Consent Procedure for Certain Hazardous Chemicals and Pesticides in International Trade (PIC): http://www.pic.int/en/ViewPage.asp?id=345 Stockholm Convention on Persistent Organic Pollutants (POPs): http://www.pops.int/documents/signature/signstatus.htm UN Convention to Combat Desertification in Those Countries Experiencing Serious Drought and/or Desertification Particularly in Africa (UNCCD): http://www.unccd.int/convention/ratif/doeif.php UN Convention on the Law of the Sea (UNCLOS): http://www.un.org/Depts/los/reference_files/chronological_lists_of_ratifications.htm#The United Nations Convention on the Law of the Sea UN Framework Convention on Climate Change (UNFCCC): http://unfccc.int/essential_background/convention/status_of_ratification/items/2631.php Basel Convention on the Control of Transboundary Movements of Hazardous Wastes and Their Disposal (Basel): http://www.basel.int/ratif/ratif.html

Acronyms and abbreviations

ACIA	Arctic Climate Impact Assessment
ACTO	Amazon Cooperation Treaty Organization
AGM	Annual General Meeting
AHEG-PARAM	Ad Hoc Expert Group on Consideration with a View to Recommending the Parameters of a Mandate for Developing a Legal Framework on All Types of Forests (of UNFF)
AMAP	Arctic Monitoring and Assessment Programme
AMCEN	African Ministerial Conference on the Environment
ASMA	Antarctic Specially Managed Area
ATCM	Antarctic Treaty Consultative Meeting
Basel Convention	Basel Convention on the Control of Transboundary Movements of Hazardous Wastes and their Disposal
BPoA	Barbados Programme of Action
CBD	Convention on Biological Diversity
CDM	Clean Development Mechanism
CEC	Commission for Environmental Cooperation
CEDAW	Convention on Elimination of all forms of Discrimination Against Women
CFCs	chlorofluorocarbons
CITES	Convention on International Trade in Endangered Species of Wild Fauna and Flora
CLRTAP	Convention on Long-Range Transboundary Air Pollution
CO_2	carbon dioxide
COP	conference of the parties
CSD	Commission on Sustainable Development
DDT	dichloro-diphenyl-trichloro-ethane
DHF	dengue hemorrhagic fever
DPRK	Democratic People's Republic of Korea
DRC	Democratic Republic of Congo
EC	European Community
ECO	Economic Cooperation Organization
EEA	European Environment Agency
EPA	Environmental Protection Agency (of the United States)
ESA	European Space Agency
EVI	Environment Vulnerability Index
EU	European Union
FAO	Food and Agriculture Organization of the United Nations
GCC	Gulf Cooperation Council
GC/GMEF	Governing Council/Global Ministerial Environment Forum (of UNEP)
GCM	General Circulation Model
GDP	Gross Domestic Product
GEO	Global Environment Outlook (of UNEP)
GHG	greenhouse gas

GM	genetically modified
GMOs	genetically modified organisms
GRID	Global Resource Information Database
HCFCs	hydrochloroflourocarbons
HDI	Human Development Index
HIV/AIDS	human immunodeficiency virus/acquired immunodeficiency syndrome
IAATO	International Association of Antarctica Tour Operators
IAF	International Arrangement on Forests
IAP	International Action Programme
IASC	International Arctic Science Committee
IEA	International Energy Agency
ILO	International Labour Organization
IMO	International Maritime Organization
IPCC	Intergovernmental Panel on Climate Change
ITPGRFA	International Treaty on Plant Genetic Resources for Food and Agriculture
ITTA	International Tropical Timber Agreement
IUCN	World Conservation Union
JPOI	Johannesburg Plan of Implementation (of the World Summit on Sustainable Development)
Kyoto Protocol	Kyoto Protocol to the UN Framework Convention on Climate Change
LAC	Latin America and the Caribbean
LME	Large Marine Ecosystem
LMOs	living modified organisms
MBRS	Mesoamerican Barrier Reef System
MDGs	internationally agreed development goals and targets, including those contained in the UN Millennium Declaration
MEAs	multilateral environmental agreements
MeBr	methyl bromide
MERCOSUR	Southern Common Market
MODIS	moderate resolution imaging spectroradiometer
MoU	Memorandum of Understanding
MOP	Meeting of the Parties
NO_2	nitrogen dioxide
NO_3-N	nitrate nitrogen
NO_X	nitrogen oxides
NADW	North Atlantic Deep Water
NASA	National Aeronautics and Space Administration (of the United States)
NEPAD	New Partnership for Africa's Development
NGO	non-governmental organization
NOAA	National Oceans and Atmospheric Administration (of the United States)
NPP	net primary production
NWME	Network of Women Ministers of the Environment

OECD	Organization for Economic Cooperation and Development
PM	particulate matter
PCBs	polychlorinated biphenyls
POPs	persistent organic pollutants
PRSP	Poverty Reduction Strategy Paper
PTWC	Pacific Tsunami Warning Center
ROPME	Regional Organization for the Protection of the Marine Environment
SAICM	Strategic Approach to International Chemicals Management
SARS	Severe Acute Respiratory Syndrome
SCOPE	Scientific Committee on Problems of the Environment (of the International Council for Science)
SIDS	Small Island Developing State(s)
SO_2	Sulphur dioxide
SPREP	South Pacific Regional Environment Programme
UAE	United Arab Emirates
UK	United Kingdom
UNCTAD	United Nations Conference on Trade and Development
UNDP	United Nations Development Programme
UNECE	United Nations Economic Commission for Europe
UNEP	United Nations Environment Programme
UNEP-WCMC	UNEP World Conservation Monitoring Centre
UNESCO	United Nations Educational, Scientific and Cultural Organization
UNFCCC	United Nations Framework Convention on Climate Change
UNFF	United Nations Forum on Forests
UNGA	United Nations General Assembly
UN-HABITAT	United Nations Human Settlements Programme
UNICEF	United Nations Children's Fund
UNIDO	United Nations Industrial Development Organization
UNIFEM	United Nations Development Fund for Women
UNPD	United Nations Population Division
WAVE	Women as the Voice for the Environment
WHO	World Health Organization
World Bank	International Bank for Reconstruction and Development (IBRD) and the International Development Association (IDA)
WSSD	World Summit on Sustainable Development
WWF	World Wide Fund for Nature
ZAMCOM	Zambezi Watercourse Commission

Acknowledgements

UNEP would like to thank the following for their contributions to the GEO Year Book 2004/5.

Lead Authors:

Overview 2004:
Global: Prisna **Nuengsigkapian**, International Institute for Sustainable Development/Earth Negotiations Bulletin, United States

Africa: Munyaradzi **Chenje**, United Nations Environment Programme/Division of Early Warning and Assessment, Kenya

Asia Pacific: Twinkle **Chopra** and Subrato **Sinha**, United Nations Environment Programme/Regional Resource Centre for Asia and the Pacific, Thailand

Europe: Mirjam **Schomaker**, Consultant, France

Latin America & the Caribbean: Eduardo **Gudynas**, Centro Latino Americano de Ecología Social, Uruguay; and Kakuko **Nagatani-Yoshida**, United Nations Environment Programme/Division of Early Warning and Assessment, México

North America: Jane **Barr**, The Commission for Environmental Cooperation of North America, Canada

West Asia: Adel **Abdelkader**, United Nations Environment Programme/Division of Early Warning and Assessment, Kingdom of Bahrain; and Mohammed **Abido**, Arab Forest and Range Institute, Syria

Polar: Kathrine **Johnsen**, GRID-Arendal, Norway; and Michelle **Rogan-Finnemore**, Gateway Antarctica, Centre for Antarctic Studies and Research, University of Canterbury, New Zealand

Indian Ocean Tsunami: Anju **Sharma**, United Nations Environment Programme/Division of Early Warning and Assessment, Kenya

Feature Focus: Gender, Poverty and Environment: Joni **Seager**, Faculty of Environmental Science, York University, Canada

Emerging Challenges – New Findings: Emerging and Re-emerging Infectious Diseases: Links to Environmental Change: Bernard D. **Goldstein**, University of Pittsburgh Graduate School of Public Health, United States

Abrupt Climate Change: Ocean Salinity Changes and Potential Impacts on Ocean Circulation: Bruce **Peterson**, Marine Biological Laboratory, Woods Hole, Massachusetts, United States

GEO Indicators: Jaap **van Woerden**, United Nations Environment Programme/Division of Early Warning and Assessment/Global Resource Information Database-Geneva, Switzerland; and Volodymyr **Demkine**, United Nations Environment Programme/Division of Early Warning and Assessment, Kenya

Participants in the Expert Group Meeting on Gender and Environment – a contribution to the Feature Focus: Gender, Poverty and Environment section: Adebisi **Adebayo**, Consultant, Switzerland; Betsy **Apple**, Women's Environment and Development Organization, United States; Srilatha **Batliwara**, Women's Environment and Development Organization, India; Sudipa **Bose**, Emirates Environmental Group, United Arab Emirates; Marie-Claire **Cordonier Segger**, Centre for International Sustainable Development, Canada; Irene **Dankelman**, University Center for Environment and Sustainable Development, Radboud University Nijmegen, The Netherlands; Jocelyn **Dow**, Red Thread Women's Development, Guyana; Monique **Essed**, Women and Environment Movement, Suriname; Sascha **Gabizon**, Women in Europe for a Common Future, Germany; Kyoko **Kusakabe**, Gender and Development Studies Centre, Asian Institute of Technology, Thailand; Doris **Mpoumou**, Women's Environment and Development Organization, United States; Fatou **Ndoye**, Network for Environment and Sustainable Development in Africa, Cote d'Ivoire; Vijay Biju **Negi**, Chipko Movement, India; Zo **Randriamaro**, Women's Environment and Development Organization, Senegal; Marcela **Tovar**, Women's Environment and Development Organization, United States; June **Zeitlin**, Women's Environment and Development Organization, United States.

Contributors and Reviewers of Emerging Challenges – New Findings: Emerging and Re-emerging Infectious Diseases: Links to Environmental Change: Richard **Alley**, Pennsylvania State University, United Sates; Walter **Boynton**, Chesapeake Biological Laboratory, United States; Wallace **Broecker**, Lamont-Doherty Earth Observatory, United States; John **Chiang**, University of California Berkeley, United States; Bill **Curry**, Woods Hole Oceanographic Institution, United States; Ruth **Curry**, Woods Hole Oceanographic Institution, United States; Terry **Chapin**, University of Alaska, United States; Suzanne **Donovan**, Marine Biological Laboratory, United States; Larry **Hinzman**, University of Alaska, United States; Max **Holmes**, Marine Biological Laboratory, United States; Nick **McCave**, University of Cambridge, United Kingdom; Jim **McClelland**, Marine Biological Laboratory, United States; Jerry **Melillo**, Marine Biological Laboratory, United States; Mary Ann **Seifert**, Marine Biological Laboratory, United States.

Abrupt Climate Change: Ocean Salinity Changes and Potential Impacts on Ocean Circulation: Robbie **Ali**, University of Pittsburgh Graduate School of Public Health, United States; Andrew **Githeko**, Kenya Medical Research Institute, Kenya; Duane J. **Gubler**, Hawaii University, United States; John **Patz**, University of Wisconsin, United States; Douglas J. **Perkins**, University of Pittsburgh Graduate School of Public Health, United States; Lilia Rivero **Rodíguez**, Ministry of Health, México; Ismail Sallam, Egypt.

Other Contributors and Reviewers:

AFRICA
Ahmed **Abdelrehim**, Centre of Environment and Development for the Arab Region and Europe, Egypt; Charles **Doumambila**, Agence Internationale pour le Developpement de l'Information Environnementale, Gabon; Fatma **El-Mallah**, Council of Arab Ministers Responsible for the Environment, League of Arab States, Egypt; Elizabeth **Gowa**, National Environment Management Authority, Uganda; Clever **Mafuta**, Southern African Research and Documentation Centre, Musokotwane Environment Resource Centre for Southern Africa, Zimbabwe; Bora **Masumbuko**, Network for Environment and Sustainable Development in Africa, Cote d'Ivoire; Rajendranath **Mohabeer**, Indian Ocean Commission, Mauritius; Richard **Sherman**, International Institute for Sustainable Development/Earth Negotiations Bulletin, South Africa.

ASIA and the PACIFIC
Neil **Ericksen**, International Global Change Institute, University of Waikato, New Zealand; Saleemul **Huq**, International Institute for Environment and Development, United Kingdom; Kanayathu **Koshy**, The University of the South Pacific, Fiji; Pradyumna Kumar **Kotta**, South Asia Co-operative Environment Programme, Sri Lanka; Irina **Mamieva**, Scientific Information Center of Interstate Sustainable Development Commission, Turkmenistan; Matthew **McIntyre**, South Pacific Regional Environment Programme, Samoa; Hideyuki **Mori**, Institute for Global Environmental Strategies, Japan; Vishal **Narain**, The Energy and Resources Institute, India; Somrudee **Nicro**, Thailand Environment Institute, Thailand; Atiq **Rahman**, Bangladesh Centre for Advanced Studies, Bangladesh; Ram Manohar **Shrestha**, Asian Institute of Technology, Thailand; Chris **Spence**, International Institute for Sustainable Development/Earth Negotiations Bulletin, New Zealand; Ruisheng **Yue**, Department of International Cooperation, State Environmental Protection Administration, China.

EUROPE
Rob **Alkemade**, National Institute for Public Health and the Environment, The Netherlands; Tom **Bigg**, International Institute for Environment and Development, United Kingdom; Barry **Dalal-Clayton**, International Institute for Environment and Development, United Kingdom; Cynthia **De Wit**, Stockholm University, Sweden; Genady **Golubev**, Faculty of Geography, Moscow State University, Russian Federation; Wilfried **Haeberli**, World Glacier Monitoring Service, Department of Geography, University of Zurich, Switzerland; Craig **Hilton-Taylor**, Species Survival Commission of IUCN – The World Conservation Union, United Kingdom; Nazneen **Kanji**, International Institute for Environment and Development, United Kingdom; Ruben **Mnatsakanian**, Central European University, Hungary; Jan-Eric **Petersen**, European Environment Agency, Denmark; Véronique **Plocq Fichelet**, Scientific Committee on Problems of the Environment, France; Jerome **Simpson**, The Regional Environmental Centre for Central and Eastern Europe, Hungary; David **Stanners**, European Environment Agency, Denmark; Elsa **Tsioumani**, International Institute for Sustainable Development/Earth Negotiations Bulletin, Greece.

LATIN AMERICA and the CARIBBEAN
José **Gerhartz**, University of the West Indies Centre for Environment and Development, Jamaica; Rosario **Gómez**, Universidad del Pacífico, Perú; Gonzalo **Gutiérrez**, Centro Latino Americano de Ecología Social, Uruguay; Edgar **Gutiérrez Espeleta**, Observatorio del Desarrollo, Universidad de Costa Rica, Costa Rica; Diego **Martino**, Centro Latino Americano de Ecología Social, Uruguay; Verónica **Quirici**, Centro Latino Americano de Ecología Social, Uruguay.

NORTH AMERICA
Sabrina **Barker**, Global Environment Monitoring System/Water Programme, Canada; Paul **Grabhorn**, Grabhorn Studio, United States; Tiina **Kurvits**, Global Resource Information Database-Arendal, c/o Canadian Polar Commission, Canada; Richard **Robarts**, Global Environment Monitoring System/Water Programme, Canada; Mark **Schulman**, International Institute for Sustainable Development, United States; Noelle **Eckley Selin**, International Institute for Sustainable Development/Earth Negotiations Bulletin, United States; Lynn **Wagner**, International Institute for Sustainable Development/Earth Negotiations Bulletin, United States.

WEST ASIA
Asma Ali **Aba Hussein**, Arabian Gulf University, Kingdom of Bahrain; Ibrahim **Abdel Gelil**, Arabian Gulf University, Kingdom of Bahrain; Mahmood **Abdelraheem**, Kadhema Scientific Counsultancy and Services, Kuwait; Yousef **Abu Safieh**, Environmental Quality Authority, Occupied Palestinian Territories; Abdul Rahman **Al-Awadi**, Regional Organization for the Protection of the Marine Environment, Kuwait; Abdullah **Al-Droubi**, Arab Centre for the Studies of Arid Zones and Drylands, Syria; Mohanned S. **Al-Sheriadeh**, Environment Research Center, University of Bahrain, Kingdom of Bahrain; Waleed K. **Al-Zubari**, Arabian Gulf University, Kingdom of Bahrain; Adel **Gouda**, Arab Centre for the Studies of Arid Zones and Drylands, Syria; Abdullah **Noaman**, Faculty of Engineering, Sana'a University, Yemen; Muthian **Thangaraja**, Regional Organization for the Protection of the Marine Environment, Kuwait.

Other UN Offices: Karin **Buhren**, United Nations Human Settlements Programme, UN-HABITAT, Kenya; Richard **Grainger**, Food and Agriculture Organization, Italy; Kenneth **Oredo**, United Nations Development Fund for Women, Kenya; Ole **Lyse**, United Nations Human Settlements Programme, UN-HABITAT, Kenya; V. P. **Sharma**, World Health Organization, India; Ulrich **Wieland**, United Nations Statistical Division, United States.

UNEP Headquarters and Outposted Offices: Johannes **Akiwumi**; Alex **Alusa**; Meryem **Amar**; Chizuru **Aoki**; Per **Bakken**; Nalini **Basavaraj**; Alberto T. **Calcagno**; John **Carstensen**; Mark **Collins**; Gerard **Cunningham**; Dag **Daler**; Olivier **Deleuze**; Salif **Diop**; Ahmad **Ghosn**; Etienne **Gonin**; Hiremagalur **Gopalan**; Elizabeth **Guilbaud-Cox**; Julia **Hagl**; Jan **Husby**; Melanie **Hutchinson**; Elizabeth **Khaka**; Sonja **Koeppel**; Angele **Luh**; Desta **Mebratu**; Salem **Milad**; Elizabeth **Mrema**; Martha **Mulumba**; Michael **Mwangi**; Agneta **Nilsson**; Theodore **Oben**; Akpezi **Ogbuigwe**; Fatoumata **Ouane**; Joakim **Palmqvist**; Naomi **Poulton**; Daniel **Puig**; Mark **Radka**; Anisur **Rahman**; Ricardo **Sánchez Sosa**; Vicente **Santiago**; Frits **Schlingemann**; Charles **Sebukeera**; Mohamed **Sessay**; Rajendra **Shende**; Surendra **Shrestha**; David **Simpson**; David **Smith**; Hari **Srinivas**; Agneta **Sundén Byléhn**; Sekou **Toure**; Brennan **Van Dyke**; Hanneke **van Lavieren**; Melanie **Virtue**; Njeri **Wamukonya**; John **Whitelaw**; Kaveh **Zahedi**; Laetitia **Zobel**; Ulla Li **Zweifel**

UNEP Associated Centres:
United Nations Environment Programme Regional Resource Centre for Asia and the Pacific, Thailand: Mylvakanam **Iyngararasan**; Jacob **Kurian**; Achira **Leophairatana**; Purna Chandra Lall **Rajbhandari**; Tunnie **Srisakulchairak**; Gulmira **Tolibaeva**; Saule **Yessimova**

United Nations Environment Programme Regional Office for North America, United States: William **Mansfield**; Felix **Wing**

United Nations Environment Programme World Conservation Monitoring Centre, United Kingdom: Carmen **Lacambra**; Lucy **Fish**; Phillip **Fox**; Harriet **Gillet**; Edmund **Green**; Jerry **Harrison**; Val **Kapos**; Igor **Lysenko**; Edmund **McManus**; Lera **Miles**; Simon **Blyth**

United Nations Environment Programme GRID-Arendal, Norway: Christian **Nellemann**

United Nations Environment Programme Brazil Office, Brazil: Hugo **Rosa da Conceição**; Cristina **Montenegro**

United Nations Environment Programme/Post-Conflict Assessment Unit, Switzerland: Aniket **Ghai**; Jon **Godson**; David **Jensen**; Hassan **Partow**; Pasi **Rinne**

Errata

The list of **Contributors and Reviewers of Emerging Challenges – New Findings** on page 96 should read as follows:

Emerging and Re-emerging Infectious Diseases: Links to Environmental Change: Robbie Ali, University of Pittsburgh Graduate School of Public Health, United States; Andrew Githeko, Kenya Medical Research Institute, Kenya; Duane J. Gubler, Hawaii University, United States; John Patz, University of Wisconsin, United States; Douglas J. Perkins, University of Pittsburgh Graduate School of Public Health, United States; Lilia Rivero Rodríguez, Ministry of Health, México; Ismail Sallam, Egypt.

Abrupt Climate Change: Ocean Salinity Changes and Potential Impacts on Ocean Circulation: Richard Alley, Pennsylvania State University, United States; Walter Boynton, Chesapeake Biological Laboratory, United States; Wallace Broecker, Lamont-Doherty Earth Observatory, United States; John Chiang, University of California Berkeley, United States; Bill Curry, Woods Hole Oceanographic Institution, United States; Ruth Curry, Woods Hole Oceanographic Institution, United States; Terry Chapin, University of Alaska, United States; Suzanne Donovan, Marine Biological Laboratory, United States; Larry Hinzman, University of Alaska, United States; Max Holmes, Marine Biological Laboratory, United States; Nick McCave, University of Cambridge, United Kingdom; Jim McClelland, Marine Biological Laboratory, United States; Jerry Melillo, Marine Biological Laboratory, United States; Mary Ann Seifert, Marine Biological Laboratory, United States.

GEO YEAR BOOK 2004 Collaborating Centres

Agence Internationale pour le
Developpement de l'Information
Environnementale (ADIE)
http://www.adie-prgie.net

Arab Forest and Range Institute (AFRI)
http://www.afri-edu.org

The Commission for Environmental
Cooperation of North America
http://www.cec.org

Centre for Environment and Development
for the Arab Region & Europe (CEDARE)
http://www.cedare.org.eg

Centre for International Sustainable
Development Law
http://www.cisdl.org

Centro Latino Americano de Ecología
Social (CLAES)
http://www.ambiental.net/claes

GRID-Christchurch
Centre for Antarctic Studies and Research
University of Canterbury
http://www.anta.canterbury.ac.nz

GRID-Arendal
http://www.grida.no

Commission de l'Ocean Indian (IOC)
Indian Ocean Commission (IOC)
http://www.coi-info.org

International Institute for Sustainable
Development (IISD)
http://www.iisd.ca

National Environmental Management
Authority (NEMA)
http://www.nemaug.org

Network for Environment and Sustainable
Development in Africa (NESDA)
http://www.nesda.kabissa.org

Southern African Research and
Documentation Centre (SARDC),
Musokotwane Environment Resource
Centre for Southern Africa (IMERCSA)
http://www.sardc.net/

Scientific Committee on Problems of the
Environment (SCOPE)
http://www.icsu-scope.org

United Nations Environment Programme
World Conservation Monitoring Centre
(UNEP-WCMC)
http://www.unep-wcmc.org

PRODUCTION

Nairobi Coordinating Team:
Marion Cheatle
Jacquie Chenje
Harsha Dave
Volodymyr Demkine
Tessa Goverse
Carol Hunsberger
Elizabeth Migongo-Bake
Anju Sharma

Regional Coordinating Team:
Adel Abdel-Kader
Munyaradzi Chenje
Kakuko Nagatani-Yoshida
Ashbindu Singh
Subrato Sinha
Jaap van Woerden
Ron Witt
Jinhua Zhang

Support Team:
Ivar Baste
Andrea DeBono
Carolyne Dodo
Mark Ernste
Kim Giese
Gregory Giuliani
Steve Lonergan

Ram Chandra Mishra
Anne Muchiri
Erika Monnati
Stefan Schwarzer
Jane Smith
Josephine Wambua
Angela Zahnisser

**Electronic References
and Internet site:**
John Mugwe
Brian Ochieng
Mick Wilson
**Public Awareness and
Outreach:**
Eric Falt
Beth Ingraham
Nick Nuttall